REGIONS *of the* HEART

REGIONS
of the HEART

The Triumph and Tragedy
of Alison Hargreaves

David Rose and Ed Douglas

ADVENTURE PRESS

NATIONAL GEOGRAPHIC
WASHINGTON, D. C.

Published by the National Geographic Society
1145 17th Street N.W., Washington, D.C. 20036

First published in 1999 by Michael Joseph, Penguin Books, Ltd., London
This edition published by arrangement with the authors.

First Printing, June 2000
Printed in U.S.A

Interior Design by David Griffin

Library of Congress Cataloging-in-Publication Data

Rose, David, 1959-
    Regions of the heart : The triumph and tragedy of Alison Hargreaves / David Rose and
Ed Douglas.
        p. cm.
    ISBN 0-7922-7696-5
        1. Hargraves, Alison Jane, 1962-1995. 2. Mountaineers--Scotland--Biography. 3.
    Woman mountaineers--Scotland--Biography. I. Douglas, Ed. II. Title.

GV199.92.H35 R68 2000
796.52'2'092--dc21
    [B]   00-028072

To Carolyn

and

To Margaret and Raymond

There is a region of heart's desire
free for the hand that wills;
land of the shadow and haunted spire,
land of the silvery glacier fire,
land of the cloud and the starry choir,
magical land of hills;
loud with the crying of winds and streams,
thronged with the fancies and fears of dreams.

Geoffrey Winthrop Young

CONTENTS

For a few moments more Alison Hargreaves lingers in the dark shelter of her tent. Her mind is racing with excitement, a free-wheel release from tension after days of bad weather have forced her to sit still at Base Camp and do nothing but fret. As though she's leaving the house to go on holiday, Alison forces herself to stop and run through the list of things she has to remember. If she forgets something now, her chance of climbing K2 may be lost. She traces the thin beam of her flashlight across the tent's floor.

She looks at her rucksack and thinks about the layers of fleece clothing to insulate her body from the penetrating cold of high altitude. She tightens the laces on her boots, battery-heated to keep the blood flowing to her toes and to protect her from frostbite. She imagines her hands inside her multilayered mittens grasping her ice ax, its shaft scratched and worn from use; sees herself looking from behind dark glasses at the glare of the sun, through half the air found at sea level. She feels the warm thickness of her down-filled suit, the thin crackle of her wind suit, the hood wrapped around her head adding to her disorientation, the strange, dreamy world of high altitude. She hears the rasp of her breathing, the constant haul of her lungs on the depleted oxygen. Sometimes she has felt that this is all she is, two desperate lungs and the will to keep going.

Every item in her rucksack has a purpose; nothing extraneous is left in. Every ounce has to be carried on her back, and she wants nothing that will weigh her down. Alison has always been practical and logical in preparing for a mountain, arranging the gear in her tent better than any man she has climbed with, so that everything she needs is close at hand. She has climbed alone for years and knows the full meaning of self-reliance.

Outside, in the indigo night, the sole remaining member of her expedition is also preparing to depart. They are committed to climbing together, but they are new friends; they have not shared a rope before this expedition. She won't be alone on the mountain, but she is prepared to be, if it means success. The sky is washed with stars and dagger cold, promising a clear dawn. They are leaving now to make good progress before the sun rises, draining their energy even as it softens the snow.

In a separate base camp close by, other climbers move about their tents, preparing to leave with them. They are part of a different expedition. Alison knows and likes them, but they are no more than affable half-friends, sharing a common interest but not a common life. They know little of what she faces at home. As she pauses inside her tent, she thinks of those closest to her, those who know her and love her best, thousands of miles away.

Her children, Tom and Kate, the center of her universe, will be asleep at home in Scotland, breathing evenly in their warm beds, unconscious of her. She has thought often, in the previous days of bad weather and frustration, about their tearful parting weeks before. She was home for only two weeks after her triumphant return from Everest, and much of that fortnight was given over to media interviews and meetings. At night she has cried in her tent, longing to be home. She can see their faces, wonders how they will have grown or changed; wonders how they will be with her when she returns. The end of the expedition is near. When she comes down the mountain, she will be coming down to them. She will be putting them to bed herself in only two weeks.

In the cold tent she thinks about her husband. Her marriage has stuttered, and she has agonized over whether and how she should finish it. The tension is there with her at K2 Base Camp, in the strained letters and faxes she has sent and received from home. Piled on top of this emotional confusion is her fear about money. She is here because she thinks she has to be, trying to climb for her living, trying to do something that will secure the new future she is planning for herself and her children. She thinks about the freedom she felt as a young climber. All these things have whirled round her mind as she sat killing time beneath the mountain, day after day, waiting for her life to start again.

Beyond the thin nylon skin of her tent, the mass of K2 soars 11,000 feet above the glacier, a huge bulk of snow, ice, and rock reaching into space. She has already climbed all but the last 2,000, so the first part of her journey to the summit will be on familiar ground. It should take her three or four days to the top and another two to come down and start on the long trail home. Less than a week. Still, she can't escape a tightening in her stomach as she contemplates the final unkown section.

In Britain she tried to shrug off K2's reputation. Now she has plenty of firsthand experience, knows how quickly the weather can change and how bad it can be on the world's second-highest mountain. Climbers coming down have been trapped by bad weather, forced to linger in the too-thin air, growing weaker, the life slowly fading from them. She knows that only four women have reached the summit, and two of them died trying to get back down. The ascent looms over her, nagging at her consciousness. Nothing can progress until she has finished with this examination she has set herself. After that she can turn to the rest of her life.

Spread around her tent are things from home: face creams to protect her skin from the strong sunlight, notes she has faxed to her children. They are the links with her other life, the one that has dragged at her heels in the long weeks on the stony glacier, her mood lifting and falling along with the capricious weather. Each time she has gone up the mountain, Alison feels closer to going home; each time she has come back unsuccessful, she feels the urge to throw it all up and go back to her children. But there are people at home who expect her to do well. She expects herself to do well. When will she have this chance again? She looks around the tent one last time. When she comes back it will all seem different. Then she zips the door shut and goes out into the darkness of the early morning to climb the mountain.

≈

CHAPTER 1

BEFORE THE FALL

T he life of Alison Hargreaves began in the early hours of February 17, 1962. The day before, as her mother felt the first signs of labor, a violent storm shook and rattled the house. The roof of the garden shed was torn off by the wind, wood splintering from nail, and hurled down the garden to smash the kitchen window, littering the worktops and an open cutlery drawer with broken glass.

The world Alison entered was a brand-new brick estate in Mickleover, a suburb of Derby, the old railway manufacturing center at the point where the English Midlands come to an end and the north begins. Her mother, Joyce, had given up her job as a math teacher 21 months earlier, when she gave birth to her first daughter, Susan. She remembers Mickleover as a "rabbit warren" filled with young families. Alison's father, John, developed computing techniques for British Rail Research, part of the state-owned railway network.

Alison was a contented baby and was soon sleeping through the night. She was lively and eager to please. By the time she was three, she would try to help her mother with washing or cleaning the floor. She was also strong-willed, and if she failed to get her way, would sometimes hold her breath until it seemed she would burst. Joyce's niece, Daphne, remembers Alison's determination very clearly. Twelve years younger than Alison's mother and 12 years older than Susan, Daphne often came to visit during school holidays. "Alison could throw the most amazing tantrums I've ever seen. If she wanted an ice cream, there was nothing, absolutely nothing you could do except buy her that ice cream." Once, when Alison was still very small, her mother discovered that she had ripped her new anorak. Allison had been out in the garden, climbing.

Joyce sometimes found full-time mothering tedious. Her intellect, she felt, was beginning to wither away. Only when all of her three children were at school—Alison's only brother, Richard, was born in 1965—did she return to paid employment, eventually becoming deputy headmistress of a girls' high school. John, meanwhile, was making advances in computing. Occasionally, he took Alison to see his laboratory. Holding his hand, her eyes wide with wonder, she watched the Elliott 402F machine, an assembly of glowing valves and cooling fans more than 20 feet long, hum and whir its way through the complex calculations required to work out railway timetables and the strength of bridges and viaducts.

John and Joyce had met as students at Oxford University, where both read mathematics. Each had been brought up in the north of England: John in Preston, then a thriving textile town in Lancashire; and Joyce, the daughter of a tailor, in Ripon, Yorkshire. Unlike most of their Oxford contemporaries who were beneficiaries of elite private education, they had been educated at state grammar schools, and both were the first generation of their respective families to go to university. They were dating by the end of their first term and soon discovered a shared passion for the outdoors. As students, they made frequent walking and cycling trips together. After graduation, while Joyce took a teaching job in Bedford, they continued to see each other most weekends. At first, while John was working for a firm in Cheltenham, they would meet somewhere halfway between their respective digs, after train journeys of formidable complexity. They were married in the Methodist chapel at Ripon, where Joyce's father ran the choir, on August 15, 1959. British Rail had already offered John a job in Derby. Mickleover beckoned.

It soon became apparent that the love for the hills that had drawn the Hargreaves together was inherited by their young family. From Alison's early childhood, the family's happiest times were spent high on the fells and mountains.

In 1970, when Alison was eight, John took his daughters up Snowdon, the craggy peak that is the highest point in Wales. John, whose knowledge of navigation was not as good as it later became, had planned to make the ascent by the easy Pyg Track. Susan was wearing her first proper pair of walking boots, while Alison was in rubber Wellingtons.

When mist unexpectedly shrouded the mountain, John and the girls lost their route and found themselves on the Crib Goch, a rocky knife-edged ridge with a steep drop on either side. Both children reveled in the exposure, scrambling happily over the rough volcanic rocks. A year later Alison climbed Ben Nevis, Britain's highest summit, a grueling, boulder-strewn slog from sea level to 4,406 feet. She skipped ahead, leaving the family behind, dancing up the track with effortless agility.

John loved all his children, but there was a special quality to his relationship with Alison. Before Oxford, he had been drafted to do his national service in the Royal Navy. He disliked military discipline, and later turned down a well-paid research job with the Admiralty when he received a letter telling him to "report for duty," a phrase that made him recoil with unhappy memories. In Alison's mischievous, testing laughter, and in her formidable determination, he recognized a kindred spirit. He understood the joy she felt in the freedom of the hills, and he shared it.

In the autumn of 1971, the family left Mickleover for a detached house in Belper, in the Derwent valley north of Derby. At the bottom of the road the river surged across a weir, past the redbrick walls of the old Strutt cotton mill, a looming monument of the industrial revolution. The house was set on a hill, and immediately beyond lay the southern margins of the Peak District National Park. Despite being sandwiched between the industrial cities of Derby, Manchester, and Sheffield, the open moors and deep-cut valleys of this upland tract have retained their grandeur and remoteness, punctuated by dozens of rocky crags where climbers have been active for more than a century. The first were a few miles from Alison's home: rough gritstone towers on the hilltops; gleaming river-cut limestone along the dales. On alternate Sundays John Hargreaves worked as a volunteer ranger on the High Peak Trail, an activity that led him to try rock climbing. He never pursued it with the single-minded obsession required to climb the hardest routes, but he enjoyed the sport, delighting in the problems posed by difficult moves—the physical counterpart to the intellectual conundrums he solved at work. Often the children came to watch and, eventually, to join in.

John and Joyce Hargreaves were not demonstrative of the love they felt for their children. Their own childhoods had been emotionally austere. John's mother died when he was five, leaving him with few memories; Joyce remembers her own mother as a cold, determined woman who liked to get her own way. As adults, they set high standards, and their children were expected to achieve. Alison—lively, confident, hardworking, and intelligent—seemed unlikely to disappoint. In Belper, after Long Row Primary School, she joined Strutt's Middle School, which took children up to the age of 13. At the end of her first term there, she was judged top of her class. She rarely got less than full marks when given a test, especially in mathematics. She won a series of awards in the Girl Guides, and helped start a school magazine. She was learning the tenor horn, which she played in local bands, as well as the piano, and was on the school netball team, a game similar to six-player girls' basketball in the U.S.

From the beginning of 1973, the year she turned 11, Alison began keeping a daily diary, a habit she maintained with few interruptions for the rest of her life. Her father had done the same thing for many years. Most days, she filled the best part of a page with her neat, round hand. Usually she would simply describe the minutiae of the day: her lessons and her interactions with her friends. As she grew older, her journal's factual tenor changed very little. She had the habit of making lists, especially if she felt a sense of achievement, in a long walk for example, when she would write down each place on the route, or later, in a tally of rock climbs, recording every route accomplished, no matter how insignificant. She loved food and recorded her diet with meticulous enthusiasm, detailing the menu at every meal and commenting on how much she'd enjoyed each dish. When she failed to write in her journal every day, she would catch up at the end of the week, a method that only encouraged the diary's general literary blandness. Occasionally, however, she would write when she could barely contain the passionate feelings she usually kept concealed, and then her true preoccupations would erupt on the page.

"I loved our childhood," Alison's sister, Susan, says. "Our parents made sure we were never couch potatoes. We were always doing things." Poor weather was no excuse: sun, rain, or snow, the outings continued. One freezing day during April 1975, the family were in Wales. "All set off up Snowdon, very snowy," Alison wrote in her diary. "It was blowing hard so just Dad and me went up a knife-edged ridge in snow to top. Everything covered with ice like coral."

That May, Alison did her first roped rockclimb. She was 13. The family drove out to the western edge of the Peak District to the Roaches, a sprawling complex of brown gritstone buttresses close to the Staffordshire town of Leek. From the road, the cliffs look like a mountain range in miniature, their precipices and overhangs dominating the flat country beyond. They walked up through the trees beneath the cliffs, the smell of new bracken growth filling Alison's head, before they broke out of the woods onto the path to the foot of the crag and the long view over Staffordshire. She learned how to uncoil the rope, running it through her fingers, and to tie an end securely round her waist, using a knot known to climbers and sailors alike as a bowline. With the family were John's outdoor friends. One of them tied the other end of the rope to his climbing harness before starting to climb, moving nimbly up the 40-foot buttress. At the top he "belayed," fastening the rope securely to an outcropping flake, and pulled up the slack. At last the rope came tight, and heart racing, Alison began to follow him. Should she fall, her father had promised, the rope would stop her immediately. But as she took her first faltering steps into the vertical world, she felt vulnerable. What if the rope should snap or slip? Her leader grinned down from the top of the cliff and offered words of encouragement. Breathing more easily, she started to relax.

As the day went on, Alison began to learn the different ways of moving on rock. Like most climbing beginners, she had a tendency to clutch at the handholds, to hang from her arms, rapidly losing strength. The crucial principle, it was readily apparent, was to use and rely on her legs: to work out how to shift her weight across the footholds in the rock; to develop confidence so that on even the tiniest ripples, her feet would stick. As she climbed, the growing distance from the ground snapped at her heels, making her increasingly nervous the higher she got. But desire was overcoming her instinctive caution. Each time she finished a climb, clambering over the edge of the crag to join her partner on the heathery moor above, she felt a deep-seated, physical sense of happiness, an idea of some anxiety within her being stilled.

The summer of 1975 was long and hot. The moorland bogs dried out, becoming brittle underfoot, while the rocks radiated heat. Smitten by climbing, Alison begged her father to take her out again. He was charmed by her enthusiasm, and almost every weekend he and his friends tried to sate her appetite, introducing her to many of the local crags. Alison had a natural ability and soon discovered that the more she climbed, the harder the climb would need to be for her to attain that profound satisfaction she had experienced on her very first day. Like her father, she loved the way climbing combined a physical challenge—the excitement of pulling on holds high above the ground— with intelligent problem solving, deciding which holds to use and how to make progress. Each new sheet of rock, however difficult it looked from the bottom, had a sequence of moves programmed into its surface, which if read correctly would unlock a kind of choreography, a way of climbing that felt not like a struggle but a glorious, floating dance. Making swift progress, Alison learned that the keys were grace and patience rather than strength and adrenalin. She developed the climber's habit of looking at cliffs not as blank and looming masses but as assemblages of possibility, teeming with lines of cracks and holds begging to be explored. A few weeks after her first rock climb, Alison kissed a boy for the first time. Unlike her climbing, the event was recorded in her diary without detail or comment.

The national park on her doorstep brimmed with crags, little ragged lines on the one-inch-to-a-mile Ordnance Survey maps that Alison poured over each evening. Up the valley from Belper were Cromford Black Rocks, weathered boulders and outcrops of abrasive gritstone. Alison learned that in order to climb on gritstone, she would have to acquire the confidence to stand with her toes on rounded edges which felt strange and insecure. The handholds weren't like the rungs of a ladder, one after the other and just above her head. Here was a flake aligned vertically, which she had to pull on sideways, her feet braced in opposition; here a rough-sided crack, where she learned to insert her hands and jam them by making a fist. On the limestone cliffs in the bed of the Derwent valley, the holds and pockets in the rock were sharp and comfortingly secure, more likely to be what climbers call "jug handles," or "jugs" for short. But limestone cliffs are steeper, rarely less than vertical, and sometimes overhanging. Alison needed greater physical strength to climb them. Even within the same rock type, there were subtle geological differences, giving each crag its own particular character, dictating the required technique. Some cliffs had loose rock and she needed to be wary; others were as solid and dependable as old friends.

In northern England in the mid-1970s, rock climbing was not widely considered a suitable sport for girls, and from the beginning, Alison's gender made her a novelty, prompting attention. She noticed experienced climbers nudging each other, nodding their heads at this young bright-eyed teenager with her shock of honey-colored hair, levering her way across overhangs and padding her feet up fine-grained slabs. She did not mind the attention. Climbing, she thought, could open up a world that seemed brighter and more independent than that of her peers.

In October 1975 Doug Scott and Dougal Haston, members of an expedition led by Chris Bonington, made the first ascent of the Southwest Face of Everest, solving a mountaineering problem that had defeated several expeditions over the preceding five years. The achievement captured the imagination of the international news media, and it had an overwhelming impact on budding young climbers like Alison Hargreaves. The siege of the Southwest Face had become a public saga, its protagonists mythical heroes whose status was only enhanced by the tragic disappearance of Mick Burke on the way down from the summit. Other girls worshipped pop stars. The only posters on Alison's bedroom walls, even then, were of mountains and mountaineers.

Years of Methodist Sunday school and Joyce's teaching at home had left their mark. Recording the climb in her diary, Alison asked God to bless the Everest team. Often her diary included little prayers, usually for her family's well-being; but despite this coy piety, she seethed with the normal ration of adolescent hormones, developing a series of unrequited crushes on boys at school. Sometimes she prayed for the courage to speak to one of the objects of her affection, or asked Him whether her feelings were reciprocated.

Belper is a very traditional northern English town of 60,000 people. Almost entirely white, its population includes hundreds of extended families who have lived there for generations, since its textile trade first boomed in the 19th century. Belper's only large buildings are its mills, blunt structures of glass and brick, nestling in the valley bottom where the power of the Derwent was tapped to drive their looms. Most of them have other uses now, artifacts of an industrial past, but they remain the town's physical focus. The rest of Belper slopes down the hillside toward them, a high street of little shops, rows of redbrick workers' terraces, and on the outskirts, postwar estates and avenues of detached houses like the Hargreaves' own, where the countryside ends abruptly amid carefully tended gardens. People know each other's business without inquiring, and they tend to social and political conservatism. After an interlude in the 1960s, when the town's MP was the alcoholic and self-destructive Labour Cabinet minister, George Brown, Belper sent Tories to Parliament with comfortable majorities.

However, in the early 1970s, the town acquired a new and far from conservative school. Belper High School's head, Michael Tucker, was an atheist, influenced by the free school movement founded by the radical 1930s educationist, A. S. Neil. Under Tucker's leadership, school assemblies were omitted and rules set down by consensus, while he asked the teachers to get their students to address them by their first names. Most of the staff were young, still fresh from college. There was no school uniform. Tucker believed in developing every aspect of a child's potential and in the importance of the self-reliance to be derived from the great outdoors. The school treated climbing, canoeing, and caving as an intrinsic part of the curriculum, with time to pursue them built into the class schedules. For Alison, who started there in September 1975, it was paradise.

Two teachers responsible for outdoor pursuits, Hilary Collins and Pete Clarke, became important influences on Alison's development. No pupil could have been more enthusiastic. "She already had a strong interest from her parents," Clarke recalls. "She knew her own mind from an early age. She would gather all her resources if she wanted something, put in a hundred percent, and then a bit more if necessary." On weekends and school holidays, Collins and Clarke drove groups of children to the hills of Snowdonia or the Lake District, to stay in hostels or climbing huts and to walk the fells or tackle longer rock climbs. In term time, there were orienteering and overnight bivouacs in sleeping bags on the tops of Peak District fells. Every week, one school day afternoon was spent rock climbing, exploring the area's limestone caves, or canoeing the Derwent rapids.

The week before Christmas 1975, the school booked a hostel in Snowdonia, where Pete Clarke led Alison and four other students on an unseasonal climb along Grooved Arête, on the east face of Tryfan. One of the area's biggest hills, Tryfan is a comb of volcanic rhyolite which dominates the surrounding moorland. With a little imagination, Tryfan's east face, as it hoves into view along the main A5 trunk road from Holyhead to London, looks a bit like the Matterhorn. Compared to the little crags of the Peak District, rarely as much as a hundred feet high, this was full-blown mountaineering. Grooved Arête requires nearly 600 feet of roped climbing; and once a climber begins to ascend its looming towers and slabs, there are no easy ways down, no easy escape routes to the summit by sneaking off to one side. It has nine separate sections, or "pitches," between ledges, each one as long as an entire Peak District rock climb. Pete led the way up each pitch, then the students followed one by one as he took in the rope. Not far from the top is a series of delicate steps across and then up a smooth sheet of rock, a sequence of moves so well known that they have their own name, the Knight's Move Slab. The angle is not very steep, but the holds are small and polished to a dull sheen by the passage of thousands of climbers since the route was done for the first time in 1911. Even with the security of a rope above them, beginners find it frightening because the pitch involves a horizontal section, a "traverse." If the second fell, it would mean swinging across the slab in a pendulum, a jolting, skin-scraping slide above a long drop before being held on the rope.

It was December and the daylight hours were short. By the time Alison and the other children had teetered their way across, it was beginning to get dark. For a moment, Clarke considered trying to fight their way to the top by flashlight. A glance at the rocks above convinced him otherwise; they were dark and dripping, covered with slime from a weeping line of cracks that drain the mountain's summit slopes of rainfall. He was forced to organize an epic retreat.

Clarke had taught the children to abseil, or rappel, in the safety of the Belper High School gym. Now they were forced to remember their technique on a wild Welsh mountainside, on a black winter night. At the top of each pitch, Clarke doubled the rope and fixed it to a spike of rock. Once each pupil reached the safety of the ledge below, he pulled one end of the doubled rope so the spike above acted as a pulley. In this way, he was able to retrieve the rope and use it again on the pitch below. In the darkness, with the wind rising, it was a nerve-racking process. The ledges were small, and as the children descended one by one and huddled at the bottom of each rappel, Clarke had to make sure they were secure and didn't plummet into the black void below. It was a dramatic introduction to a technique Alison would use years later to descend great mountains in the Alps and Himalaya. Little by little, the party came down safely, not reaching the road until nearly 9 p.m. By then, Hilary Collins had put the mountain rescue team on alert.

Alison enjoyed every minute of what others might have found a daunting experience. As she told her friend Bev England, she loved the feeling of controlling danger, of being tested and staying calm. "Abseiled 1,000 feet then walked down in dark for 8.40 p.m.!" she wrote in her diary, as if this was the most normal thing in the world. The following day, while the other children rested, she insisted her teachers take her climbing again.

Meanwhile, she was beginning to immerse herself in the canon of mountain literature. One book that made a deep impression was *The White Spider*, Heinrich Harrer's account of how he and three companions made the first ascent of the north face of Switzerland's Eiger Peak in 1938. Their success was preceded by a long saga of failure and tragedy, which made the mountain internationally notorious, and Harrer omits few details—the deaths of Sedlmayer and Mehringer, who froze to the mountain on a ledge known forever after as Death Bivouac; the grisly end of a party of four caught in a storm in 1936, the last of whom expired less than three feet from the grasp of his would-be rescuers, unable to move as he dangled, frostbitten and exhausted, from a frozen rope. Alison read the book in her bedroom late into the night, inspired by the eventual triumph, not repelled by the horror of its cost. Like thousands of embryonic mountaineers before her, she imagined herself picking her way up the ice fields to Death Bivouac, daring to overcome her doubts and break through the north wall's gloom onto the summit snows above.

Early in the new year, 1976, she went to a lecture by Doug Scott, one of the 1975 Everest Southwest Face summiteers. After a long, arduous climb from the last camp on the face, Scott and Dougal Haston reached the highest point on earth moments before sunset. Their way down was too difficult to attempt in darkness, and they were faced with an unplanned bivouac at 29,000 feet, in the penetrating cold of the Himalayan autumn. After digging a snow cave on the mountain's South Summit, they avoided frostbite by placing their feet inside their clothing on each other's stomachs, but suffered altitude-induced hallucinations. It is one of the great survival stories in climbing history. Again, Alison was inspired. "Dear God, it all seemed too wonderful," she wrote in her diary. "I would really like to go, but know my chances are one in a million." Climbing was rapidly coming to dominate her inner life. By the beginning of February, she was drawing her rock-climbing boots as a still life in the school art class.

Her interest in climbing did not completely subsume her attraction to boys. Throughout this period, Alison had a powerful crush on a fellow pupil, Rob Hutton. She reflected deeply over any conversation they had, discussing him endlessly with Bev England, and suffering agonies when he seemed to be interested in someone else. She posted him a Valentine's card, then panicked in case it offended him. She dwelled on the relationship with the same intensity she gave to climbing and all the serious commitment of youth. On Valentine's Day another student, Sharon Gregory, had a party, and Alison tried to work up courage to approach Rob by drinking a martini and two glasses of cider. Finally, he came over to talk. Just for once, the subject of his conversation left her disappointed—not romance but rockclimbing. In something close to despair, Alison wrote: "Rob may not love me, but I know God does, and he knows what is best for me. I still have the mountains to love, and somewhere a boy to love."

At the beginning of April 1976 the Hargreaves' cheerful equilibrium was suddenly disturbed. Susan, an accomplished musician, had come home after a viola exam. She kept dropping things, and seemed to have lost all strength in her hands. The following morning she could not move one arm; within another couple of days, she had lost the use of a leg and her speech was slurred. At first the doctors were uncertain what was wrong. Susan—nearly 16—spent four weeks in the Derbyshire Royal Infirmary being tested for a range of infections and nervous disorders, including a possible brain tumor. Her symptoms eased quite quickly, and when she was allowed to go home, she was overjoyed. But as Sue recalls, "My parents were obviously less happy. They told me a day or two after getting home, I had multiple sclerosis and might relapse at any time."

Alison seemed to have had little awareness of the potential seriousness of her sister's condition. She visited her in hospital only a few times, and carried on with her busy climbing and social life. Her diary shows no trace of introspection, no intimation of her sister's sudden confrontation with mortality. Susan, however, was left in no doubt: "I was devastated, distraught. All my dreams had gone out of the window. I thought it was the end of my life." As the years passed, Susan was to suffer periodic relapses, but at the time of writing in 1999, the disease remains at bay. Susan was able to graduate from Oxford and Lancaster universities and pursue a successful career. She is now the mother of two children, the younger named after her sister, and Susan's health is usually good.

Her illness led to a definite, albeit temporary, cooling of her relationship with Alison. She could not help feeling slightly let down. Perhaps Alison's lack of support at this critical period in Susan's life can be explained by her youth; she was still only 14. Yet in the minds of the rest of her family, there was a sense of unease, that her interest in climbing was turning into a kind of monomania.

While Joyce had stayed at home to look after her children, money had been relatively tight. Now, however, she was back at work, and John's career with British Rail was thriving. For the first time the Hargreaves had spare disposable income and they chose to spend it on trips to the mountains. That August the family went on holiday to the Austrian Alps. For Alison, the first sight of mountains on a scale to dwarf anything in Britain was a moment of revelation. They were traveling by train, and as they entered Austria from Switzerland, sparkling peaks more than 11,000 feet high, dusted with recent snow, loomed above the tracks. The train went through a valley with soaring pinnacles and 2,000-foot rock faces, and Alison told her diary: "It was marvellous." At Innsbruck, where they changed trains, she glimpsed real alpinists, men with crampons and ice axes on their rucksacks. It wasn't only the mountains. Everything thrilled her, even the continental quilts in the hotels, an exotic contrast to the sheets and blankets she was used to at home. Each night she faithfully recorded what she ate for dinner.

One day Alison and her family walked up to a mountain refuge, where John mixed his beer with her lemon to make shandy. Then she and her father went on alone, reaching 7,000 feet and more. Alison was thrilled as they gazed across the seemingly endless mountains. Then they made the long descent back to the valley and to a delicious supper of ham, potatoes, and grapes: "It was absolutely gorgeous." On some days the family visited local railways where steam was still in use. Alison preferred hikes in the mountains, long scrambles along the ridgetops, and the sight of climbers tackling faces harder and higher than any she had seen. Once they were caught in a sudden downpour. As the thunder rumbled around them, she rolled up her trousers and rolled down her socks, and continued in a state of sodden ecstasy.

When the time came to board the sleeper train home, Alison didn't want to leave. Nineteen years later, speaking to the New Zealand climber Matt Comeskey, in an interview conducted at K2 Base Camp, she recalled her reactions as the train pulled out from Innsbruck: "I rolled up the couchette blind ... and peered out and there were these fantastic, mega limestone rocky walls, and I just burst into tears. I felt that was home, and I wanted to stay there." The morning after departure, Alison woke up in northern France. "It was, I thought, a very boring country," she told her diary. "No hills."

The end of that summer seemed to her family to mark the end of Alison's childhood. She was 14 and, like most adolescents, striving to create her own identity, a process that created frequent conflicts with her parents. Obsessed as she was with climbing, it was climbing that became the focus of their increasingly frequent rows. Alison's parents feared she was beginning to neglect her schoolwork. In some subjects she was still at the top of her class, but it was climbing, not scholarship, that dominated her thoughts and dreams. If she was not out on the crags, she was planning the next trip, attending climbing lectures, or reading climbing books and magazines.

The worst arguments were with her father, as if their very closeness made the emergence of conflict between them harder to bear. After a row, Alison tended to go to her room and shut the door, making it harder to resolve the frustration. Innately stubborn, she would not let them see a sign of weakness; only her diary knew that sometimes she lay awake into the small hours, weeping with both sadness and frustration. "To the rest of us, it seemed as if she were starting to withdraw from the family," Susan says. "She would shut herself in her room for hours at a time. We all felt hurt."

One source of trouble was an invitation, posted on the school noticeboard, to apply for a Derbyshire schools' expedition to the mountains of Norway in 1977. Alison and Bev England both wanted to go, and so did Susan. But the risk for a sufferer from multiple sclerosis, of spending several weeks in strenuous activity remote from hospitals, was too great. For weeks Alison badgered her parents to let her go, arguing that while it might not be fair on her sister, Susan would not mind. Finally they agreed, and at the beginning of December, Alison and Bev learned they had been chosen. Susan very much *did* mind. She was, Alison recorded, "very upset."

The strength of Alison's passion is common to many young rockclimbers. Almost by definition, climbing is an obsessive activity. At the most basic level the euphoria experienced on overcoming a difficult route is physically addictive, and the sense of well-being and achievement at the end of a great day on the crags or mountains is impossible to replicate by other means. At the same time, to climb well requires regular outings. To climb infrequently, almost invariably, is to climb clumsily, badly, and in a state of apprehension.

It is hardly surprising that experience as intense as this has created its own seductive subculture. When climbers aren't on the rock face, they love to talk about it, to show off, to establish hierarchies of skill, to share and relive the simple joy of climbing. They mark their territory in pubs and cafés, and learn to recognize each other at a glance and then to sink rapidly into their private world's argot. Like fighter pilots after a sortie, they discuss and relive the intensity of hard moves and difficult routes, often demonstrating them graphically with apparently bizarre arm movements. Other people, uninitiated into these mysteries, may wonder and disapprove. What could be less responsible or less productive a way of consuming precious energy? Secretly, the young climber thrives on this censure. In the late 1970s, before climbing's potential was noticed by the glossy style magazines and big business, its exponents liked to think of themselves as radicals, outlaws, and anarchists who had chosen to reject the shackles of bourgeois mediocrity.

For a rock climber, the crags of the Peak District, seldom more than a hundred feet high, offer an opportunity for exploration as satisfying as the conquest of an unclimbed peak is to a mountaineer. The region's pioneers, the first rock climbers who emerged toward the end of the 19th century, were happy to find the easiest ways to the top of each cliff, scrambling up deep gullies or easy-angled slabs. Soon, however, they and their successors realized that every cliff held numerous possibilities—alternative, more difficult routes on parts of the cliff that were steeper. Over the years, these new routes were spotted, climbed, and named, and then recorded in guidebooks for others to follow. Gradually, the new climbs being done became harder and more challenging, with each generation taking a fresh look at what was left.

Alison's teenage years in the 1970s were a period when exploration of this kind was unusually active. Climbers had begun to train in gyms and on the first indoor climbing walls, maintaining their fitness when the weather was poor and developing the strength in their fingers to pull themselves up on tiny holds on long sections of overhanging rock. In the hierarchy of climbing, there is no way of establishing superiority more conclusively than to climb a hard new route; and on the walls of the Peak District, new climbs were being made almost every week at a level of difficulty that bettered anything managed by previous generations.

Some of Alison's heroes, those who had reached the top of big mountains in the Himalaya, were also well known to the non-climbing public. At the same time, she worshipped the new rock athletes, whose exploits were less widely publicized. Their new routes were chronicled in the specialist magazines that Alison devoured each month—not just their climbs but their social lives, too. When Ron Fawcett, then Britain's best rock-climber, announced his engagement, Alison read about it as a news story in *Climber and Rambler*. But there was also an intimate accessibility to rock climbing. She could see these men—and they were all men—in action whenever she liked on the cliffs near her house. She could visit the places of their triumphs, touch the holds they had used, and try to work out the first few moves. "We were in total awe of people like Ron," Bev England recalls. "Yet at the same time, we felt we were on the fringes of the same scene."

It was not so much a café society as a greasy-spoon society. Climbers would hang out in transport cafés like the Lover's Leap in Stoney Middleton, a village in the heart of the Peak District. When it was raining at a weekend, the grim, narrow room would be packed with climbers drinking pint mugs of tea, telling each other about their latest climbs or craning their necks to see who was the big name queuing at the counter for a bacon sandwich. During the week, the hard core—dressed in weathered down jackets or well-worn pile sweaters—would eke out their dole money, rolling match-thin cigarettes and talking, always about climbing. At night the climbers would wander down the street to pubs like the Moon, where they switched from tea to beer but kept up the same topics of conversation: extreme deeds and wild behavior. It was a male, hierarchical, and unforgiving world, but an anarchic and exciting one as well, where the strictures of society were relaxed to the point of abandonment.

In London fashions this was the era of punk rock, when new designers like Vivienne Westwood were attracting international attention with their radical approach. Alison and Bev, however, had no interest in the look that was being paraded on Chelsea's King's Road. The objects of their deepest desire were the new Javelin fiber-pile jackets, cozy, rather shapeless zip-up garments made of a revolutionary artificial fabric, which in the climbing subculture were suddenly de rigueur. "To own one was a statement that you were a climber," says Bev. The firm's production was not up to the demand, and for weeks, Alison and Bev vied to be first in getting one. With local shops out of stock, Bev even went to London for the day scouring the capital's outdoor shops, but returned empty-handed. The prize fell to Alison, but when Bev got hers a few weeks later, Alison was dismayed to find that her own was already showing signs of wear. Even worse, the all-important Javelin trademark began to peel away from both girls' garments. Ever resourceful, they stuck them back with superglue. Their fastidiousness was in contrast to most young climbers growing up in the Peak District, who considered keeping tidy or clean as intolerably middle class.

But then most young climbers attracted to the sport at the end of the 1970s weren't female. Some women went climbing with their boyfriends, but Alison and Bev weren't interested in being led around by men. They often climbed together, and from the beginning the phenomenon of two girls sharing a rope attracted attention. One day they hitched a lift to a gritstone cliff above the village of Hathersage, Stanage Edge. To their delight, the driver who stopped turned out to be Paul Nunn, a famous veteran of the Himalaya.* "It's great to see two lasses climbing together," he said. "Keep it up." They should consider climbing in the Alps, he added; their obvious ability meant there were many routes they might reasonably consider tackling. Until then, Bev says, it had not occurred to them that their gender made them unusual; there was little, if anything, to distinguish the motives impelling her and Alison from those that drove their male contemporaries.

In the summer of 1977, after weeks of preparation on long training hikes, carrying heavy rucksacks, Alison and Bev went as planned to Norway. The party, drawn from schools all over Derbyshire, sailed from Newcastle to Stavanger, then took the train up the rugged coast. Their base camp was in the Rajo national park inside the Arctic Circle, and within a few days they

---

* Paul Nunn was tragically killed in August 1995, in an accident on Haramosh II, a mountain in the same range as K2.

had established a remote advance camp on a glacier, beneath vast sweeps of granite. Alison had been thrilled by her family holiday to Austria the previous summer. But here, there were no mountain restaurants, hotels, or continental quilts. They lived under canvas, on freeze-dried rations cooked on Primus stoves at the end of each exhausting day. It was Alison's first taste of wilderness, and soon she was reveling in the emptiness and isolation, bathing in freezing glacial lakes and basking under the midnight sun. Alison and Bev found a supply of fresh food in trout from the lakes, a welcome addition to the monotonous dried rations.

Nominally, the expedition was supposed to be measuring glacial recession, recording the weather, and looking for ancient Lap settlements. Its main effect, as far as Alison was concerned, was to reinforce her love of mountains still further. The only drawback were the clouds of ferocious mosquitoes. Alison brought home several taped into her journal, stained with their diet of human blood. The expedition ended with a hike from advance camp down to a mighty fjord. "For 15-year-olds," says Bev, "it was an overwhelming experience." Two days after getting home on August 9, Alison was chosen to talk about the trip for an interview on Radio Derby. The following afternoon she was back on the crags, climbing with Pete Clarke at Black Rocks—a far cry from the mountains of northern Norway, but the object of as much enthusiasm as ever.

She was beginning to feel grown-up, and sometimes in her diary would refer to herself in the third perso as "a woman." Indeed, at 15, she looked very much as she would as an adult. Her great strength was concentrated in a slim, boyish frame. Like many good climbers, she was far from tall at five feet four inches. Her hair, with its natural wave, was a rich dark blond, and her eyes were blue. But it was her warm, ready smile that drew attention, prompting those who met her to assume that her character was open and straightforward.

After weeks in the wilderness, the parts of her life that were vexing, the pressures of school and the tension with her family, had receded into the background, and Alison felt something close to perfect happiness. It was not the last time in her life that the mountains provided an emotional escape. In a prayer in her diary written shortly after her return from Norway, she looked forward to the coming academic year, when she would take the O-level (ordinary) examinations on which her sister had done so well. Yet, at the same time, she implored the Almighty to give her the time to improve her climbing. Somehow, she thought, she would achieve a balance.

In assuming that her parents worried about her devotion to climbing largely because of the threat it posed to her schoolwork, Alison was partly mistaken. The main root of their fears was more visceral; they were scared she might hurt herself badly, or worse. Like most beginners, on her early outings with her father or with the school, Alison had climbed as a "second," with the rope being taken in above her. Climbing as a second is essentially safe; provided the leader is concentrating, any fall will be arrested by the rope. But it had not taken long for Alison to begin to lead, inevitably a more dangerous but also more exciting activity. As leader, the rope, tied securely to a harness, trailed behind her as she climbed, while her second, usually at this period in her life Bev England, paid out the slack.

When rock climbing began in the 19th century, there was a simple principle that the leader must not fall. To do so was to hit the ground. But over the years, climbers have developed equipment to stop this from happening, "protection" for the leader to limit the length of a fall. The simplest type is a sling draped over a spike or flake of rock or wrapped round a stone wedged in a crack. In the Alps, popular climbs are often strewn with pitons, steel blades hammered into the rock. In Britain, pitons are relatively rare, and climbers usually use wedge-shaped tapered aluminium "nuts," threaded with short lengths of rope or high-tensile wire. Lead climbers place protection wherever it is available and clip the rope to it with a carabiner, an aluminium link with a spring-loaded gate. At the bottom of the pitch, the second feeds out the rope through a special friction device, and if the leader falls, she will hold the rope tight. As long as the leader's rope is clipped through a carabiner attached to a secure piece of protection, she will not fall far.

Yet leading remains a serious activity. It might be that a leader has just managed to arrange protection, and if she slips off the rock, she will not fall more than a foot or two. Sometimes, however, there is no protection near a difficult move, because the rock is blank, devoid of cracks in which to place a nut. In that case, the leader will fall as far as the highest piece of protection, always assuming the force of the fall does not lever it out of the rock, and then the same distance again. In fact, that is an underestimate. Climbing ropes are strong enough to hold the weight of several cars, but in order to reduce the shock of arresting a fall on the human body, they are made very stretchy. A typical nylon rope will stretch 40 percent when first loaded. Thus the falling leader 10 feet above a good piece of protection will fall at least 28 feet, assuming she is more than 28 feet above the ground. It takes time and experience to learn when a crack is the right shape to provide security and what size of nut to use. At the same time, the second must always be attentive. If the second responds slowly in stopping the rope, the leader will fall much farther than necessary. Good climbing partnerships require a degree of trust that goes well beyond that needed in other sports, and in the most literal sense, to lead a climb is to take responsibility for one's future.

The paradox is that it is precisely this element of responsibility, this awareness of what gravity may do if things go wrong, that makes climbing, and especially leading, such an intoxicating activity. Seconding a rock climb can be highly enjoyable, but it can never equal the pure exhilaration of making demanding moves at the "sharp" end of the rope. As a means of relaxing, climbing is unique. Whatever preoccupations a leader may have had before starting a climb, within a short distance of leaving the ground they will have been pushed to the very back of the mind. It is the ultimate displacement activity. Before long, Alison wanted to lead whenever she could, and as she did so, a word with a very particular meaning for climbers entered her vocabulary—"commitment." Being committed, whether it is on a 50-foot crag or a mountain wall two miles high, means going beyond the point where retreat is feasible, where it is almost certainly easier to go on up and reach the top than to climb back down. The point where commitment occurs will vary between individuals, according to their ability. Whatever the level of difficulty, most climbers find the most satisfying routes are those that need commitment, an approach toward a personal limit. The best climbers are those with the skill and determination to push that boundary forward, qualities that Alison had in abundance.

Climbs of all types, on rock, ice, or big mountain walls, are graded. Under the somewhat confusing system used in Britain, the easy climbs Alison was introduced to by her father were graded Difficult or Very Difficult. Most reasonably fit people would manage to second climbs of this level. Before long, she graduated to the next grade up, Severe. By the spring of 1977, Alison was regularly leading routes that were considerably harder, in the Very Severe category. To lead a gritstone VS you have to climb it properly, responding to the rock's choreography, or you will fall off. Some of the handholds will be little more than rounded bulges, enough to steady the balance but useless to haul yourself up on. The footholds will not be comfortable ledges but, sometimes, mere ripples; to stand on them, you must trust the friction between the smooth, sticky rubber soles of your climbing shoes and the rock. Often, protection on gritstone is sparse, and as Alison learned, leaders must be confident in climbing hard moves with the nearest "gear" well below their feet, knowing that if they fall, it may not stop them from hitting the ground. Limestone VSs are generally less dangerous, but they are also mostly longer and steeper, and require more weight to be taken on the arms. The leader needs the strength to finish a climb before getting "pumped," that agonizing condition when arm muscles flood with lactic acid and the fingers, suddenly powerless, uncurl.

To the alarm of her parents, Alison's confidence was so great that she seemed not to notice the potential risks, assuming, like many climbers, that her own awareness of her personal limits would keep her safe. During Easter 1977, she planned a climbing trip with Bev to North Wales, reacting with piqued frustration when John and Joyce vetoed the idea on the grounds that they were not sufficiently experienced. In Wales, they pointed out, many of the climbs are hundreds of feet high, far from roads or habitation. Despite Alison's resentment, her parents' concern was justified. A few weeks later at Lawrencefield, a gritstone quarry near Sheffield, Alison found herself in trouble leading a VS. Unable to reach the next handholds, she tried to climb a different line up the crag to the one the guidebook described. She was well above her last protection. As she committed herself to the hardest move, her feet slipped, and she fell 20 feet, swinging back into the rock below, slamming into the unforgiving slab headfirst. Only a few weeks earlier, her teacher Hilary Collins had nagged her repeatedly about her failure to wear a protective helmet. This time she was wearing one, and it saved her from serious injury.

The first fall as a leader is a heart-stopping moment, especially when it is not expected. There is the sudden shock of parting from the rock and an involuntary yell of fear. Time seems to slow down, and in the intense adrenalin charge of falling, there is a moment to wonder where and how you will come to a stop. If all is well, there is a flood of the purest relief, laughter even, and reassurance to one's friends. Only in her diary did Alison express her customary prayer and how she really felt: "Very shocked and embarrassed. Thank you I wasn't hurt. Thank God for my helmet, definitely broken skull otherwise."

Three months later, on July 10, she fell again, from near the top of Sunset Slab, a badly protected VS on the gritstone of Froggatt Edge. This time she twisted the ligaments in her ankle as she hit the ground, a painful injury that was to dog the first part of her trip to Norway. But she was becoming more insouciant, less prepared to dwell on the horrifying might-have-been. There were some expert climbers at the crag that day, tackling some of Derbyshire's hardest routes, and after her fall Alison concentrated on trying to impress them, basking in the sun. That night she composed another prayer: "Thank you for letting me fall and get away with it—I must be more 'careful'."

And then, on September 18, came something close to nemesis. Alison was at Stanage, climbing with a group from school. She warmed up with a couple of easy climbs, then turned her attention to a well-known classic—Hargreaves' Original Route (named after a climber who is no relation) — a VS on the imposing Black Slab, a series of awkward steps up between spaced, rounded footholds. Alison had no protection at all, nothing to stop her hitting the jagged boulders at the base of the climb if she came off.

As she climbed upward with her usual confidence, trailing a rope for Bev, John Sellars, another Belper student, was playing around on the rock face, traversing horizontally across the slab beneath her. When she was more than 30 feet up, he slipped and fell. For John, it was only a short jolt. But as he fell, he got caught in Alison's rope. His whole weight was suddenly tugging at her waist. "It really did look like slow motion," Bev says. "She had no chance. She was just being peeled off the rock."

There was no sudden bounce as the rope came tight on her harness because there was no protection, and with a few scrapes on protruding edges, Alison went the distance. In one sense she was lucky, landing on the only patch of grass below the entire section of cliff, winded, stunned, but conscious and alive. "If she hadn't done that, I'm sure her injuries would have been much worse," Bev says. "The ground was soft, and absorbed a lot of the impact." Nevertheless, she was in agony. Both legs were twisted beneath her and painful to touch. While her friends tried to keep her warm, burying her shocked body under piles of climbing jackets, someone ran to call the rescue service. Within half an hour she was being stretchered across the moorland to a four-wheel-drive ambulance, then taken to a hospital in Sheffield. There she endured a miserable wait for her parents to give permission for a general anesthetic so that her bones could be set in place. They were enjoying a long hike across the moors somewhere else and could not be found. Finally, at the end of the afternoon, John and Joyce were traced, and the surgeons could do their work. Alison had broken both bones in her lower left leg and cracked her right heel. She would be in plaster for months.

~

CHAPTER 2

THE MISTRESS OF MEERBROOK LEA

Alison prodded the frozen ground with her crutch, searching for purchase in order to swing her injured leg, and trying not to let her toes, emerged from her hated plaster cast, drag in the snow. The path was steep as well as icy; once she had to drop to a crouch and steady herself with her crutchless hand in order to prevent a fall—like a rock climber, she thought to herself, using all four limbs to stay in balance, but on an easy walker's track. At last she reached the top of the natural citadel, with its muffled, wintry view of farms and drystone walls. She turned with a smile to her mother. Anxious as she was, Joyce Hargreaves had known better than to offer assistance during the short climb from the road. In happier times, Alison had swarmed all over the citadel's sunny front face, the pitted limestone towers of Harborough Rocks, regarding their little buttresses as no more than training exercises, too short to need a rope. Now, in the flat light of mid-November, reaching their summit by the path up the side was some kind of triumph.

For weeks she had lain inactive, first in the hospital, then at home, and had hobbled no farther than her mother's car, an infant again. Like any climber with the smallest ration of imagination, she had always accepted the theoretical possibility of getting hurt. But once the adrenalin charge of the fall was over, the reality of her long confinement caught her unprepared. "Alison was a free spirit," says Bev England, "and her freedom—and something of her sense of self-worth—had been taken away." Day after day she filled her diary with the record of her frustration. "Oh for rock," she lamented. "[I] feel short-tempered at the moment. Oh, a woman is so missing snow, ice, rock." Rooted to the sofa in her parents' living room, she spent her evenings annotating her climbing guidebooks, immersing herself in the recollected glories of the previous spring and summer. Aware of her depression, John and Joyce promised her a new rope for Christmas. But however hard she wished to fight her injury, there was no escaping her incapacitation and melancholy. At the end of January, shortly after what should have been her final release, Alison took a tumble on the way to school. In agony again, she was taken back to hospital in an ambulance and was told she needed another month in plaster.

Almost as soon as she could walk unaided, Alison asked Mick Kelly, a friend from school, to take her to her nearest crag, Cromford Black Rocks. With a lot of gentle encouragement, he helped her to second Railway Slab, a route she had once climbed solo without a rope. It was, she told her diary, "so excellent to be climbing again." If she felt any apprehension or fear, she betrayed no sign of it, and over the next ten days, a school holiday, she managed to go climbing five times.

John and Joyce Hargreaves knew their daughter and wanted her to be happy. Her accident had only underlined her need for independence. So it was that as she finally began to recover in the spring of 1978, they suggested she take a part-time weekend job— as a sales assistant at a climbing shop a few miles up the Derwent valley in Matlock Bath, the Bivouac.

Festooned with rucksacks, tents, and sleeping bags hanging from the walls and ceiling, the Bivouac was a dark, cozy place, and both Hargreaves sisters had been visiting it with their parents for years. It sold a wide range of equipment for every kind of outdoor sport: boots and waterproofs for hiking; lamps and flexible ladders for exploring caves; ropes, protection, and harnesses for climbing rocks. Alison and Susan were on first-name terms with its proprietor, Jim Ballard, and when Susan bought a copy of the local caving guidebook he had written, Ballard proudly inscribed his name. For climbers visiting the crags of the southern Peak District, the shop's location was ideal. The limestone crag of High Tor rose opposite the shop front across the Derwent, making the Bivouac a magnet for the local climbing scene. Often young hotshots would drop in after making the first ascent of a new route. "Jim would ply them with tea, get them to describe the climb move by move," a contemporary habitué recalls. "His other customers would be standing round, agog. On those occasions, the place really buzzed."

Jim Ballard, a small, round-shouldered and heavily bearded figure in his mid-30s, made an immediate impact on Alison. Even when there were no famous climbers present, he loved to hold court, showing off his knowledge of climbing's rich literature, casually dropping the names of his more famous customers so that he seemed on first-name terms with Alison's greatest heroes. The

Bivouac, which he had started in 1972 with his wife, Jean, was prospering; they had recently opened a second branch, and as Ballard liked to remind people, he was a self-made man. He was the son of a steelworker, and his upbringing, in a small terraced house in one of the poorer parts of Sheffield, had been extremely tough. He had had none of the educational advantages granted Alison's parents, and had started adult life as an engineering apprentice at the age of 15.

Jim readily agreed to the Hargreaves' suggestion that he take Alison on. By the end of March she was on the mend, and her natural exuberance and optimism flooded back. Her irrepressible presence in Ballard's shop each Saturday could only be good for business. It would also be relatively cheap. Rather than be paid her wages in cash, she asked if she might save them up and take them in kind, in items of climbing gear from the Bivouac's stock.

In her later teens Alison was quick, keen, and humorous, impossible to ignore. Others who knew her at this time still speak of her with undimmed affection. "I've got this image of her in the shop, wearing a ski sweater, her hair piled up in a topknot and spraying out, smiling and sparkle-eyed," says Dawn Hopkinson, a Derby educationist who met her through the Bivouac and later accompanied her on some difficult climbs. "She seemed mad, brave, always going for it, laughing. I just thought she was great, a superb person."

Alison's job at the Bivouac gave her access to a different, adult world, peopled by climbers, some of them well-known, who drove their own cars and didn't have to worry about what time they got home. On her first Saturday she struck up an acquaintance with Paul Howarth, the shop manager. The following weekend, after work, he drove Alison and Bev England to North Wales, where he had reserved space at a climbers' club cottage in Nant Peris, in the heart of the mountains. They arrived in time for a drink at the Padarn Lake Hotel, one of the hubs of the Welsh climbing scene. There sipping pints were two of Alison's heroes, the bluff, straight-talking Don Whillans, author of desperate first ascents from the Derbyshire gritstone edges to Himalayan giants, and Ron Fawcett, then thought of as being the best rock climber in the world.

From the moment of first acquaintance, Alison wanted to be part of that world, to be known and accepted by it as a climber to be reckoned with in her own right. She saw none of its insularity or sacrifice, the way in which those who dedicated their lives to the sport so often seemed to have turned their backs on most of the rest of society and culture, to the extent that they seemed unable to hold a meaningful conversation about anything else. Nor did she dwell on the ghosts who hover round the fringes of every popular climber's social venue, the absent friends remembered and mourned. To Alison, climbing seemed the most glamorous and important thing in the world, and her energy and enthusiasm were accompanied by a certain impatience, a sense that she had to get things done before life passed her by.

As school began again in the autumn of 1978, she found another way of realizing her ambitions in the shape of the Derwent Mountaineering Club, a small but highly motivated group of climbers who lived nearby, some of whom had climbed big and difficult mountains. Like dozens of similar clubs across the country, the Derwent organized climbing trips almost every weekend. They would stay in one of the numerous climbing huts in North Wales, the Lake District, or Scotland, basic accommodation with communal bunk beds and gas rings, designed for people for whom material comforts, at least during their leisure time, are not highly valued. Most of the Derwent climbers were years older than Alison, but she appeared to find no difficulty in holding her own with them. Soon she was attending their weekly meeting at a local pub, joining them on other weekdays for training sessions on the cliffs or in the gym, and going off with them at the weekend whenever she could.

Alison was leading a strange double life. In her diary she still dwelt at length on the concerns of an ordinary schoolgirl: which lessons had interested her; that afternoon's sports schedule; which kind of chocolate she had bought at morning break. Her evenings and weekends were a voyage of discovery into an adult world, in which almost everything she did was related, one way or another, to climbing rocks and mountains. By now Susan had started her first year at Oxford University, where, like her parents, she read mathematics. One weekend in February 1979, Alison was due to visit her and then, at short notice, postponed the trip. She had had a better offer, the chance to spend a week learning to climb on vertical ice in the snow-clad Scottish mountains with her older friends.

They saw none of the conflict that Alison sometimes experienced at home, nor her failing attempts to interest herself in academic work. Many of them were at least a little in love with her. "She was so very excited, and extremely competent, tough and quick to learn," says Gerry Lidgett, her partner for most of the week in Scotland. "She was almost fearless, always perky, bubbly, bright. Her whole passion was climbing."

The Derwent had rented a chalet in Glen Coe, the sombre, claustrophobic valley in the West Highlands, where the Mac-Donald clan had been massacred by the Earl of Argyll's regiment in 1692. The mountains were deep in snow, and their crags, the tallest more than 1,000 feet high, were seamed with ice. Each day started early, well before dawn, with the beep of alarm clocks and hot, greasy breakfasts forced into bodies that wanted still to be sleeping. Then came the struggle through knee-deep snow to reach the base of the cliffs, every step a wearying effort, weighed down by heavy rucksacks full of climbing gear. Instead of the fluid, balletic grace needed to move well on rock, winter climbing requires determination, endurance, and immunity to cold. Strapped to Alison's thick leather boots were crampons, steel claws that are kicked into the ice to get a purchase. Each crampon had two front points, which stuck out horizontally. On steeper sections, Alison learned she had to kick the front points in and trust her weight to them, though sometimes they penetrated less than half an inch into the ice. In each hand she clasped an ice ax, swinging each alternately and then hanging off their curved blades as she brought her feet up and kicked them back into the ice. Sometimes the ice was brittle and shattered on impact; sometimes rock lurked close to the surface and the ax would jar her arm and bounce back out. She learned to listen for the solid *thwunk* of a strong, secure placement, and happily pulled up.

Most of the climbs followed narrow gullies, ice-choked gutters sunk deeply into the rock. They acted as natural channels for snow being blown down the mountains from the powder-laden summit slopes, and for the frozen debris Gerry dislodged with his axes and crampons as he led. Huddled on the belay ledges, Alison tried to retreat into the warmth of her thick pile jacket and anorak, shivering and ducking beneath the bombardment of falling ice, remembering to remain attentive in paying out the rope. Her hands, despite thick woolen mitts and undergloves, would slowly freeze.

As the rope came tight and she started to follow each pitch, she felt a fierce, hot aching as blood seeped back into her fingers.

Yet as she climbed, the blue-and-white vista of the Highlands unfolded like a glittering vision of the Arctic, and the air she sucked into her lungs took on the cold, dry brilliance of champagne. In the grip of a real winter, Britain's mountains grow in both stature and beauty. In summer, a climb like the Aonach Eagach, a crenellated ridge that forms Glencoe's northern rim, is an undemanding scramble, often spoiled by crowds. In winter, it becomes an expedition on an alpine scale, a traverse over icy pinnacles above vast, snowy drops, with long views across neighboring peaks and over the sea lochs to the west, strips of gold in the sun.

Exhausted and as content as she had ever been, Alison arrived home to find her parents away in North Wales. She spent the afternoon before their return cooking them an enormous meal: roast pork with four vegetables, gravy, and apple sauce, followed by Baked Alaska. Despite solemn promises before her departure, in her week away she had not so much as looked at a school textbook. This was a meal marinaded in guilt.

In Scotland, on the summit of Stob Coire nan Lochan, Alison met Nigel Shepherd, a trainee mountain guide from Wales in his early 20s. They spent an evening together, and after the trip was over, he wrote to her. "Grand, ta, overwhelmed," she told her diary the day his letter arrived, "HAPPY." A few weeks later, at the end of March, John and Joyce agreed to let her stay the weekend at Nigel's house in Snowdonia. He met her on the Saturday evening at Bangor station, where Alison was thrilled to be offered the pillion seat on his motorbike. The following day they roared across the hills to the crags at Tremadog, and when it began to rain after only one route, they ducked inside the small café at the base of the cliff. Run by Eric Jones, the first Briton to climb the north face of the Eiger solo, it was decorated with pictures of climbing stars in action, several of whom sat at its bleached pine pews. To Alison's delight, Nigel knew them all. Confident and good-looking, he was in some ways similar to Alison, but closer to achieving the ambitions they shared.

After another idyllic visit, Alison believed she was in love for the first time. Until now, the best surviving record of her inner life, her diary, had not dwelt much on romance. She had developed a few teenage crushes, and one or two uncommitting relationships with climbers, but this was different. She went to stay with Shepherd for a few days during the school holidays, delighting herself with domesticity. While Nigel worked at his new job as a climbing instructor, Alison went shopping and cooked him huge meals.

When the relationship ended, Alison was overwhelmed by a sense of loss. She had arranged to see him again one weekend in April, and managed to organize a lift back to Wales with Geoff Douglas, a member of the Derwent Mountaineering Club. When Alison arrived at Nigel's house toward the end of the evening, the only sign of him was a letter, addressed to her, in which he explained that he was still involved with someone else. Fortunately for Alison, Geoff was waiting in the car outside. They drove in silence across Snowdonia and the Isle of Anglesey, where they pitched a tent at midnight in a gale, above the sea cliffs at Craig Gogarth, on the edge of the Atlantic. There they climbed the following day, the sky a deep and unremitting gray, the dull ocean pounding the foot of the gray-green cliffs. The following day she met Shepherd in a café and they went for a dispiriting walk. It was over.

For weeks she refused to accept the inevitable, clinging to the hope that Nigel would choose to be with her after all. She wrote him long unhappy letters to which he never replied, bit her fingernails to the quick, and spent her evenings guzzling biscuits and Coca-Cola. Her diary became a record of anguish deeper than any she had known. "Nigel's a swine and he's hurt me," she wrote one day, "felt unwanted, unhappy, lonely and generally undesirable." Slowly, as he maintained his silence, grief was replaced by resignation: "For last time—looked for post—nothing. Upset. Today —this evening—I wept." Alison tried to forget Shepherd with her usual frenetic activity: working, climbing, and going to climbers' parties. Eventually, months later, he made contact, and they took up an awkward friendship. Their brief affair had exposed a vulnerability that she neither liked nor understood. She hated wanting something she could not have, and as she had loathed the helplessness caused by her broken leg, so she cursed not only her loss but her sense, as she saw it, of becoming emotionally dependent and vulnerable.

As in 1978, she spent much of the summer working in Jim Ballard's shop. Almost every evening she was out climbing as well. In North Wales, Ron Fawcett had climbed an important new route called Lord of the Flies, starting a fresh wave of interest in Welsh climbing, and most weekends Alison found herself a part of this vibrant scene. She was a regular visitor of its central venues: Eric Jones's café at Tremadog; Pete's Eats, a diner for climbers with gargantuan appetites, at Llanberis, the old slaters' village at the foot of Snowdon; smoky, no-frills pubs like the Padarn, also in Llanberis. The crags in North Wales are on a grander scale than in Alison's native Peak District, and the best of them lie in the mountains, high above screes and lonely lakes. She loved these bigger challenges, where the weather, and loose or greasy rock, might leave the outcome in doubt until the very end. For Alison, the Peak District, with its short cliffs near the road, was only a training ground; Wales was true climbing.

Almost recovered from her broken leg, Alison was getting noticed, partly because of her gender but also for her obvious determination and ambition. She was tackling harder routes of widely differing types: smooth, easy-angled slabs with tiny holds, which she padded up using just the friction of her soles on the rock; steep, brutally strenuous crack-climbs found in abundance on Peak District gritstone, where the key to success is sheer muscular effort; the intricacies of limestone, with its tiny edges and pockets, which demand steel-like finger strength. There is no mystery to the addictive allure of climbing. Provided the route is accomplished in good style, the equation is extremely simple: the harder the climb, the greater the pleasure and satisfaction in doing it. All too easily, the goals and ambitions of conventional life begin to fall away. When school began again in September, her concentration was suffering. "HAPPY. In love with Welsh 'scene'," she wrote one Monday. "BAD during lessons ... In love with Wales/climbing, I can't settle to life at school."

Apart from her obsession with climbing, there was nothing to distinguish Alison from thousands of other sixth-form schoolgirls the length and breadth of the country. She had applied to read geography at several universities, all chosen for their proximity to good rock-climbing areas, and had been accepted, conditional on achieving good results in her A-level examinations the following summer. She spent much of December rehearsing a minor part in the school play. After spending Christmas at home, she flew to Spain with the Derwent Mountaineering Club to climb on the sunny limestone of the Costa Blanca. None of her friends noticed anything unusual about her demeanor. However, she was only weeks away from a decision that would profoundly change the course of her life.

From the day Alison began working at the Bivouac in April 1978, Jim Ballard found himself taking a keen interest in his new Saturday girl. He had climbed for years, albeit without great distinction, and the mere fact that here was a girl with such strength and determination made her an object of curiosity. Like many older men she had met, he found himself trying to impress her.

The face Jim Ballard showed to the world was blunt and confident. He liked to describe himself as a "professional Yorkshireman," proudly endorsing a stereotype in which macho plainspeaking could be taken to extremes. This persona hid some deep insecurities. He had, for example, suffered intermittently from agoraphobia, which at its worst prevented him from leaving his house for days at a time. He often spoke of what he had achieved without the benefit of higher education, and if he discovered that one of his staff had a degree, he would dwell on it endlessly, as if the graduate in question must be a towering intellectual. "He used to tell sales reps he was used to big orders and large sums of money because he'd worked in the aircraft industry," one of his staff recalls. "In fact, the closest he'd come to aircraft parts was when he worked in a factory." Jim was a member of the Derwent Mountaineering Club, but much as he liked to hold the floor with his customers, in more sociable situations he was ill at ease. He was seen only seldom at the weekly club meetings, and even more rarely on their outings to the crags.

To Alison, Ballard's insecurities were invisible. She saw only his apparent confidence, and his acid comments on departing customers could reduce her to hysterical laughter. One day, as she was about to sell two expensive ropes, Jim interrupted her, shouting across the shop that the buyer had better beware, because these were "Mickey Mouse ropes." To the customer's bewilderment, Alison responded with helpless, giggling mirth. She was also impressed by what she saw as Ballard's personal freedom. He had money but, unlike her parents, could be his own boss, and he took frequent trips to ski or climb in the Alps, sometimes with his wife, Jean. As Alison told her diary, he seemed to have an enviable way of life.

Within a few weeks of her starting work, when she was still barely 16, a friendship sprang up between Jim and Alison that went beyond business. With breathless excitement, she told her diary how he had offered to take her climbing, and throughout the spring and summer of 1978, they visited the Peak District crags together. Often they ate at pubs afterward, and she returned home very late, creating another source of conflict with her parents.

Nevertheless, if there had been an element of mutual attraction in her relationship with Jim, by the time Alison fell for Nigel Shepherd in the spring of 1979, it appeared to be over. She had never written in her diary explicitly of her feelings for Jim, whatever they might have been. Now, after months of frequent mentions, he virtually dropped out of the record. Nor did they climb together. Right through the autumn of 1979, Alison's journal maintained its humdrum tone. Then, at the beginning of 1980, for the first time in seven years, she ceased writing in it altogether.

Alison's 18th birthday, on February 17, 1980, the day she legally came of age, fell at the start of the school half-term holiday. The previous evening, a Saturday, John and Joyce took her out to dinner at Ramsden's in Derby, a favorite local steak house. They passed the time pleasantly, reminiscing about her childhood. Next morning Alison arrived at the breakfast table with a packed overnight bag. Jim's wife, Jean, had left him, she announced, and she planned to keep him company at his house in the hills a few miles away, Meerbrook Lea. She would be spending the night there, she said. Her parents may have had misgivings, but their daughter was now an adult. "We knew she had to have her own life," Joyce says. John gave her a lift to her job at the Bivouac, expecting to see her at home the following night.

The following day John and Joyce went to work as usual. They got home about half past five. There was no sign of Alison. They remained unconcerned; it was hardly exceptional for their daughter to be out. But as the evening wore on without her sending word, they began to wonder where she was. Finally, at about nine o'clock, Joyce decided to telephone Jim Ballard and ask if he knew. He passed the telephone to Alison. Her words struck her mother like hammer blows. Alison said she had been unhappy at home for many months. Jim was her lover, and she intended to stay with him permanently.

Jim came back on the line and offered to come to Belper to talk to Alison's parents. Joyce covered the receiver with her hand, and after a hurried conference with John, she told Ballard that they would drive up to Meerbrook Lea. "As Joyce put the phone down, we felt shattered," John says. "We were both in tears."

They prepared for their encounter with Jim and Alison in a state of bewildered shock. But as John and Joyce made the short drive up the valley to Alison's new home, they knew two things were paramount. The first was that Alison, wherever she lived, must somehow finish her education. The second was that while they might recoil from her new situation, they had to accept both Jim and what their daughter had done or risk losing her forever.

Jim, Alison, and her parents talked in the living room at Meerbrook Lea for almost two hours. "Jim took the initiative," John recalls. "He seemed to do most of the talking. She seemed in awe of him, almost under his thumb. He wasn't objectionable or rude. But he was very forthright and firm." Alison, he told John and Joyce, was an adult, and had every right to do as she wished. She had made her decision, and it was final. For a short while John and Joyce tried to persuade Alison that she ought to come home. Before long, however, they saw that this was futile. "It was a very emotional exchange," John says. "She started to realize how much she was upsetting us. It hadn't really dawned on her. It was the sheer suddenness of it; we'd had no idea she'd been as unhappy as she said she was. We both wept."

The following morning, she wrote John and Joyce a letter. Written neatly in blue ink, it was free of changes or crossings-out, and they suspected it was the product of several drafts. As an account of her emotions and of the events preceding her departure, it was far from illuminating. Indeed, Alison began her letter with an apology for her inability to communicate: "I suppose it's my problem/weakness cropping up again, but I find it very hard to explain myself." The tone of much of what followed was also apologetic. She was sorry to have acted deceitfully in having concealed her relationship with Ballard; sorry for hurting them and for causing "inconvenience." The previous evening, she went on, had been "very daunting for all of us." But she hoped it marked a new beginning, as well as the end of the first stage in her relationship with her parents. Above all, it had "opened my eyes to how much I really love you, for all you've done and given me." In the future, she wrote, she hoped she would be able to return her parents' love, as they had always deserved. There was only one phrase that hinted at her true mental state: "I'm not trying to escape from the family for good, just becoming the independent person I feel I need to be."

Some of its unstated meaning was uncovered some time later by Alison's cousin Daphne when she visited Alison at Meerbrook Lea. In her own way Daphne had been as rebellious as Alison, resisting the censure of her mother—Joyce's sister—much as Alison had done. "I understood her and what she was doing." As they sat in the garden outside her new home, Alison told Daphne that what she craved was free will, a sense that she could be the agent of her destiny. Daphne still recalls the words Alison used to describe her decision to leave home: "I had to go, I couldn't stand the expectation." According to Daphne, "She felt there was a whole world out there and she was going to have it." Her sudden, secret action was both a rebellion against the future her family had envisaged for her, and also a means of realizing her ambition as a climber. It took the explosive form it did because Alison and her family seemed to have no means of defusing the tensions between them. They had built to the point where Alison believed they could only be resolved by a radical decision to break free.

At the same time, Alison thought that having made the break, it was irrevocable. She knew how deeply she had disappointed her parents' expectations. She did not appreciate how far her parents' love was already pushing them to reach an accommodation, the extent to which they remained determined not to create an unbridgeable gulf. Until Easter, she continued to spend the weekdays at her family home, as agreed. It was a strange time. "We carried on as normally as we could," Joyce says. "We just didn't talk about what had happened. It made us too upset, and it made

Alison angry." "It was a traumatic time for them all," Daphne recalls. "But Alison dealt with that trauma by being even more determined to make things work. She had made her bed. Now she would show everyone else how determined she was to lie in it."

She had kept her relationship a secret not only from her family but from her closest friends. When she told Bev England, her first reaction was astonishment. "My God, woman," she said, "with all these hunks out there, why in the world do you want to go off with him?" Jim Ballard, 36 years old, who smoked heavily—a habit Alison always loathed—seemed a surprising choice. Bev remains convinced that Jim's practical assets were much more important to Alison than feelings of romantic love. "Even at the very start, when she first told me, she didn't say she was in love with him. She was intoxicated with the idea of becoming an adult: of having her own kitchen, with no one watching over her, telling her what to do. And she was desperate to climb, and she thought that living with Jim would give her the freedom to follow her desire."

Bev's judgment is too harsh. Alison did believe she was in love—albeit that this time, unlike with Nigel, she had also convinced herself she was in control. A passage in her diary—which she resumed a few weeks after moving—serves to confirm the depth of her affection. Toward the end of August, Jim was away for a few days at a trade fair. Alison missed him deeply, and when he returned home in the middle of the night, she leaped out of bed as soon as she heard him fumbling with his key. Inside the house, they went into the dining room, where there were "more nice surprises in the way of presents, lots and lots."

Jim showered her with gifts and gave her the use of his car. Her fellow pupils would watch in amazement and envy as she drove through the school gates in his Renault 25. A few weeks after Alison moved in with Jim, Paul Howarth married his girlfriend, Sally. For the wedding Jim bought Alison a red-and-black designer suit. He gave her some Chanel No. 5, a perfume he remembered noticing during his own impoverished childhood, when it seemed like a symbol of fabulous, unattainable wealth. Many months earlier Alison had expressed her envy of Hilary Collins, who had a man, a car, and a job. Now she herself had the first two.

She had, however, missed the opportunity of higher education. By the time she began to live with Jim, her zest for book learning had been fading fast. Alison took her A-level exams but failed physics altogether, and in maths and geography achieved grades below the standard required to gain a place at university.

To John and Joyce this was a bitter disappointment, and for a long time relations between Alison, Jim, and her parents were uneasy. "She became very self-contained," Joyce says. "It was as if she had a shell round her. Sometimes you'd see a crack in it, and you'd almost get through; then it would close up again." When the four dined together, they usually played cards. "It was a way of easing the atmosphere. It meant we didn't have to make conversation." Alison's regular walks with her family, which had gone on even in the months immediately before her departure, ceased.

Instead, she took to her new life with relish. Meerbrook Lea is an attractive stone-built house, set amid woods and meadows, with views across rolling hills. It is a secluded place, removed from the bustle of Matlock and the traffic on the A6 trunk road threading its way down the Derwent Valley. There are roses round the door, a huge lawn, flowerbeds, apple trees, and a tall copper beech by the front window. Inside, the rooms are a little gloomy, but a spacious kitchen floored with earthenware tiles looks out to the garden, the green fields of the surrounding hills filling its big windows. The bedrooms are cozy, with dormers built into the eaves. The contrast with suburban Belper could hardly have been more marked. It was an extraordinary demesne for a girl of 18 to possess.

She made a striking impression on her new farming neighbours, Ted and Jackie Johnson. "I liked her straightaway," Ted says, "she had so much energy and joy. She'd run up and down that garden with an industrial-size Flymo, wearing a sweatband and her little shorts. Jim would be watching, reading a book." From the very beginning they noticed that it was Alison who did most of the physical work.

In her resumed diary Alison's authorial voice was almost unrecognizable. Previously, it had been the unselfconscious record of a passionate and lively teenage girl. Now it was arch, mannered, with more than a hint that she was sending herself up, littered with phrases like "taking luncheon," "depositing the cleaning lady," and "a leisurely drive was undertaken." Alison might still have been spending her weekdays at school, but Alison the schoolgirl was gone forever. In her place was the mistress of Meerbrook Lea, a freshly minted grown-up trying to conceal her naivety. Four years earlier Alison had been thrilled by the continental quilts and scrumptious meals she found in Austrian hotels. Now she felt a similar excitement for the novelties of an unfamiliar domestic routine.

In July, and again in October, Jim, Alison, and John Cook, a friend from up the valley who had worked with Jim at the engineering works, spent two fortnights in France, touring various sunny crags. The sun shone, the rock was warm, the food and wine a considerable distraction. Now she became the English lady abroad, slipping into a swanky Franglais. The ingenue escorted by the older man, Alison was touchingly unaware of her own unworldliness. At Buoux, in Provence, Jim took her to see "naked lady friends" having their lunch at a "pique-nique site." Later, on a visit to the Calanques sea cliffs near Marseilles, they walked to "Port Miou and Port Pain to see where naked bathing takes place." Others, such as Jim's staff, stunned by Alison's sudden rise from Saturday shop assistant to boss's girlfriend, saw through the pose without much difficulty. "She had led a very sheltered life, and all she had really done was climbing. It wasn't surprising she didn't seem old for her years," one of them recalls. "But I was a little surprised when we were in the car one day and she pointed to a building, and asked if this were a terraced house."

Generous as Jim was, his pending divorce from Jean and her share in the business involved paying a heavy financial price. He had always supplemented his income from the shops with a little manufacturing, mainly of the steel-wire and aluminium ladders used by cavers for descending vertical drops. In the autumn of 1980 Alison took the first steps to start manufacturing other products for climbers. They bought an industrial sewing machine and various materials, and she began making gear items: bags for the magnesium carbonate chalk powder climbers use to absorb the sweat on their fingers; nylon gaiters to seal walking boots when crossing wet terrain. Later, as Alison's business grew, there would be climbing harnesses, small rucksacks, and clothing. From the age of 17, Alison had signed her name with a big, flamboyant lowercase *a*, embellished with a smiling face, like a personal trademark. She used the same motif as a label, and *Faces* became her trading name. She now had something of her own to develop into a potential living.

Yet even at the beginning, some believed that Alison's relationship with Jim had its negative side. The next member of the Hargreaves clan to visit Alison at her new home was Susan, who returned to Derbyshire at the start of her Easter vacation. "Jim tried hard to create a good impression. I got on with him very well. But Alison seemed subservient, the servant. She was already doing everything around the house. Jim loved to show her off, he was incredibly proud he had this attractive younger girl hanging on his arm. But Alison had missed her youth. Jim seemed opinionated. He used to joke about her lack of political knowledge. You could see him trying to bring her under his control. She seemed sort of tame, compared to how she used to be."

There was another unforeseen consequence for Alison of moving in with Jim. As a schoolgirl and a member of the Derwent Mountaineering Club, her social life had been extremely busy. She had many friends of both genders, and as many invitations to parties as anyone could have wished. By comparison, Jim was a virtual recluse. Aside from John Cook, he had few friends, and almost his only social contacts were with people he knew through his work. He saw no reason why Alison's arrival meant he ought to change. Instead, it was her social horizons that shrank to conform with his. After February 1980, few of the Derwent climbers ever saw her again. She kept in touch with Bev England, but only intermittently. And although the climbing world itself is highly sociable, Jim and Alison were strangely removed from its mainstream, living their isolated, pressurized life at Meerbrook Lea.

By the summer of 1982, Alison's diary had lost the mannered tone she had used in the aftermath of leaving home. At the same time, the heady, sweet romanticism with which she had once expressed her feelings for Ballard was rarer and less voluble. She felt Jim expected too much of her and that everything she did was wrong. Life had become too serious, without the moments of fun that had characterized their early relationship. All she seemed to do was cook and clean for him. Little by little, Alison was becoming less the moneyed country wife, more a common drudge.

In the autumn there were the first signs of what was to become a recurring theme. On several occasions Jim accused Alison of not pulling her weight with the business, usually on days when his own work had not been going well. On November 2, she had a typical day. She did all the household chores, sewed Faces gear until five o'clock, then made Jim's tea. Her best, she wrote, was apparently not good enough.

Two days later they were still not on speaking terms, but as the year drew to a close sales in the shops picked up, and Jim and Alison seemed to forget their differences. On New Year's Eve Alison prayed that 1983 would "be just as good" as the year that had passed. For Christmas, Jim and her parents clubbed together to buy her present, a Kenwood Chef food mixer. "Ta very much," she wrote in her diary. "It's grand." She was still just 20 years old.

CHAPTER 3

ROUTES TO THE TOP

Alison Hargreaves may have been unusual, but she was not yet breaking new ground. A woman had climbed Mont Blanc as early as 1808, albeit as a publicity stunt for her local business. The first famous woman mountaineer, the French aristocrat Henriette d'Angeville, overcame the opposition of the Catholic Church and wrote a book about her ascent of the same mountain in 1838. In fact, women were involved in mountaineering as a sport from the very beginning, although in small numbers. Lucy Walker started climbing in the Alps in 1859, wearing heavy skirts and surviving on a diet of sponge cake and champagne. Her great rival, the American Meta Breevort, climbed throughout the range with her dog Tschingel. By the early 20th century, women were climbing in Britain as well as in the Alps; in 1937 Berridge and Clare Mallory, sisters of George Leigh Mallory, who was killed near the summit of Everest in 1924, took part in the first ascent of Sunset Crack on Clogwyn Du'r Arddu, a huge, brooding cliff on the north side of Snowdon. Other women, such as Nea Morin, were prepared to lead new routes long before the days of good equipment, on cliffs that were covered in loose rock and greasy vegetation.

But despite this long history of women's involvement in climbing and mountaineering, the numbers of women actually doing it were small, and their standard generally modest. The idea of a woman mountaineer joining one of the attempts on Everest between the world wars was ridiculed; the social attitudes of the period would not have allowed it. When a Frenchwoman, Anne Bernard, applied to join the 1922 expedition to Everest, the selection panel responded: "It is impossible for the Mount Everest Committee to contemplate the application of a lady of whatever nationality to take part in a future expedition to Everest. The difficulties would be too great."

The assumption that women were not prepared for or able to cope with the physical and mental demands of the more difficult routes prevailed until the 1970s, when women started climbing the world's biggest mountains. Everest was first climbed by a woman, a Japanese housewife called Junko Tabei, in 1975, 22 years after the first ascent by a man. But it was the Polish mountaineer Wanda Rutkiewicz who was the real innovator, organizing women-only expeditions to Himalayan giants such as the 26,660-foot Nanga Parbat and later becoming the first woman to climb K2. She was tough, charismatic, driven, and successful but even she believed that women lagged behind men physiologically, comparing top women climbers to track athletes who couldn't reach the standards of their male counterparts. However, her example inspired many others, and the numbers and standards of women mountaineers have increased exponentially in the last 20 years.

In the early 1980s, however, women were still hugely outnumbered by men, and in the macho Peak District climbing scene, Alison was isolated from other female climbers and barely aware of their activity. All that was about to change. News of her ability had reached the Manchester office of the British Mountaineering Council, and Alison was invited in June 1982 to join a group of about 20 women in the first international women's climbing meet organized in Britain. For a fortnight she and the other participants would be driven around the country, visiting a variety of crags, fêted and subsidized by the climbing establishment, with the express purpose of giving impetus and focus to women's climbing in Britain.

For Alison this was recognition, and on opening day, she had her first taste of national publicity as the women were photographed and interviewed by a national tabloid newspaper, the *Daily Mail*. Alison probably learned more as a climber in that fortnight than during any comparable period in her life. Inspired by her companions, she led several climbs significantly more difficult than any she had previously attempted. For years now, she had been happily leading routes rated Very Severe, and the next grade up, Hard Very Severe. Above that category is a whole new realm of difficulty: Extremely Severe. Climbing with some of the Bivouac's male staff and customers, Alison had seconded plenty of extremes, but she had never led one. She knew what they entailed: extremes were either more difficult or more strenuous or both; resting places were less frequent and the holds smaller. To place protection might mean hanging from the fingers of one hand, with the feet smeared on tiny excrescences. The psychological barrier for any climber is daunting, but for a woman in a world where very few women climbed extremes, it was nerve-racking. Early on during the international meet, she realized there was a handful of women for whom leading climbs of this standard had become a regular occurrence. It didn't take long before she resolved to try one herself.

Her debut was audacious. Climbers speak of routes which are a "soft touch" at the grade, climbs where the guidebook writer has perhaps been a little generous. Alison's first extreme lead, the Quartz Icicle on the Craig Gogarth cliffs of Holyhead island, was no soft touch. It starts in the depths of Wen Zawn, a giant-size bite from the coastline, its base washed by the sea, the rock sometimes loose. Merely to reach the start involves an exposed scramble down steep grass banks along the edge of a 300-foot drop. Next comes an awkward, diagonal rappel to what the guidebook describes as a ledge but is, in fact, a few good footholds, less than 12 inches wide, 100 feet above the sea.

Here Alison's French partner, Meije le Cottier, slotted two protection nuts into cracks in the rock, clipped them with carabiners, and attached herself to them by the rope tied to her harness. Now she was safely belayed, and if Alison fell while leading, at least she would not pull Meije into the ocean. She clipped Alison's ropes through the friction device on her harness and waited for her leader to start climbing. Alison breathed deeply, smelled the tang of ozone, noticed the way the top of the crag, so distant, reared up against the sky. She dipped her fingers into the bag of chalk dust hanging from her waist, drying her anxiously sweating fingers before grasping the first handholds. "Okay," she said. "Climbing."

Quartz Icicle is the kind of route that requires a cool head, a climb where a leader who fails to suppress her fear will fail or fall. The rock is quartzite, bleached from green to brilliant, grainy white, which runs to thin, sometimes wobbly flakes. Each move involves a delicate shift from one flake to the next, a calm, unhurried transfer of weight. The angle is just less than vertical, and it is vital to stay in balance, not to lunge. On the huge slab at the back of Wen Zawn, there are few cracks, few opportunities to place protection, and the sea has left the rock slippery with accumulated salt. Often, a slip would mean a fall of 40 feet or more.

Alison saw nothing but the rock in front of her toes and fingers and the next move. She ran out 120 feet of rope until she reached the shelter of a broken rocky chimney running down the slab. Here she belayed, taking in the rope while Meije climbed to join her. There was another long pitch to go. Alison led this too, and then, as the sun glinted on a family of seals at the foot of the Wen Zawn, she lay back in the warm grass, dry-mouthed, smiling, flooded with joy and relief.

The international meet exposed Alison to people and values from worlds very different to her own. She struck up an instant friendship with Catherine Freer, a practicing psychologist from the Pacific Northwest of the United States. Freer, urbane, vibrant, and highly educated, was open to ideas and subjects that Alison had barely noticed. She was also 13 years older, and Alison, always hungry to learn from her elders, found her greater experience very impressive. Catherine was one of the first Americans she had met, and she discovered an attraction for Americans' outlook on life; their apparent self-confidence and ease in discussing their emotions, qualities that Alison was well aware she lacked.

For her part, Alison impressed Catherine by her general mountaineering skills. Catherine was a talented performer on rock, but unlike Alison, she had spent little time trudging across wild hills. One day, when the meet had moved to the Lake District, Alison guided her round the fells that ring the Langdale Valley, all the way navigating by compass, scrambling through the drizzle and cloud. Both women had similar dreams for the future of climbing big mountains, perhaps in the Himalaya, and after the meet they remained in regular contact.

One thing Alison was not was politically aware. Others she met that June had pondered their place in climbing very seriously, with a developed feminist perspective, and for them, the meet had a significance beyond the opportunity to climb a few routes in pleasant female company. They found Alison difficult to understand. Even during the meet, Jim Ballard often made appearances, chauffeuring her from crag to crag, hanging around to take pictures. By contrast, the British climber Jill Lawrence, one of the meet's leading figures, was an academic lesbian feminist, witheringly critical of women who held traditional gender attitudes. She found Alison immature and naive, materially secure, and free to go climbing simply because she had moved in with a man 16 years her senior. During the meet, Lawrence began a relationship with the American Rosie Andrews, arguably then the leading woman rock climber in the world, and their energy and ambition percolated through the group, even if their opinions were not universally popular.

At the end of the meet, Rosie, Jill, and Alison visited a Peak District gritstone outcrop, Higgar Tor. The two older women set about a notorious extreme, the Rasp. The names of rock climbs sometimes give a clue to their nature, and the Rasp is one such example. Continuously overhanging for 50 feet, the route is a long, abrasive struggle, where a leader must hang in space from her arm, and fight to place protection. Rosie tried first and got halfway before falling. When she had been lowered back to the ground, Jill took over and pushed a little farther before she too ran out of strength and retreated. When it came to Alison's turn, protection had been placed most of the way up the cliff and she could concentrate on simply climbing, without having to stop. She reached the top where the other two had failed.

News of Alison's ascent spread rapidly through the climbing grapevine, and Jill Lawrence was furious. Climbing might appear to be a noncompetitive sport, but many of its participants spend a high proportion of their time trying to work out their ranking in relation to others. When two climbers meet for the first time, they undertake a ritual, a series of questions, asked in apparent innocence, tailored to discover which one has tackled the harder routes. As important as their difficulty is the style in which these routes were accomplished: did the climber make progress only using the rock's natural holds, for example, or did she use "aid," assist the ascent by pulling on a piece of protection? Inside the subculture, cheating or claiming a route unfairly is a serious offense, and the punishment for persistent offenders is exile from the tribe.

It was clear that Alison hadn't led the Rasp purely on her own efforts but had built on the groundwork, the line of protection, laid by the others. It is unlikely Alison overstated her own contribution, but if someone had been broadcasting her "victory" over Lawrence and Andrews on the Rasp, it is possible she was content to let the mistake go. Whatever the truth, some of Lawrence's friends believed Alison had gone too far by attempting to overshadow her elders and betters. She was forcefully criticized, mainly in her absence. As time went on, the story grew in the telling, becoming the start of a largely undeserved reputation for hyperbole among some climbers, which Alison would find extremely difficult to lose.

The argument was an unfortunate end to Alison's brilliant fortnight, and her self-confidence, so recently inflated, crashed. A few days after the women's meet ended, she tried to lead an awkward crack climb at Froggatt Edge, but fell, ripping out the protection she had placed and landing in a heap in front of several Sheffield climbers she perceived as being influential. They probably thought nothing of it, but Alison noted in her diary: "I'm frightened that people expect me to climb so well all the time and I can't cope." Having left home and turned her back on university, she now felt doubly compelled to succeed as a climber.

At the same time, she faced the additional pressure that Jim was as vicariously ambitious for her as she was herself. As far as he was concerned, Alison was, or at least soon would be, the best female rock climber in the world. To the staff at the Bivouac, to customers and friends, he sometimes seemed to have one sole topic of conversation: Alison's astonishing prowess. "He seemed to worship the ground she walked on," says Sally Skinner, Jim's finance manager. "He put her on a pedestal." Jim didn't confine his admiration to the shop, persistently telephoning climbing magazine editors and demanding coverage for his girlfriend. Sometimes it worked, and one or two magazines asked her to write articles. But Jim's overzealous efforts at publicizing Alison's achievements did not always succeed.

Alison was beginning to see herself as a professional climber, who would one day make a good living from her sport. Her diary reveals the extent to which she had taken Jim's assessments at face value. She needed, she wrote one day, to think about developing some kind of systematic training regimen in order, as she put it, to "stay at the top" of world climbing. As it was, Alison was certainly fit, but her training consisted of nothing more scientific than regular runs over the hills behind her house and frequent visits to crags. But she had little idea of how difficult it was and still is to make even a poor living from climbing; how difficult it is to achieve the necessary media profile. At the beginning of 1983 Karrimor, a manufacturer of rucksacks and other equipment, offered her free gear in return for her posing for their catalog. They dressed the proposal up a little, announcing that Alison and their other models were part of a so-called "Hot Rock" team, and she was delighted, believing she had her first commercial sponsor. But she was not going to get fat on free rucksacks.

Jim was proud of Alison's progress in other ways. Julianne Dickens, a climber married to an engineer who later became one of Jim's business partners, remembers that when she met Alison for the first time, Jim asked her to guess her age. She looked at this handsome woman in a cashmere skirt and calfskin leather boots, and suggested she must be at least 28. Her overestimate, eight years out, seemed to give Jim great pleasure. His gifts of clothes and cosmetics had made Alison look sophisticated, older than her years: he had taken a teenager and turned out a mature woman.

As time went on, Alison began to feel the weight of the expectations upon her, both her own and others. The paradox was that the more she felt she had to succeed, the more difficult it was to reach the relaxed but focused frame of mind required to lead hard routes, and the more likely she was to fail. To be able to climb rock well is as much a mental as a physical trial, and slowly she was losing its most vital component, confidence. Like most climbers,

Alison had days when she simply wasn't going well, when the moves refused to fall into place, when she felt clumsy and apprehensive. She found it very hard to shrug such days off, and they triggered sharp crises in which she questioned whether she should be climbing at all. Jim saw himself as Alison's coach, and his ambitions for his partner could produce agonizing scenes. Sally Skinner remembers a day in the spring of 1983 at Chatsworth Edge, a gritstone cliff in the estate of the Dukes of Devonshire, when Jim talked Alison into trying to lead a route she did not feel ready to do. "She was actually in tears," Sally recalls. "To me, it looked as if he was pushing her, making her climb harder than she wanted."

There were other sources of unhappiness between Jim and Alison at this time, principally their business. Alison had started Faces as a way of making a little money and occupying time between climbing trips. Now, fueled by a boom in walking and climbing, the firm was taking off rapidly, and extending its range of products. Jim had had to struggle for most of his life, and he found the prospect of commercial success intoxicating. It was no longer feasible to produce everything at home or in the back of the shop, so Jim leased a small workshop in Matlock. Alison, who had grown up in much more comfortable circumstances, never shared his excitement. But she felt that Jim expected a similar commitment from her, which she was not prepared to make. Rows, often triggered by her desire to spend some time climbing abroad, alternated with sweet reconciliations. Alison complained in her diary that Jim took her for granted and expected her to fit in with his plans, and to fulfil his needs. There were times when he must have felt much the same about her.

At least her relationship with her parents, which had been so badly undermined by her sudden departure from home, was beginning to recover. One sunny February day in 1983, two days after her 21st birthday, John and Alison trekked to the base of Kinder Downfall, the series of steep cascades that drain the black peat bog of the Peak District's highest fell. The waterfalls had frozen solid, leaving a cataract of gleaming ice. Father and daughter strapped crampons to their boots and she led him up the Downfall's center, dividing it into two pitches, tying herself to a huge icicle halfway up to protect them both. The roles they had played when John introduced Alison to rock climbing as a child were reversed; it was his first time on ice. But he liked it so much that above the main waterfall, he led a pitch himself. As night closed the short winter day, they returned to the valley across the top of the ghostly summit plateau, navigating by compass. Years later both would remember this day together as one of luminous brilliance, when the weather, the climbing, and their partnership had all been perfect. Afterward Alison's regular walks with her parents, which had stopped on her 18th birthday, were resumed.

In May she was invited to a second women's international climbing meet, this time in the south of France. Its base was the village of La Palud, above the sunny, vertiginous walls of the Verdon Gorge, a limestone canyon more than 1,000 feet deep. Climbing in the Verdon ought to be terrifying. For much of its two-mile length, the lower part of the main cliff, the Grande Falaise, is made of crumbly, yellow rock, and so the routes begin from ledges halfway up. The only way to reach them is by rappelling over the rim, above exposure so great that the mature trees that line the river at the bottom of the cliff look like little sprigs of broccoli. Once embarked on a climb, the only way to safety is to finish it.

In the early 1980s the Grand Canyon du Verdon was part of a climbing cultural revolutionthat was changing the sport's image forever by removing most of its risk. In the Verdon and at other cliffs in southeast France, a group of European rock climbers with no interest in big mountains was pioneering new climbs that were harder, in terms of the physical effort required, than any in the world. The revolutionary difference was that while these routes were very difficult, they were also completely safe. Unlike earlier generations, the new wave of French climbers thought it acceptable to place drilled steel expansion bolts wherever they wanted protection. Their routes were studded every few feet with points of shiny steel to which a leader could clip a rope and fall from as often as she liked without risk of serious injury. In this way, climbs could be practiced, like gymnastic routines. That old climbing adage, "The leader must not fall," was being rewritten. Now the leader ought to fall frequently, because falling off proved a climber was pushing her personal limit.

As rock climbing became safer, its popularity surged, boosted by a glamorous, sexy image promoted in the French media. For the first time climbers could be fashionable as well as talented. In the not very distant past, magazines and television had stereotyped climbers as grizzled, bearded, scruffy men with the faraway look that comes from having spent too long on frigid north walls. The new wave wore revealing, brightly colored Lycra, displayed their tanned muscles, and posed for photographs in *Paris Match*. They were being used in advertising campaigns, not just for outdoor sports equipment, but for confectionery and cars. One climber in particular was the center of much of this attention, a charismatic Parisienne, Catherine Destivelle.

However modish her image, as a climber Destivelle was extraordinary. While still in her teens, she had climbed some of the hardest routes in the Alps: the forbidding, creaking ramparts of the

Ailefroide north face, raked by frequent falling stones, and the Petit Dru near Mont Blanc, a perfect conical spire that could have been drawn by Walt Disney. There was no questioning her determination; she had toughened herself for these early expeditions by spending nights in the middle of winter sleeping on her parents' balcony, exposed to the cold. Now in her early 20s, she was proving equally adept on the new-style limestone routes of Provence.

Her character and background contrasted sharply with Alison's. The eldest of six children, she was gregarious and cosmopolitan, and had lived a wild life in Paris, giving up climbing for a time to stay up all night gambling at casinos. Her image was of someone carelessly brilliant. Bleary-eyed after a night on the tiles, she could step on to rock and transform herself in an instant, climbing with a flow and athleticism that was a joy to watch.

Where Catherine was chic, Alison seemed provincial and gauche. While Alison struggled for recognition, Catherine was as skillful at using the mainstream media as she was at climbing overhanging rock, and knew how to flatter the egos of male journalists. In the mid-1980s, an opinion poll found that Catherine was the most recognized woman in France; she was more well-known than the then prime minister Edith Cresson. Alison, by contrast, was famous only to the Derbyshire climbing subculture. One day in 1983 she was thrilled when two youths asked for her autograph at a climbing festival in the Lake District. Pleasant as this was, it did not compare with the advertising posters on the stations of the Paris métro that featured Catherine Destivelle.

Catherine had also been invited to the Verdon meet, and Alison spent most of a day with her, climbing some of the shorter routes below the canyon's rim. It was one of only a very few occasions they would meet, but Alison at least would never forget it.

Catherine, she realized, harbored ambitions very similar to her own. Both women wanted to make an impression not only as rock climbers but as mountaineers on the world's greatest peaks, and both wanted to be the best. In years to come Catherine often loomed large in Alison's mind, and if she had a personal competitive project, it was to beat Catherine at the game each had chosen.

If Alison was beginning to direct her ambition toward the Alps and Himalaya, this was partly because she was beginning to understand that her talents and physical abilities were more suited to big mountains than short rock climbs. As the Verdon meet suggested, the best rock climbers were climbing overhanging limestone on holds no wider than the first joint of a finger. To a greater extent than ever before, the crucial factor limiting the level of difficulty a rock climber could reach was the ratio between strength and body weight. Alison was strong and slim. But the very best climbers had to be more than that. They had to have almost no fat at all, and to be shaped disproportionately, with thin, spindly legs and powerful upper bodies. A few had this strength and power naturally, like Catherine Destivelle. Most others in this austere arena tended to behave like catwalk models, watching their caloric intake and training obsessively, not in the old haphazard ways but systematically, on artificial climbing walls and in gyms, repeating circuits with weights, long sequences of pull-ups, and balletic stretch routines derived from yoga.

Even had Alison been prepared to submit to such a grueling regime, it is unlikely she would have succeeded. As it was, she was well aware that there was a measurable gap between her best performances and those of other leading British women rockclimbers, let alone the best men. The grade Extremely Severe covers a broad range of difficulty, and has been subdivided, the easiest extremes being E1, and the hardest, by 1983, E7. Alison's first extreme lead, the Quartz Icicle, was E2. At her best, she managed to lead a handful of E3s. But other women, like Jill Lawrence, often led E4s and occasionally E5s. Gill Fawcett was about to lead an E6, a standard Destivelle attained regularly. As the best climbers developed more effective training aimed at specific muscles, the ceiling of difficulty continued to rise. By the end of the 1980s, Britain was studded with E8s. The gulf between Alison and those at the sport's physiological frontiers was as great as that between her early days fumbling up easy routes and the standard she had now reached.

At the same time, she knew that proficiency on extreme rock was no indicator of how someone might perform in the rather different activity of mountaineering. The physical strengths and skills required for big mountains are just as demanding, but they are also more diverse, less specialized. There may well be sections of difficult rock on a high mountain route, but there will also be glaciers split by deep crevasses, requiring a whole range of techniques to be crossed safely. How to climb pitches of steep ice, learning to cope with the debilitating effect of thinner air, and the determination to carry a heavy weight of equipment are all extra abilities that the rock climber doesn't require. Above all, mountaineering needs stamina. In the Alps, a worthwhile route will last at least a long day. In the Himalaya, mountaineers must expect to keep going for days or weeks at a time. Some of the greatest British mountaineers have been mediocre rock climbers. While Alison climbed in the Verdon sun, Alex MacIntyre, one of the best British mountaineers of her generation, was completing a bold first ascent on Shishapangma, a 26,418-foot peak in Tibet. On crags in

Britain, MacIntyre, who was later killed on Annapurna, would struggle to lead straightforward rock climbs.

For some time now Alison had climbed in the Peak District with Ian Parsons, who had recently become a partner in Jim's business. Nine years her senior, Parsons came from a wealthy family in Redditch, and had several years' experience climbing around the world. His experience was as varied as it was extensive. He had tackled some of the "big wall" routes of the Yosemite Valley in California, grueling expeditions on rock faces up to 3,000 feet high, requiring up to a week's continuous climbing. He'd done a number of hard and lengthy routes in the Alps, including the American Direct on the Petit Dru. Most impressive of all, he had made a fast, lightweight ascent of the huge Cassin Ridge on Denali, North America's highest mountain. Parsons had known Jim Ballard since the early days of the Bivouac. Reserved, almost shy, he was wary of making unsupported statements, and among his fellow climbers he was as popular as he was respected. Alison could have chosen no one better as her partner for her first climbs in the Alps.

She had no experience climbing anything bigger than the hills of the Scottish Highlands, but Ian Parsons' attitude was somewhat unconventional. Most mountaineers taking someone to the Alps for the first time would have chosen to start with something very easy, a walk up a snow peak. Ian, however, had done enough climbing with Alison to trust her ability, and throughout his own career he had always made a point of "climbing the routes I wanted to do, not the routes people told me I ought to be doing." He says: "I tend to think that doing big routes is all about acquiring the right mindset. You can learn the different technical skills quite easily. But the mentality, if you haven't got it naturally, is more difficult. If you do possess it, it doesn't matter very much what sort of route you go for: a big rock wall in Yosemite or a north face in the Alps. Mountaineering is really about getting stuck in and committed — once you do, you tend to get on with it, and get up the route." At the end of September 1983 Ian and Alison headed for the Alps. His first objective was ambitious: a hard and beautiful climb on the north face of the 13,000-foot Aiguille du Midi called the Frendo Spur.

Ian drove along French autoroutes all night and much of the following day, and when they arrived in Chamonix, tired and hungry, he wanted only a bed. But the weather forecast, pinned up on noticeboards outside the mountain guides' bureau, was perfect. Alison lifted her eyes from the tawdry commercialism of the town's ski boutiques and bars, gazing at the towering skyline above, a mighty parapet eight miles long from the dome of Mont Blanc to the snow-flecked daggers of the Chamonix aiguilles. She could not bear to wait a single night. Overwhelming Ian's protests, she insisted they pack their rucksacks and take the cable car out of the valley.

Their destination was the Plan de l'Aiguille, the halfway point on Europe's highest cableway, which continues almost vertically above to the Midi summit. While the tourists changed cabins, Alison and Ian began to climb old snow toward the looming face, a cold, chaotic jumble of granite and ice. The autumn day was well advanced, the pure blue of the sky acquiring the paler, milky quality that heralds an Alpine dusk. Beneath them, pine trees faded into the turquoise deeps of the Chamonix Valley.

As they trudged, the last cable car of the day hummed overhead. The smooth surface of the snow became irregular and broken, and they scrambled over the blocky remains of an old avalanche, tons of debris that had swept down from the over-hanging band of ice cliffs—"seracs"—near the summit. Where the slope finally met the gray, speckled granite, their path was barred by a dripping, gloomy chasm of unknown depth—a *rimaye* or *bergschrund*, the crevasse formed in the angle between the wall and the glacial slopes below. Here they paused, took off their ruck-sacks, and rummaged for helmets and ropes. Ian found a bridge of hardened snow and began to teeter across, probing with his ice ax. Alison stamped out a hollow in the snow and tried to feel secure, paying out the rope. The shadows were lengthening, and she felt the temperature fall.

The Frendo Spur is named after the French climber Edouard Frendo, who led the first ascent in 1941. In the prosaic jargon of the French mountain guidebook, the *Guide Vallot*, the Frendo is a *grande course*, a big route which few beginners would contemplate. Its salient features draw the eye from the streets of Chamonix, cleaving the irregular oblong of the Midi north face in two. The first third comprises a broad, pear-shaped fan of rock, spotted with snow, which stands proud of the face on either side. The pear's stalk is the start of a steep and sinuous granite rib, curving steadily to the right. Above, an ice ridge glistens like a fold of frozen linen before a last rocky buttress that bars the way to the summit. As Alison crossed the *rimaye*, Ian was already scrambling up a snowy ramp beyond.

At twilight they found a ledge, the size of a coffee table. They clipped their sacks to pitons driven into the rock and snuggled into sleeping bags, still wearing their climbing harnesses, using the rope to tie themselves securely to the mountain. They half-lay, half-sat on a bed of sharp stones, brewing tea from snow and munching their supper, sardines, cheese, and chocolate. There was no wind and they barely spoke, gazing at the lights of the town that twinkled up from the valley floor, the bottom of the 7,000 foot chasm at their feet. The moon came up with preternatural brightness, disturbing Alison's attempts to sleep.

Ian's digital watch alarm shattered the predawn silence. Alison started, and twisted her head so her eyes emerged through the neck of her sleeping bag. The valley was a bed of gray cloud, still deep in shadow. To the east, the limestone towers of the Dents du Midi were rimmed in cold pale pink. She shivered, stiff and aching, forcing herself to light the stove and shovel snow into the mess tin, and enamelware pot, for drinks. The purr of the burner was the only sound. After an hour they were ready to climb: sacks packed, boots laced, equipment at the ready.

Alison was used to climbing rock in a state of terpsichorean grace; to feeling the rock's every wrinkle through lightweight, rubber-soled shoes; to the sensuous pleasure of sun-warmed stone on her fingers. Now she was shod in brand-new, unresponding, double-skinned plastic boots, and over them, crampons. She could not feel the nicks and ledges where she had to place her feet: only by looking at them could she tell if she was secure. The rock of the Frendo was cold, sharp, abrasive: it was like starting to learn to climb all over again. Her balance, normally so certain, was thrown. Between her shoulders the weight of her rucksack and its contents bore down. Her usual confidence was gone, and she felt uneasy and unsure.

What staggered her most was the scale, the distance that had to be traveled. Before leaving the valley, Alison had studied the guidebook. It looked a long way to the top, but the book said it was only 1,100 feet — no farther than some of the bigger climbs she had done in Scotland. In fact, she had misread the description. The Frendo Spur is more than 1,100 meters, nearly three-quarters of a mile of vertical height. The morning passed in a blur of effort. At eight o'clock the cable cars began to whir overhead. Ian and Alison barely noticed them, absorbed in a universe that had shrunk to a single line on a mountain face. They took turns to lead, trying to make sense of the bewildering maze of ramps, cracks, ribs, ridges, and overhangs, which the clean shape of the Frendo's pear becomes at close quarters. Alison wasted precious time by climbing for a 160-foot rope's length up a blind chimney, which ended at an impassable overhang. She had to retreat, lowering herself on the rope from a piton. A third of the way up, at the top of the pear, she felt instinctively that they ought to have reached the top. The difference between feet and meters was suddenly very clear.

The route stretched out indefinitely, the summit apparently no nearer than it had been hours earlier. Beyond a deep notch, the climbing became almost vertical as they followed the curving rib, a succession of steep cracks and chimneys, partially choked with ice. They climbed with legs spread wide, balancing upward, always looking for the next foothold. Once Ian slipped and started to fall stopping only when his toe caught a piton. Flooded with adrenalin, he lunged for a flake of granite and steadied himself. Unacclimatized to the altitude, dehydrated by the arid air, Alison was becoming exhausted, lurching, ungainly. Ian was doing most of the leading. Each time she caught him up at a ledge, she gasped that she needed a rest.

Yet as the climb unfolded, Alison saw things of which she had previously only dreamed. The glacier slope up which they trudged from the cable car seemed so far below, they could have been in an airplane. She could see over the mountains on the northern side of the valley, over newly revealed lakes and meadows, and to the west, far into the vastness of rural France, until the ground met the sky in a haze of dark blue. To her right, the needle summits of other mountains, the Aiguille du Peigne and the Aiguille des Pèlerins, were beneath her, their granite golden in the sun. Above their peaks, in the lee of the huge west face of the Aiguille du Plan, a big bird, maybe a lammergeier, rode a thermal, its wingspan black against the snow.

The rock rib ended at a platform the size of a single bedroom, the biggest level space for thousands of feet. Alison and Ian sat for a while, sipped water, nibbled chocolate. Beyond lay the ice ridge, where they had to make their own holds, kicking the crampon spikes on their feet into the surface and swinging the axes they clasped in either hand. The ridge is not steep, no more than 55 degrees, but after a long dry summer, it was iron hard, so that the steel hardly pierced its surface. Halfway up the first pitch, her insecurity amplified by the 3,000-foot drop to the glacier, Alison realized she had forgotten to put on her mittens and her fingers were freezing. Balanced precariously on her crampon points, she had to let go of her axes, and fumble in her pockets to find the gloves. Her heart pounded in the thinning air; her breath ragged with effort and fear.

Still, the spur stretched upward. The afternoon was ending, and the most difficult section, the final rocky buttress, was still to come. At its base, lashed to the rock above the sickening drop, Alison shivered uncontrollably, frightened and demoralized, waiting for Ian to reach the next tiny ledge. Then he grappled with the hardest pitch of all, an open book of granite where he had to resort to climbing with artificial aid, probing the blackness with his head lamp, searching for pitons left by previous climbers to pull himself up. It was no place to stop for the night. As Alison paid out the rope, her stance was a single foothold, and she shifted her weight from leg to leg to stop them going numb. The wind was rising, and clouds were beginning to fill the sky. At last she heard Ian shout that he was safe, and it was her turn to climb. She struggled up the last rocks of the buttress and flopped over the top onto snow. She could lie down and rest.

She had reached the ridge that links the Midi with its near neighbor, the Aiguille du Plan. In winter the ridge is protected by a rope handrail, and hundreds of skiers descend it every day to the start of the run down the Vallée Blanche to Montenvers. On the last night of September it was wild, dark, and windswept, with the temperature far below freezing. Ian, no less tired than Alison, plodded on ahead. At first she felt resentful, angry that he had left her there alone. But then she looked to her left and gazed on a new, starlit world, the interior of the range. Jagged giants gleamed through the darkness: the great prow of the Grandes Jorasses; the steep minarets of Mont Blanc du Tacul. Suddenly she was exultant, possessed by the certain knowledge that this was the world she craved. As she entered the tunnel leading into the cable car station, Alison smiled.

The following morning, after a night in the cable-car station, they took the first cabin back to Chamonix. Over the next ten days Ian and Alison completed another five climbs. Most of them were rock routes on the golden granite with which the Mont Blanc massif abounds, but the last was a short, steep wall of ice, the north face of a peak on the French—Italian border, the Tour Ronde. Afterward they spent the night in their tent, high in the Vallée Blanche glacier basin. The previous few days had been almost unbearably hot, and Alison had climbed in a T-shirt despite the altitude. After the Tour Ronde, however, the Indian summer broke with a vengeance. As they descended from the climb toward their tent, the sky filled with clouds, and snow began to fall. Soon they were caught in a full-fledged mountain storm. All night the wind tore at the tent fabric, the guylines snapping one by one until it seemed certain it would collapse on top of them. The following morning they packed and readied their gear in a gloomy maelstrom, drawing the strings of their anoraks tight around their faces in an attempt to minimize the area of flesh exposed to the wind. In the Mont Blanc massif, the magnetized rock renders compasses virtually useless, and as they fought their way across the Vallée Blanche, linked by the rope, navigation was mostly luck. The previous morning the glacier had seemed peaceful, benign. Now it was lashed by a howling snowstorm.

At first Alison felt uneasy. But once the familiar crags of the Midi appeared through gaps in the clouds, she began to relish the experience. She still had to climb the exposed, knife-edge ridge she had reached on completing the Frendo, but she found herself delighting in her strength and sense of balance as she teetered upward, bent against the wind. Now she was fully acclimatized, both to the mountains and the altitude; she felt confident and in control.

There was no chance of descending to Chamonix in such conditions—the cable car doesn't run in high winds—and they settled down for another bivouac in the warmth of the generator room. The following morning, the storm had blown itself out. Alison and Ian watched the sunrise from the station terrace, marveling as the view unfolded, the mountains plastered with fresh snow, glowing pink in the morning sun. In her diary she reflected on the experience, and on the lessons of the trip as a whole:

I had experienced/survived an Alpine storm, now the mountains were showing their glory: if in the Alps one is humble, can survive and adjust, then one is rewarded. Stubbornness, and pigheadedness, I fear will lead to disaster. There is a lot to be learnt about, but with a good amount of care and time put in, even greater rewards can be gained. . . . I feel with more and more time and routes, I shall acquire exactly the right gear for my needs, the right "know-how" for routes, and with time be able to minimize all dangers by an acute awareness, attention and respect.

She was right to emphasize the need for flexibility; nothing is more deadly in mountaineering than a determination to achieve a particular objective, whatever the conditions. In the Alps and other glaciated mountains, it is vital to climb efficiently, to minimize exposure to danger by keeping to recommended times. Even if conditions are not so bad as to make a route unclimbable, they may make progress so slow that this in itself constitutes a major risk. Climbers who arrive at a mountain base with an objective in mind may live longer if they show themselves ready to choose another if circumstances so require. It is also true that experience can reduce risk. Nevertheless, Alison seemed close to believing it is possible to develop one's judgment to the point where danger is virtually removed—that in theory all mountain accidents could have been foreseen and are therefore avoidable.

At a trade fair in Munich a few days before leaving for Chamonix, she had been introduced to a man who had lost his fingers through frostbite after being caught in a storm on the Matterhorn. Alison found this deeply upsetting; she was horrified that anyone could suffer so much from the sport she loved. She commented: "Things like this should not happen. I will take all possible care that nothing like that should fail for me. With caution, care and respect, things like that should not occur." Among mountaineers who push the sport to its limits, the idea that they will not make the mistakes of others is common, a way of coping with a level of danger that even most climbers do not find acceptable. But it is a fallacy. With intelligence and planning, risks can be reduced, but a residual danger will always remain. Weather forecasts are not infallible, and storms break from what had been clear skies. Sometimes snow slopes that had seemed stable avalanche. Serac bands suddenly collapse, bombarding those beneath with ice blocks the size of cars, and stones—from pebbles to blocks weighing several tons—are loosened by the constant interaction of sunshine and frost. The great mountain ranges of the world are places where the planet's surface is in motion, where tectonic plates collide, and human beings, no matter how experienced, may get caught by the consequences. Mountaineers call these unpredictable hazards "objective dangers." As the name implies, they are nobody's fault.

Alison returned from Chamonix in a state of beatific grace. She felt utterly relaxed, and savored both her memories of the mountains and the reassertion of normality: Derbyshire's clear autumn air, her mother's baking, and the routines of the Faces workshop, where Jim had hired two full-time workers to cope with rising demand. She went for walks with Jim and scrambled happily at Harborough Rocks.

Alison was not the only British woman taking mountaineering seriously. Jill Lawrence had climbed in Yosemite and on Baffin Island in the Arctic Ocean; Brede Arkless had been guiding professionally in the Alps for years. Nevertheless, in the early 1980s, the number of women attempting routes like the Frendo Spur was small. For Ian Parsons, her gender was simply not an issue: "It always seemed secondary. After all, she was never fazed by it. It wasn't something she talked about, either. I do think it made it harder for her to succeed as she did, simply because it was then so unusual for a female to be doing the things she was—independently, not being dragged up by a bloke. But I can never recall her saying she wanted to go down, that she felt uncomfortable, even though we climbed several routes—including the Frendo—which were obviously not in perfect condition."

It was already clear that Ian and Alison worked unusually well as a climbing team. She was the neophyte, he the calmer, steadying influence. Like all partnerships, they had their disagreements, but they were easily resolved, and they enjoyed each other's company. Above all, each made the other feel safe. Over the next nine months, a period of prodigious activity, they made two more trips to the Alps, and completed a remarkable tally of routes of increasing difficulty. In May 1984 Alison and Ian climbed the Supercouloir on Mont Blanc du Tacul. Once considered one of the hardest ice climbs in Europe, this gloomy, vertical runnel, in all 3,000 feet high, etched deeply between the mountain's granite pillars, took them two long days. It was Alison's first *extrêmement difficile* or ED, a much tougher psychological barrier than leading her first extreme rock climb. It was also the first of many first ascents by a British woman. Two others followed within a few weeks, the north faces of the Aiguille de Triolet and Les Courtes, glistening sheets of ice above the Argentière Glacier.

After the Courtes, they retreated again to Chamonix, where Ian ran into a friend from New Zealand, and the two spent the evening getting drunk. While Ian celebrated, Alison planned their next route: the north face of the Matterhorn, above the Swiss town of

Zermatt. They had already approached this great face twice and been rebuffed by bad weather. This time there would be no mistake. Alison telephoned Frau Biner, who ran the Hotel Bahnhof, a climbers' refuge for more than a hundred years. The face, she said, was in good condition, and the weather forecast was good.

In was, nonetheless, a huge challenge. The Matterhorn's north face was first climbed by the brothers Fritz and Toni Schmid as early as 1931, but the intervening years have done little to reduce its difficulty. More than 3,600 feet high, it is a vast expanse of ice and rotten rock, where some of the steeper sections have all the reliability of an old drystone wall. On some of the harder pitches there are no belays or reliable protection, nowhere to slot a nut or hammer in a piton. Here, neither leader nor second can afford to fall. By the same token, retreat would be very difficult since there is nowhere to anchor a rope for abseil. Nor are there ledges suitable for an overnight bivouac. The face must be climbed fast, or not at all.

To Alison's disgust, Ian was suffering the following day from a severe hangover, and they were forced to stop twice during the four-hour car journey from Chamonix so he could be sick. When they arrived, Ian crept off to sleep, only to be woken two hours later by Alison, kitted up and ready to go. "She wasn't very impressed," Ian recalls. "When she wanted to do a route, she could be quite businesslike."

Alison told him that she was going to walk to the Hörnli hut, the mountain cabin at the foot of the face. If Ian was capable of following her, they would climb the north face the following day. If not, she would do the easier Hörnli ridge on her own. Shamed into action, Ian packed up and staggered after her, first to the cable-car station, and then up the steep and sweltering path above.

This time the face was in perfect condition. They left the hut at 3.30 a.m., and started up the face at five. The steep snowfield, which makes up its lower third, was firm and well consolidated, and the rocks above were dry. Ian took his crampons off at the end of the snowfield and led the harder rock pitches, while Alison kept hers on, taking the lead where ice predominated. Near the top they were faced with a confusing array of gullies and chimneys, only one of which led to the safety of the easy final slopes. Ian had some anxious moments crossing bands of crumbling vertical rock, but by eight o'clock that evening they were on the summit. As the darkness closed around them, they climbed down to the shoulder of the Hörnli ridge, and bivouacked at 13,100 feet. The following morning, chilled to the bone, they were woken by the first guided parties climbing past their frozen aerie.

At the bottom of the Matterhorn, their descent complete, Ian and Alison slept for a while by the Schwarsee, a lake, before continuing to Zermatt, where the magnitude of their achievement began to sink in. Frau Biner came out to meet them, flanked by some of the local guides, who queued up to shake Alison's hand. Alison's climb on the Matterhorn was the first by a British woman and one of very few by a woman of any nationality. Later, Frau Biner asked them into her parlor for homemade cakes and tea. It was, Ian suggested, a sign that they had done something really special. In her diary Alison could afford to be nonchalant. "Climbed north face of Matterhorn," she wrote. "Very chuffed."

CHAPTER 4

KANGTEGA

As Alison's flight made its descent into Kathmandu, one of the world's most hazardous international airports, lightning flickered across the hills immediately above the Nepalese capital and thunder rolled across the valley. The plane banked right for its final approach, the Himalaya hidden by a wall of black cloud and rain, but any sense of dread Alison felt was overcome by her excitement at reaching a world she had dreamed of visiting as a teenager, when climbers like Doug Scott had seemed like distant heroes. It was her first direct contact with the developing world, and she felt a typical mixture of confusion and excitement as she drove from the airport through the crowded streets of Kathmandu in the back of a rickety taxi. For a young woman whose range of experience was confined to her home in Derbyshire and mountains across Europe, "this strange mixture of people, animals, life," as she described it in her diary, was the start of an education in life that she had so far missed out on.

The following morning she rushed out for a visit to the temples and palaces of Kathmandu, and climbed the long flight of polished steps to the Buddhist temple Swayambhu. Monkeys ran alongside her, performing tricks and sliding down the railings; beggars waited in the hot sun, victims of leprosy and tuberculosis, their hands held out for a few rupees. At the stupa on top of the hill, Alison looked out across the city and watched pilgrims spinning prayer wheels as monks in their maroon robes lounged in the shade. Afterward, she walked back through the squares and alleys of the old city, determined to miss nothing despite the midday heat. Her only anxiety was her stomach: "I am very nervous as to what I should eat [so I] stuck with hot cooked food."

Tourism, however, was not Alison's purpose for being in Nepal. While she delighted in the exotica of Kathmandu, she was also waiting for the rest of the expedition she was joining to arrive from the United States. Soon she would be taking a plane into the heart of the mountains, close to Everest itself, for an attempt on a new route on a mountain called Kangtega. Until the last few weeks, she may have known little about the peak she was hoping to climb, but the men she would climb with, especially Jeff Lowe and Tom Frost, were among the most famous mountaineers in her world.

Climbing in the Himalaya takes time, money, and commitment, and most never manage it or even want to bother. In the Alps, you can climb comfortably half a dozen routes on half a dozen different mountains in a fortnight. In the Himalaya, it often takes a week or more just to reach the bottom of the one mountain you choose to climb. Even then you cannot guarantee to get much climbing done if the weather proves fickle or conditions on the mountain are dangerous. Special equipment has to be collected and food organized. Then there is the extra cost of flying halfway round the world and dealing with the bureaucracy that can tie up mountaineers for days. You have to find porters to carry your gear to the mountain, and a cook to feed you at base camp. The scale of such an enterprise is vast in comparison to tossing a rucksack in the back of the car and driving to Chamonix. For Alison, however, that commitment was never the problem; in her mind the Himalaya were a natural progression of the journey that had started on the small crags of Derbyshire. Alison's problem was finding an expedition she could join. Living with Jim had restricted the number of climbers she knew. Ian Parsons was the only real mountaineering partner she had had and his time was absorbed by his helping run the business. While the end goal remained a trip to one of the Himalayan giants, until February 1986 it seemed like a distant prospect. And yet, in a matter of weeks, she had graduated from being an accomplished Alpine mountaineer to fulfilling her dream of climbing in the greatest mountain range of all. In one apparently effortless jump, she was where she wanted to be, stepping off a plane in Kathmandu.

How she made that jump is typical of both her fierce determination to achieve and the pressures and conflicts of her relationship with Jim. Throughout her life, despite periods of doubt and prevarication, Alison grasped the opportunities that came her way with both hands. But at this point, as a rather sheltered woman in her early 20s, she didn't understand how to make things happen, how to realize her ambitions, assuming that her life would simply unfold in the correct and desired fashion. When life proved more complicated than the plotline in a movie, her thwarted hopes and Jim's conflicting aspirations tightened the spring of frustration inside her.

After her triumph on the Matterhorn's North Face in 1984, Alison didn't visit the Alps for another 15 months. Even allowing for a period of satiated ambition, this was a surprising length of time for someone of her age and passionate drive not to follow up on her success. The reason, according to her diary, was Jim. There had been a time, she lamented, when he had seemed happy to let her go climbing when she wanted. Now, she wrote, he was insisting she had to "pay her way," and that she was not to use his money to subsidize holidays in the Alps. "I'm getting to the prime of my climbing—this is my only achievement in life," she wrote in one of many entries on the subject. "I feel if Jim stops me, like he wants to, I'm not sure what will happen to my future."

It wasn't just the cost that Jim cited as a reason for her not to go, it was her time away from the business. By definition, climbing mountains meant absences from home, for a couple of weeks at a time in the Alps and, if she wished to make her debut in the Himalaya, then more than a month. She could spend her evenings on the Peak District crags as often as she liked, Jim said, but if she were to take a long leave of absence, the business could not cope. Alison resisted his opposition. If Jim would not "help" her go to the Alps, then she would, as she wrote, "find my own source of income, and not drain off his resources." She appeared to have forgotten that it was she who had founded Faces, the most successful part of the business, and that she was also a partner in both the factory and the shops, legally and morally entitled to a share of their profits; they were not just "Jim's resources." Each time Alison went to the Alps, she grew and achieved more, and did so independently of Jim. The confidence she took from climbing mountains may have seemed like a threat. Then, after telling Alison throughout the summer of 1985 that she could not go to the Alps, Jim finally relented, though he still maintained that she ought to stay at home and work. At the end of September, as excited as she had ever been, Alison was on her way back to Chamonix with Ian Parsons.

For once they accomplished an easy warm-up climb before committing themselves to a big route. Then, after a night in the valley, they headed toward the Leschaux refuge and the north face of the Grandes Jorasses. For many climbers, this is both the most inspiring and at the same time most daunting face in the whole of the Alps, framed at the end of the Leschaux Glacier and apparently vertical. The north face of the Eiger may be more famous, but the elegance of the Grandes Jorasses, its architectural lines and solid granite, give the mountain a special appeal; and like the Eiger, the Grandes Jorasses has attracted the best climbers and the wildest stories, which have only added to its allure. Alison and Ian had their sights set on a spur of rock and ice that rises 4,000 feet to the mountain's central summit, the Pointe Croz, and as they trudged up the rubble-strewn glacier, the vast face filling the sky ahead, they had the mountains to themselves.

The weather was clear, cold, and still, but the autumn days were short. The climb began with a snowy gully, that sneaks up the lower slopes of the mountain behind a rocky tower. They had expected this to be easy. Instead, Ian found himself teetering on his crampon front points on almost vertical frozen rubble, interspersed with occasional blobs of ice. Halfway up he dropped an ice ax, and only made it to the top of the slope after taking off his rucksack and leaving it behind for Alison.

After several rock pitches on the crest of the spur, it began to get dark. They searched for a place to bivouac, but the mountain dropped away without a pause. At last they stopped on a narrow block of granite, a flat surface just large enough for their buttocks, their feet swinging over the abyss. They were getting ready again before sunrise, sipping hot drinks as the first rays crept over the neighboring peak to the east. The climb did not relent as they slowly picked their way up cold granite, steep ice, and intermittent rubble. Nightfall caught them still far below the summit, insects on a darkening mirror. This time there was no ledge at all, and Alison hung from her harness inside her sleeping bag, her body almost vertical against a wall of stones, and yet somehow she managed to maintain their intake of nourishment, working the stove despite her discomfort.

"We didn't talk much," Ian recalls, "we just got on with it." On their earlier climbs, he had been the leader with the experience to get them out of trouble, Alison the promising apprentice. On the Croz, they climbed as equal partners. There was no latitude for error.

The following morning, their third day on the face, Alison led the first pitch, a steep runnel of ice. Below her, attached to the mountain by a pair of wobbly pitons, Ian paid out the rope. Bleary with exhaustion and fumbling in the half-light, Alison had failed properly to attach one of her crampons. It was the sort of mistake she thought she could avoid, but suddenly she was in mortal danger. Halfway up the runnel, the crampon worked itself loose from her boot and dangled uselessly from its safety strap attached around her ankle. Without the crampon, the toe of her naked boot slid against the ice, unable to gain the least purchase. She could not move up or down. If she fell, it was likely that the jerk of the rope coming tight would pull Ian hard against his belay, that the pitons to which he had tied himself would rip out, and both of them would fall the length of the face. Alison felt herself hyperventilating, her heart thumping against her ribs as she gripped the shafts of her ice tools in sheer terror. She knew she had to bring herself back under control, and quickly, or her strength would fail.

Taking a series of deep breaths, she imagined herself not 3,000 feet above the Leschaux Glacier, but playing around on the Bossons Icefall, a popular training ground a few minutes from the Chamonix valley road. Slowly, taking care not to lose her balance, she half-bent down, half-raised her leg, until she could reach her boot and the dangling crampon. She slipped off her mitten, stuffed it into her pocket, and gently replaced the crampon's catches on her toe and heel. She stood up and tested the crampon to make sure it was firmly placed. At last she resumed her upward progress, her heart again pounding, but this time with relief.

The Croz Spur wasn't giving up easily. The next section, a horizontal traverse, should have been ice, but most of it had melted, leaving smooth slabs of granite. After a final rocky chimney, they were on the summit, a perfect right angle separating the wall from flat snow. Exhausted, they sat down. In the freezing autumn air, 14,000 feet above sea level, they prepared their third bivouac.

The Croz was the last big Alpine route Alison climbed with Ian. This was not his choice; by any standards, they had enjoyed a remarkable partnership. The reason, he says, was the demands

made on his time by his business involvement with Jim. In the
following seven years he had a total of six weeks' holiday. "I
wasn't running a business," he recalls. "The business was running
me." For a long time Ian had spent months each year climbing
abroad. Now, as he tried to pursue the dream of success Ballard
had created, he found himself tied to the shops and factory, shack-
led by Jim's demanding ethos: "If you weren't there, you were going
to have to employ someone else to do the work." Alison, on the
other hand, would escape this restriction.

Shortly after her 24th birthday on February 17, 1986, Alison
and Jim were in Munich for a trade fair. Among the hundreds of
exhibitors, they saw Jeff Lowe, a famous mountaineer from the
United States who ran a climbing hardware company and had
come to Europe to market his products. He and Jim were old
acquaintances, and Alison had come across Lowe in Chamonix
the previous autumn, just before she climbed the Croz Spur.
Aware of the difficult conditions, he had been impressed by
Alison's performance.

For Alison and Jim, Jeff Lowe had a glamorous appeal, traveling
and climbing all over the world and living a life of apparent freedom. A few weeks after the trade fair, Lowe told them, he was planning to go to Nepal to attempt a new route on Nuptse, a near
neighbor of Mount Everest. It was possible one of his partners
might drop out, he added, and if so, Alison could take his place.
Even if that were impossible, she could join his party on the mountain he was planning to climb first, a beautiful, double-summited
peak called Kangtega, overlooking the Buddhist monastery of
Tengboche in the homeland of the Sherpas. For a first Himalayan
foray, it was a tempting prospect. At just under 22,000 feet

Kangtega was significantly lower than the region's true giants, Everest and Lhotse, but it was much, much higher than Alison had been before. The chance to climb a new route in the company of Jeff Lowe was too good an opportunity to miss.

Many climbers would have been intrigued, flattered even, and let the issue drop. Alison, on the other hand, saw her opportunity and took it. In the space of a brief conversation, she had committed herself to going to the Himalaya. In a literal sense, it was a childhood dream come true. Only a few years earlier, her contact with the Himalaya had been limited to attending lectures by those who had climbed there. Even Jim, who the year before had been complaining about her wish to climb in the Alps, was caught up in the promise and excitement of Lowe's suggestion, and he offered no resistance. It was now the end of February. Alison would be leaving at the end of March.

Back in Britain, she launched herself into organizing her trip, applying for grants, arranging tickets and insurance. Less than a fortnight before leaving for Kathmandu, she spent an evening with her parents, talking about her trip. They gave her £1,000 toward it, more than half the eventual cost. Alison's emotions were in turmoil, a mixture of excitement and fear, but she reveled in the sudden attention. The *Derby Evening Telegraph* sent a photographer, and she appeared on the newspaper's front page. A local woman climbing in the Himalaya was big news. Alison would be gone for more than two months, the longest period she had been away from Jim since she moved into Meerbrook Lea; but if Jim had reservations about her abandoning the business for mountaineering, they were left unspoken. He now seemed as swept up in her sudden entry to the big time as she was. On March 30 they woke to a heavy snowfall. She gave Jim an Easter egg, then went for a walk in the snow, "her choice," she told her diary, of activity for their last hours together before she left. Later, one of Jim's colleagues arrived to drive them to the airport. There was time for dinner, and Alison cried a little, feeling the contrasting appeal of home and adventure. Then she gathered her belongings and disappeared into the departure lounge. Not since the day she walked out of her parents' house in 1980 had her life promised so much.

After her day's sightseeing round Kathmandu, Alison took a minibus out to the airport to meet the rest of the team. Jeff introduced her to Mark Twight, who at 24, was only a few months older. An intense, rebellious young man, Twight had only limited experience but was highly ambitious. Bruce Roghaar was not an accomplished climber and had come simply for the experience of being in the Himalaya. Two other expedition members had arrived in Nepal some time earlier. Tom Frost, now in his mid-40s, had been to the greater ranges many times before, and was already trekking with his family in the foothills of Everest. Henry Kendall, a famous research physicist, had made the first American ascent of the Walker Spur on the Grandes Jorasses. He too was already in the Khumbu region, preparing for the climb.

Alison showed no sign of being overwhelmed by such company. They spent the next few days in Kathmandu while the Nepalese authorities processed the expedition's paperwork. There were occasional sightseeing tours, but Alison and her new friends spent most of their time talking and drinking beer. The first restaurant Alison went to with Lowe was the Rum Doodle, named after the fictitious mountain in the satirical climbing novel by W. E.

Bowman. The restaurant holds a book signed by almost every person to climb Everest and survive. Nine years later Alison would be back to add her own signature.

The team left Kathmandu on April 5. Like hundreds of expeditions before them, they flew to Lukla, an airstrip carved into a mountainside, the gateway to the Everest region. As the twin-engined Otter left the confines of the Kathmandu valley, they rose above the dust and smog. Beyond lay the gorges, forests and lime-green paddy fields of Nepal's middle hills. Alison pressed her camera to the window, taking photographs as she gazed at the Himalaya for the first time, the pyramids of the Jugal Himal, Gauri Sankar, and Menlungtse, then the squat bulk of Gyachung Kang and Cho Oyu, two of the highest mountains in the world. A little farther off, at the head of the Dudh Khosi canyon, almost hidden by the colossal Nuptse-Lhotse wall, she could see Mount Everest itself. At the end of the 40-minute flight, the plane suddenly dived into a side valley and banked toward the hill on the opposite side and the narrow and steeply inclined airstrip scratched into it. It was an exhilarating introduction to the Himalaya.

Jeff had left on an earlier flight and was already organizing porters to ferry equipment up the valley toward Namche Bazar, the Khumbu region's capital. For the next few days, the expedition made its way up the valley, slowly gaining altitude. It was not an orderly procession. Alison's fears for her digestion proved well founded. She, Jeff, and Mark were all suffering from stomach ailments of various kinds, which at times left them debilitated. The path clung to the hillside, high above the river, passing wooden trekkers' lodges and Sherpa restaurants. Pausing in Namche Bazar, a bustling town full of trekking lodges, they continued to the monastery at Tengboche, set in a meadow more than 13,000 feet above sea level. Inside the monastery, shaven-headed monks chanted and lit butter lamps. Outside, above the torrent that drains Mount Everest, were peaks which had once seemed as remote and enticing as Shangri La: the fluted spire of Ama Dablam and the shimmering flanks of Thamserku.

In this beautiful place the climbers rested. Alison was completely absorbed. On April 12 she remembered it was Jim's birthday. It was the first time she had mentioned him in her diary since leaving home, and the last for several weeks. The Sherpas managed every aspect of the day-to-day running of the expedition, leaving the climbers to acclimatize to the rarefied air and relax. For a few days the most demanding thing Alison had to do was work out how to wash her hair using water heated over the fire. She felt relaxed, even spoiled, liberated from the usual chores of cooking and washing up.

Soon enough the time came to move to the base camp for Kangtega, another two days' walk away. It was set in the wild Omoga valley, well removed from the main trekking route to Everest, which the expedition had followed thus far. The climbers were above even the roughest pastures now, on the very fringe of the mountain walls they had come to climb, a remote tented community. Jeff celebrated their arrival by sharing a bottle of whisky, and they talked, eating and drinking, far into the night. All the climbers were over their gastric illnesses. A fortnight after leaving England, Alison was ready to face her first real test.

Before attempting Kangtega, Lowe wanted the team to climb an easier, lower mountain, Lobuje Peak, to give their bodies more time to adjust to the reduced level of oxygen. There is an easy route to the top that novice climbers regularly attempt, but on earlier visits to the region, he had picked out an unclimbed route on the steeper east face. It meant another day's walk, away from the unspoiled Omoga campsite to Lobuje village, a collection of summer homesteads and tourist hikers' lodges. As Alison walked, she played out future trips in her mind, tracing imaginary new routes on the flanks of the mountains on every side. Lobuje lies at the snout of the Khumbu Glacier, the river of ice that flows from Everest's South Face, and thousands of trekkers stay there every year. "Obviously once a nice place, now just a rubbish heap, scarred by westerners," Alison commented. "We've ruined it for ever."

Lowe climbed Lobuje Peak with Henry Kendall, followed a day later by Alison and Mark Twight. The new route was technically a good deal easier than some of her climbs in the Alps; the climb took less than a day, and for much of the time they felt happy to do without a rope. But the mountain is more than 20,000 feet high, almost 5,000 feet higher than Mont Blanc, Alison's previous highest summit, and the air is appreciably thinner, containing less than half of the oxygen at sea level.

Above around 3,000 feet, unacclimatized humans compensate naturally for the decreasing level of oxygen by breathing more deeply and more often, delivering more oxygen into the alveoli of the lungs, which transfers the oxygen to the bloodstream, a process called the hyperventilatory response. Pressure in the pulmonary artery also increases, forcing open capillaries in the lungs, which are usually closed while at rest at sea level, again allowing more oxygen into the bloodstream. Eventually, after a week or so, the cardiac work rate actually falls as the body adjusts to the new altitude. The number of oxygen-bearing red blood cells increases, although changes in the blood's biochemistry are more important. The manufacture of an enzyme called diphosphoglycerate, which allows the release of oxygen from hemoglobin to tissues, is increased, as are other enzymes involved in the absorption of oxygen. The number of capillaries within an individual's muscles also grows, allowing more oxygen-rich blood to reach them. Most of these changes are more or less complete after six weeks, although the breathing and biochemical changes take place in as little as six days. Until the body is acclimatized, trekkers and climbers coming from low altitude feel breathless and notice their heart racing at altitudes as low as 9,000 feet. They may develop headaches and nausea and have trouble sleeping at night, and if they gain altitude too quickly, they risk life-threatening conditions such as pulmonary or cerebral edema. Gradually, as the body adjusts to the new altitude, climbers feel fit and relaxed again, but while some make this adjustment with few symptoms, for others it is always a struggle or even impossible no matter how fit they are beforehand. In fact, physical fitness is not a reliable guide to how well an individual will adjust; it is often a physiological lucky dip.

Alison was beginning to discover that for her, acclimatization was no great problem. She was in a buoyant mood, self-assured and optimistic. The complexity of life at home had been replaced by a set of simple physical demands, and she found it easy to be happy. In this she was not unique. Most climbers find this liberating, escapist side to mountaineering one of the most attractive reasons for doing it.

Reunited at base camp, the climbers began their final preparations for Kangtega. They anticipated being on the mountain for ten days. All their food for this period, their tents and sleeping-bags, their stoves and personal items, had to be carried on their backs for that time. Furthermore, they also had to carry all the climbing equipment, the pitons, carabiners, ropes, and other gear needed for a technically challenging ascent. In the past on difficult routes in the Himalaya, mountaineers fixed rope up their route, establishing a series of well-stocked camps until they had a continuous supply line to within striking distance of the summit. As the expedition progressed they would push the route a little farther, then return to base camp for a rest. Some expeditions are still organized in this way. On Kangtega, however, the climbers were planning to reach the summit in one continuous effort, just as they might have done in the Alps. This alpine style of mountaineering is more demanding, psychologically as well as physically. It means being isolated from Base Camp, without the comfort of a line of ropes reaching down to safety. In the Himalaya, on mountains largely above the operating ceiling of helicopters, rescue is unlikely. Despite this, most leading mountaineers find the simplicity of alpine-style climbing more rewarding and even safer, as climbers are on the mountain for a shorter period of time. In the words of one of its first exponents, the Tyrolean Reinhold Messner, they see it as climbing "by fair means."

For Alison and her four companions, Jeff Lowe, Tom Frost, Bruce Roghaar, and Mark Twight, the need to carry everything in their rucksacks made cutting down weight a high priority. They laid out all their gear in front of their tents at base camp, and considered the value of every item. Then the loads were divided up equally. As Alison tried her sack for size, she could not help a feeling of apprehension. It would have felt heavy on a gentle walk at sea level, but she was going to have to cope with it on steep rock and ice on unknown ground in the rarefied air of the Himalaya. "Alison was real solid," Lowe recalls. "She did her share as well as being technically strong. She was climbing with us on an equal basis, no question. She pulled her weight." His view is shared by Mark Twight: "She had a strong, do-it-yourself ethic, which I admired. She wasn't content to follow on the coattails of others. I hadn't met that many guys who were comfortable climbing with packs that big."

Both men attest to her near-obsessive personal organization, both in camp and while climbing. She made sure that the things she would need during the day were easy to get at, and in the evening she made herself comfortable quickly, with everything at hand, so that time spent not climbing was as relaxed as possible. Domestic competence at high altitude seems a slight and mundane skill, but a lot of Himalayan climbing centers on the ability to do things efficiently and to maintain good morale. Each individual's energy levels are limited climbing in the Himalaya, and success can often come from simply lasting long enough.

Tom Frost and Bruce Roghaar had spent the previous two days preparing a track up the slopes above base camp, but the team still moved slowly. The weather was wet and cloudy, more reminiscent of Scotland than the Himalaya, but Alison was too excited for it to matter. The climb on Lobuje had been merely a warm-up. This was the real thing. At 6 p.m. they set up their first camp on the edge of a glacier.

For the first three days they made slow progress. The weather had cleared, and the climbing was not difficult, but as they struggled up snow slopes and steeper sections of ice, the sun made their loads almost unbearable. On the second day Bruce Roghaar, tired and overawed, decided to descend to base camp; Lowe had a painful cough, and the rest of the team were exhausted. On day three, they felt so tired they spent the morning resting.

To those who have never tried to climb a Himalayan mountain, the intensity of the hardship involved in simple existence is difficult to convey. The overriding need is to maintain the body in reasonable physical condition, but the obstacles are formidable. Living and climbing at altitudes burns thousands of calories, but when every morsel has to be lugged up the mountain inside a rucksack and altitude blunts your appetite, they cannot be adequately replaced. In order to avoid altitude sickness climbers need to drink at least four liters of liquid a day, but gathering the snow and melting it on a stove is a lengthy, laborious process. Merely to leave or enter the tent is far from simple. If snow comes in, it will melt, and soon clothes and sleeping bags will be sodden, useless against the penetrating cold. A short trip outside must be followed by a painstaking session of brushing snow from clothes and boots. The disposal of bodily waste becomes a persistent nuisance. It is vital not to pollute the area of snow around the tent doorways being quarried for drinks. But if, as is usually the case, climbers are perched above a terrifying precipice, moving the requisite distance away from camp will need protection from a rope. Simply getting out of the tent to urinate, especially at night, can be a major effort. Male mountaineers solved part of this problem long ago. They carry empty plastic bottles, which can be used even inside a sleeping bag, then tipped away discreetly. For women, as Alison noted pointedly in her diary, there is no equivalent.

On the third afternoon they decided to climb a short distance to a col, from which they would be able to see the rest of their proposed route. Soon they were there, without encountering difficulty. Above the col, their unclimbed ridge snaked upward toward a flatter plateau area beneath the summit. Suddenly Lowe launched himself at a pinnacle of ice 60 feet high, which sat on top of the col. Without a rope, he swung his axes and kicked his way up, yawning space at his heels. There was no reason for his behavior other than sheer exuberance, or perhaps a desire to demonstrate that he still had reserves of strength, but Alison, determined to match his easy confidence, set off after him. Twight thought her action irresponsible. "She had a competitive thing going with Jeff. Soloing the ice cliff struck me as pretty stupid. She wasn't negative about it, she didn't want to win at someone else's expense. She just wanted to keep up. She was tremendously driven."

Beyond, the ridge steepened, and the climbing became more difficult. Two days after reaching the col, they found an excellent campsite just below a final headwall that barred access to the summit plateau. Keen to prove her competence, Alison rushed to assemble one of the tents. But she stuck one of its poles carelessly in the snow, then watched in despair as it slid down the mountain. The tent had become a useless fabric sack. The only means of shelter now was to dig a snow cave. Determined to atone for her error, Alison threw herself into the excavation, tunneling into the freezing snow with her hands and ice ax, and tended both stoves throughout the evening.

The following day they had barely started to climb before the sky clouded, the wind rose, and snow began to fall. By early afternoon the climbers were back in their snow cave, enduring a freezing, joyless afternoon. It was a remote and lonely place to be, far above safety. But as Alison wrote up her diary, stuck in a storm which might last for days, she declared herself merely "chilly and a little disappointed, unsure how many further delays we're going to get." She remained determined to see the positive aspect of the situation: "Still—for me it's a good rest day—both for my body to recover and acclimatize." After a cold, cramped night she "awoke keener and fresher . . . felt ready for action."

The next section began with a horizontal traverse to the base of a rocky crack. It was far from easy, and Lowe took a short fall. He was unhurt, but as Alison followed she felt nervous and exhilarated. On Kangtega, just as much as in the Alps or a British crag, it was her ability to lead that would count. It was then that her life would depend on her skill at climbing and placing protection, then that she could demonstrate her value to the team. So far she had led only relatively easy ground. Now she faced a pitch that looked as if it was at the limit of her ability.

She took a moment to compose herself before launching up a groove in the headwall. Here and there were thin patches of ice interspersed with flaking, frost-shattered rock. This was awkward, technical climbing, requiring the same cunning twists and shifts of balance she had mastered on sunny Peak District crags, except now she was at 21,000 feet in the Himalaya, wearing heavy plastic boots and crampons, clutching a pair of ice tools. The hardest move came right at the end. She was crouched at the top of a smear of ice beneath a rocky overhang, the front points of her crampons barely biting. Slowly she stretched out an arm above the overhang, feeling for the next smear, and swung her ax. It thudded into solid, white ice, and before her nerve failed, she pulled up with all her strength. "Alison did a fantastic job on the headwall," Lowe recalls. "She really impressed me with her lead. She was strong, stronger than Mark at that point." A short distance farther lay the next campsite, a narrow bridge between two ice cliffs, but after a week on the mountain, the climb was taking its toll. Alison was suffering pains behind her eyes, and Jeff retched and coughed all night. Their bodies were becoming progressively weaker.

They were climbing as usual next morning. They were close to the summit plateau now and sensed the top of the ridge was near. From below it had looked as if a notch dividing the ridge from the plateau might present a last, formidable obstacle. But their worries were groundless. As Alison and Lowe were clearing gear left behind the night before, they heard Twight shout that he was at the notch. There was a single awkward move, and he was through to the plateau. Sprawling in the sun, at last they could relax, dry their sleeping-bags, and dig a more comfortable snow cave. It seemed as if the summit were in the bag. During the night, however, Lowe's condition worsened. He was still determined to reach the summit but feared he had pulmonary edema, a condition brought on by altitude, in which the lungs' cells leak fluid; it can be fatal within hours, sufferers literally drowning as their lungs fill up. Had Lowe really contracted edema, his only chance of survival would have been immediate descent. From the high Kangtega plateau, this would have been difficult to arrange.

The casual jollity of the previous day had evaporated. The weather was clear, but cold and windy, and the mountain's higher, southern summit was still a long way away. As they rounded an easy snow slope and got a full view of the final summit pyramid, it became obvious it was going to take a long time. In Lowe's weakened state, reaching the summit and descending would be too much. Frost offered to accompany him to the lower, easier north-west summit, and then start the descent. Alison and Mark could go to the top alone. They agreed to meet at the snow cave on the plateau where they had spent the previous night, and descend from there together.

Alison and Mark soon realized that they had seriously under-estimated the scale of the climb they faced. They had imagined the top was only four rope-lengths away. As they drew closer to the steep, icy runnels that marked the line of the final ascent, they realized they would have to climb more than double this distance. If they kept going, they would have little chance of reaching the summit and getting back to the snow cave before nightfall. Nei-ther hesitated: They wanted the prize of finishing a major Himalayan first ascent too badly, and felt certain Tom and Jeff would understand.

They reached the top at 5 p.m. The sun was ready to set. Mark took a picture of Alison sitting in the snow, her face hidden by a bal-aclava and glasses, her shadow lengthening out of shot. Behind the flat summit of Kangtega, the top of Everest emerged from a bank of cloud. The roof of the world was suddenly a very lonely place to be.

Climbing down is always harder than up, and as twilight crept up the mountain, Alison and Mark agreed that the line of their ascent was far too difficult. In the scant light remaining they peered down the mountain's sweeping precipices, looking for an easier route. They could just pick out the line of a snowy ridge, that wound downward above the upper part of the north face. It looked as if it led to an easy way back to the plateau, 2,000 feet below, where they had left Jeff and Tom so many hours earlier. The ridge was fringed with heavy cornices, curls of snow blown by the wind, which hung over the dark void beneath. Alison and Mark knew they might not support their weight.

"We were totally unprepared," Twight recalls. "We climbed down the ridge for a couple of rope lengths, and then one of us accidentally punched through the cornice." They were staring through a hole at emptiness. It was a moment of pure danger. They moved back from the ridge crest and quickly found an alternative line. Now they had to rappel, creating bollards by cutting the ice with their axes and draping their ropes over them. "I'd never chopped a bollard in my life and neither had she," Twight says. "I'd seen pictures in a book. And it was pitch dark by now. Alison and I really hung it out." At the bottom of the steep section, back on the gentler slopes of the plateau, they ate chocolate and drank water before plodding slowly back to the snow cave. They got there just before midnight.

They had hoped for a welcome from Tom and Jeff, but the cave was empty. Lowe and Frost had decided not to wait, and Mark and Alison had to fend for themselves. In the morning their stove ran out of fuel after melting one small pan of water. They were hungry and dehydrated, but until they reached the safety of base camp, there would be no relief. From the snow cave they rapelled to the notch, and then, instead of retreating down the route of their ascent, they followed an easier gully. Climbing down and rappelling for over 1,000 feet, they came across a half-dug cave where Lowe and Frost had spent the previous night, and followed their tracks toward a gap in the ridge. On the other side they had hoped to find an easy walk to safety. Instead, another steep gully dropped away. They were forced to start rappelling again, their return to camp further delayed.

They abseiled down the ropes more than 20 times to get to the bottom of the gully. At the end of each rope length, they would pull the ropes through, thread the next anchor, and throw the ropes down again, their hands and fingers battered from the days of climbing and the cold nights. Finally they reached easy-angled snow fields and waded through deep snow, sometimes sinking to their chests. Base camp lay beyond. In the mess tent the others were waiting to congratulate them.

'FANTASTIC!" Alison wrote in her diary. That night, in complete exhaustion, her toes aching from painful blisters, her wrist throbbing from a sprain, she was still too excited by the climb to relax. She lay shivering in her damp sleeping bag, a blistered toe throbbing with infection, and waited for sleep.

Yet even now her ambition was not entirely sated. With the Kangtega phase of the expedition over, the team began to break up. Tom and his family left to return home to the United States; and Mark and Jeff started planning for their attempt on Nuptse. Alison had always known that for them Kangtega was only a preparation for this even bigger objective. Now she began to feel frustrated. Her diary betrays no sign of a desire to return home, just an urge to carry on her blissful existence. When the team broke camp four days after getting off Kangtega, she walked with Jeff and Mark to their new base at the foot of Nuptse's south face.

There was friction in the air. She complained to her diary that Mark had become aloof; for his part, Mark found Alison increasingly condescending. "It was never malicious," he says. "More a difference in culture or humor." In contrast, she had an easy rapport with Lowe. The fact that he respected her as a climber was a powerful boost to her self-esteem. It was obvious, Twight says, that Alison wanted to join them. Nevertheless, they had planned their attempt on Nuptse as strictly a climb for two.

At the same time, Alison was formidably fit and almost fully recovered from Kangtega. Reluctant to go home without trying something else, she cast around for someone to climb with. "There is no way I can sit around base camp and watch someone else climb. I have to get away and do my own thing," she wrote in her diary. Mal Duff, whom she had met soon after flying in to Lukla, was still in the area after giving up on Lhotse Shar, a giant outlier of Everest. Duff was ill and planning to fly home, but Alison caught up with one of his team, a Scotsman named Sandy Allan. He agreed to go back to the mountain with Alison and make another attempt. The climbing on Lhotse Shar is much easier than on Kangtega, but the mountain is also much higher. At 27,000 feet, its summit is well into the "death zone," the region where oxygen in the atmosphere is so depleted that the body can no longer compensate and begins to deteriorate irreversibly.

Alison returned to the base camp below Nuptse to tell Lowe and Twight what she was planning, and to collect her gear. That evening they made cheesecakes and chocolate puddings, prompting Alison to wonder at her appetite. "Never before have I had so many consecutive evenings when I've eaten so much and felt so full," she wrote in her diary. "I only hope there'll be some climbing to take away this excess stodge I've been tucking away for the last two weeks."

With only ten days until her flight was due to leave Lukla, she knew that the weather would have to be perfect for a realistic chance of success, but after little more than a day on the route it was obvious that conditions were not right. Deep, soft snow slowed them down and the wind was strengthening, lightning playing around mountains in the distance suggesting that the weather would break. As the slopes steepened, the soft snow became deeper, and they made the decision to descend. Turning round and going down was so much easier.

Disappointed but convinced they had done the right thing, Alison returned to Nuptse base camp to wait for Jeff and Mark, while Sandy Allan walked out to Lukla and a flight to Kathmandu. She lazed in the sun, writing letters to Ian Parsons and Bev England. "I'm very lucky to have such good friends," she noted in her diary. She knew she would be seeing Jim soon enough not to need to write.

For four days she spent her time scanning the mountain, watching Jeff and Mark climb, tiny, brightly colored dots amid the vastness of Nuptse. At last they too turned round, defeated by the heavy snow that had thwarted Alison and Sandy Allan on Lhotse Shar. They rappelled quickly down the face, arriving back in base camp on May 27. The three of them talked for hours about the Americans' climb, forming a plan to come back in the autumn. Alison confessed that she would like to try Nuptse as well, and considered asking Catherine Freer to accompany her. The months she had spent in Nepal had been lived at high intensity and not to return seemed unthinkable. Jeff and Mark did come back in the autumn of 1986, but after ten days' effort and mounting tension between them, they abandoned their attempt. But Alison was not with them, and although she would meet both men in the years to come, they never climbed together again.

Two days after Jeff and Mark reached base camp, they dismantled their tents for the last time, turned their backs on the mountains, and walked down to the airstrip in Lukla. In Kathmandu they had time to buy presents and hold a series of farewell meals. "A sad day today—expedition over," Alison wrote on June 2. "Washed real well in a great hot shower—so nice to have clean sheets last night!" Lunch that day was "our last meal together. No time to linger, just an hour of eating, taxi back to Tibetan Guest House to load their bags, and goodbyes. Hugs and tears all round. Two great friends. I felt lonely." The following morning she stepped off the plane at Heathrow airport to be greeted by Jim, Ian Brown, and her parents. As Alison caught sight of them, she cried again. The great escape was over.

CHAPTER 5

NEW LIFE ON THE WALL OF DEATH

At the beginning of the second week of September 1986, three months after Alison's return from Nepal, the staff at the Faces factory in Matlock heard a terrible shouting from the office at the back. They knew the summer had been a difficult time for Jim Ballard: first Alison's long absence; then business cashflow problems, which led to threats from vital suppliers. They were used to hearing flashes of temper, but this was something different, and the target of Jim's anger was Alison.

"It sounded serious," says Ian "Hovis" Brown, an outdoor wholesaler who had joined the business as a partner. "He was getting very abusive—normally, when he shouted, he was still reasonably polite, if you know what I mean. So I went into the office and intervened. I came up to him from behind and put my arms round him, holding him tight. I tried to calm him down. I think I told him: "There, there, things can't be that bad.""

It isn't surprising that the incident remains imprinted on Ian Brown's memory, partly because it seemed so unexpected. He was used to Jim's talking up Alison's achievements, to his praising her strengths and abilities; for many years he described her as a climbing "genius." Alison's journals make clear that their life together was often harmonious, and there were long spells of happiness. But when conflicts arose between them, there were times Jim found himself incapable of resolving them.

At his worst, the man who placed Alison on a pedestal, who broadcast and worshipped her every deed, could also behave like a tyrant. One freezing January day a few months after the incident in Matlock, Ted Johnson, the farmer who lived next door to Jim and Alison, saw just how hard Jim could be. Jim had a meeting to go to, and was insisting Alison dig out his car from a snowdrift, a job that was proving impossible. "Alison was shoveling, but it wasn't fast enough for Jim," says Johnson. "He had really upset her. She was crying."

The anguish such incidents caused Alison is palpable. There were times when, to judge by her diary, they triggered periods of depression, which could last many weeks. And yet for years she told no one of these experiences, and made no serious attempt to leave. On the very rare occasions when people noticed a visible injury, she would explain it away. Once, shortly before Christmas 1984, she met her old schoolfriend and climbing partner, Bev England. Bev noticed she had a black eye. "She sometimes spoke of Jim 'getting nasty,' without ever saying what that meant," Bev says. "She told me the black eye was an accident. She said she'd poked her eye with a twig."

She probably came closest to talking about it with Daphne Chalk, her cousin. In the mid-1980s Alison often spent time working with

Daphne as an instructor at a Peak District outdoor center, teaching young people from deprived backgrounds how to rappel, canoe, and climb. One of the courses came shortly after she sustained the black eye, and several nights that week Daphne and Alison were up until the early hours, talking with a frankness that for Alison was rare. For the first time Alison admitted there were times she was unhappy and felt oppressed by Jim's demands and aggression. Alison knew that Daphne's first husband had abused her physically for years, and Daphne says she seemed on the verge of disclosing the violent side of her own relationship. "We skirted round it a few times," Daphne recalls. "She said a few things, which I tried to follow up, but she wouldn't give anything away. It was as though I was too close to home to discuss it. But I felt she was giving me signs that she was going through the things that I'd been through."

Alison's reactions to these incidents changed over time. In the earliest explicit reference to an assault, in April 1983, she described what transpired as "an enormous row and a fite [sic]." Alison's spelling was competent, and we must assume her use of "fite" was deliberate. It suggests a retreat into an infantile, little-girl-lost persona, as if the only way she could cope with what had happened was to accept that she had been "naughty"—a word she used at other times in their early years together in describing purely verbal rows with Jim. In those days she appeared to accept his assessments of her supposed shortcomings at face value. One senses her relief at the reconciliation that followed, and the return to normality as she describes the routines of tea, bathing, and an early night. From now on, her diary would record Jim's infrequent but regular assaults, but it was only in the last year of her life that she felt capable of confiding to those closest to her about the physical abuse she had suffered.

As Alison matured, she wrote of the bad times between her and Jim with a mixture of anger and resigned despair. By the summer of 1986, after Jim had criticized her in public, she could record that he had treated her "like a piece of dog dirt"; he should "get stuffed, show some respect for me."

It would have been remarkable, given the difference in their ages and experience, if the balance of power between Jim and Alison had been equal, especially in their early years together. The problem arose when Alison got older, becoming less and less ready to accept his direction, and increasingly resentful of the way he tried to order her life.

Some aspects of this behavior, though irksome, were extremely petty. For example, Alison adored working with Daphne at the outdoor center, delighting in sharing with the children the inspiration she derived from the mountains. To Jim, however, the courses were a frivolous diversion from what should have been Alison's real work, making and selling climbing gear at their business; and he made it as difficult as he could for her to participate. Daphne recalls: "It was very difficult with something as logistically complex as one of those courses, knowing that Alison had to be back at a certain time. If we were 15 minutes late, then he'd go berserk."

Others were more complex and, in Alison's terms, more significant. Long before he met her, Jim had tried to foster other climbing protegés, young men who had worked at the Bivouac and who showed promise, and who suddenly found themselves with a self-appointed "manager." Now Jim saw himself as Alison's coach, the mentor who would guide her to international climbing fame. The consequences could be positive. There were times when her climbing seemed to collapse, when she lost all confidence, and then it would be Jim who would nurse her back to form, coaxing her on to easy routes he knew she would "cruise" with ease, until she was ready to tackle more difficult challenges again. At such times she felt a deep gratitude. At others, however, she felt oppressed by the weight of his expectations. "JB was funny when I felt I needed a day to rest from climbing," she wrote in May 1984, "he seems to expect me to be a 'climbing machine'."

Even when she was far away, he still sought this managerial role. In the summer of 1984, at the beginning of the trip to the Alps, which ended with their ascent of the north face of the Matterhorn, Ian Parsons, and Alison made an attempt on the Walker Spur—a huge and challenging route on the north wall of the Grandes Jorasses, one of the greatest of Alpine objectives. On their first day on the face they climbed 18 pitches: nearly 2,000 feet of hard climbing on both rock and ice. But after Ian and Alison set up their tiny bivouac tent for the night, the cloud came in. There was a terrifying display of lightning and thunder, and it snowed all night. The following morning the firm gray granite, which had to be dry to be climbable, was thickly coated with white. The weather stayed bad all day, with wind and snow flurries buffeting their tent. Wisely, they decided not to try to move, and spent their time dozing, nibbling chocolate, and making drinks. The following morning the weather was still damp and very cold, the route impossible. Ian and Alison felt chilled and stiff, loath to make the effort to leave their sleeping bags, don protective clothing, and commit themselves to the elements. But it had to be done. After 18 nerve-racking, icy rappels, they were again on the glacier, relieved to be safe.

Back in Chamonix the following day, Alison was desperate to speak to Jim on the telephone and seek consolation, but his reaction left her dismayed. Instead of offering sympathy for their necessary and difficult retreat, she told her diary he was "mad cos we'd not done the Walker."

A few days later, after the weather improved, Ian and Alison climbed the north faces of the Courtes and Triolet—two hard and exhausting *grandes courses* in consecutive days. On the Triolet the ice was gray, brittle, and hard; and for much of the route, they climbed in the shadow of a serac, a giant overhanging ice cliff, which could have fractured at any time, sending car-size fragments raining down on their heads. It was six in the evening before they reached the summit ridge, and searching for the way down the southern flanks of the mountain, they lost their way more than once. They did not stumble through the door of the Couvercle refuge until 9.30 p.m., 20 hours after leaving the Argentière hut on the mountain's opposite side. When Alison called Jim, he was as nonchalant as before. Now they were fit, he said, it was time they "tried a big route."

Of course, they did just that with the Matterhorn. "He was quite harsh with her," Daphne Chalk says, "and in his own, rather different way, expected her to follow a certain path, just as her parents had expected her to go to university. Finding she had moved into a relationship where the expectations on her were just as great was very hard to come to terms with."

Paradoxically, although Jim was ambitious on Alison's behalf, living with him had a further consequence for her place and reputation within the climbing world. Socially awkward, he did not move in the circles where such reputations are consolidated and, as a result, neither did Alison. Climbers less able than her were better known, more widely respected, because they drank with the "right" people in the "right" pubs, the nodal points of the mountaineering grapevine where a few influential opinion-formers, some of them connected to the two main climbing magazines, decided who was worth taking seriously. Jim and Alison were not. Her ascents of the Supercouloir, the north face of the Matterhorn, the Croz Spur, and Kangtega ought to have established her in the British climbing public's mind as her generation's most technically accomplished female mountaineer. She was not unknown, but among climbers, if not the world at large, she should have been very famous. As time went on, Alison's sense that she was not getting her due recognition nagged at her, driving her further.

Jim might also reasonably have felt their incompatibilities were only deepening with time. Much as he reveled in Alison's success, his own ambitions were also being fulfilled. The business, which by 1986 was employing 11 people, was for him a childhood dream come true. Deprived of every natural advantage, he had transcended his origins, and could not understand why Alison— whose childhood had been materially secure—did not share his excitement. Worse, she often seemed to be really happy only when she was hundreds or thousands of miles away.

There were signs that he too sometimes felt depressed. He would complain of stress and overwork, and lacked the enthusiasm to do anything at weekends but drift around the house. One Saturday not long after Alison's return from Kangtega, he spent most of a weekend in bed, although he was physically fit. He was grumpy and irritable, behaviors that are often symptoms of male depression. His relationship with Alison was not the only external cause. Sales at the shops were beginning to fall, and cashflow was beginning to suffer. A few days before the incident in the factory witnessed by Ian Brown, he had traveled to Munich for an outdoor trade fair. There he was humiliated when a French ski-wear manufacturer, whom Jim had considered a personal friend, refused to take his order unless he paid for the goods in advance.

Time and again Alison wondered if the time had come to end the relationship; repeatedly she concluded that it had, only to change her mind the following day. Sometimes she plunged into gloom for weeks at a time, and wept with loneliness and frustration. Always she drew back from taking decisive action to change the way she lived. One bleak entry from December 1986 conveys both her periodic sadness and indecision:

> Depressed again at the moment. I need a goal again. At the moment I feel I'm lost, caught up in mid-flight, not sure if I want to crash land and start again or keep fluttering on and hope it stays all right. Any enthusiasm I had too has been battered out of me; it's easier not to bother. I need some independence — to do and create something, achieve something myself.

The depression behind her words shows how vulnerable Alison had become to Jim's bursts of temper. Her attitude, so positive and hopeful in the early months of their relationship, had been undermined by the physical and emotional abuse she had suffered, and she wondered again whether she should seek a new life outside of his control.

Yet within a few weeks, during a largely unsuccessful winter trip to the Alps, she would be writing both of her joy at the mountains and how much she missed and needed Jim. It was a pattern repeated many times. She might sometimes waver, but overall, Alison's determination to make her life with Jim succeed was almost as great as the will that drove her up mountains, perhaps because she found it difficult to envisage an alternative. She had never lived alone, never acquired a degree or professional qualifications. She had long been accustomed to the affluence that Jim and the business provided: much as she craved independence, she also feared it, and above all, she could not bear to acknowledge that those who questioned what she had done in leaving home on her 18th birthday had been correct in their doubts. At the same time, there were less prosaic reasons for their staying together, an underlying love, which had not all been worn away. After her return from Kangtega, they had discussed having children, an idea that then she rejected out of hand—motherhood, she wrote, would "blow all plans." As the months went by, however, she began to consider it again.

In the spring and early summer of 1987, Alison tried to bridge the gulf between the two emotional centers of her life by involving Jim more in her climbing. After years in which she had visited the local Peak District crags mainly with others, they began to climb together again. They had both been asked to join a second Himalayan expedition to attempt Ama Dablam, a 23,000-foot spire of elegant beauty in the lee of Everest, that autumn. Yet even on the crags and mountains, they no longer seemed compatible. Their weekend outings often ended in rows. In May they drove to France, their first holiday abroad for many months. They visited the limestone towers of the Calanques sea cliffs, an idyllic place above the beaches of the Côte d'Azur. But when Jim tried and failed to lead a route there, their climbing was over for the day and in the ensuing argument, he assaulted her.

A few weeks later, in early July, they went to Chamonix for business and spent an evening with Patrick Gabarrou, a famous mountain guide, who persuaded them that conditions were ideal for the Shroud, a huge ice field on the north face of the Grandes Jorasses.

For Jim Ballard, whose recent Alpine experience was negligible, it was an imposing ambition. The Shroud is long and demanding, and hugely exposed—in every sense a *grande course*, but Alison was overjoyed at the prospect of their climbing a significant route together and rushed round Chamonix getting food and sorting out their equipment. They took the mountain train to Montenvers and scrambled down to the frozen waves of the Mer de Glace but, an hour and a half later, as they walked up the glacier toward the gloomy north face, the enormity of what he was planning finally brought Jim to a halt. In the middle of the creaking, shifting ice they talked briefly, then turned round and headed back to the valley. In Chamonix they met an acquaintance in the street and Jim confessed that he lacked the "bottle" to pursue both business and mountaineering. Alison felt a rush of compassion, sad that he had been made to face his limitations, yet proud of his honesty in doing so.

She was thus already in an emotional state when a little while later she met Bill O'Connor, leader of the forthcoming expedition to Ama Dablam. He had devastating news. Catherine Freer, Alison's friend and role model, who had first inspired her at the women's climbing meet back in 1982, had been killed in an accident on the Hummingbird Ridge of Mount Logan, a route of great length and difficulty in the frozen wastes of the Canadian Yukon. Alison crumpled, sobbing and weeping. Only a few weeks earlier she and Catherine had been in touch by telephone, excitedly making plans to climb together in the Himalaya. As Alison looked up at the familiar shapes of the Mont Blanc Range above Chamonix, the mountains suddenly seemed hateful, malevolent. That evening she and Jim drove away south. They spent the next few days canoeing on the river Ardèche, the tensions between them dissolved by Alison's grief.

Catherine Freer's death touched Alison like nothing in her life before. The previous summer she had followed an unfolding tragedy on K2, the world's second-highest mountain, on the border of China and Pakistan, which until 1986 had been climbed only by men. In July, the Polish climber Wanda Rutkiewicz made the first female ascent and returned safely to base. Later the same day a Frenchwoman, Liliane Barrard, repeated Wanda's achievement, but died, together with her husband Maurice, after being forced to bivouac near the summit. A third woman, the British climber and filmmaker Julie Tullis, reached the summit on August 4, in the company of the Austrian mountaineer Kurt Diemberger, shortly after another Briton, Alan Rouse, had made the first British ascent. On the way down Tullis slid nearly 1,000 feet on snow slopes near the summit; she recovered, but she and Diemberger failed to find their highest camp and were forced to spend a dreadful night in the open at almost 27,000 feet. When they reached the tents of Camp IV the following day, guided by the shouts of other climbers, Julie was in a severely weakened state. A furious storm was already beginning to batter the mountain. It blew continuously for several days, keeping the climbers pinned down. Their food and gas ran out, and in the thin air their bodies deteriorated quickly. Julie Tullis succumbed on August 7, sinking into a deep sleep from which she did not awaken. By the time the storm eased three days later, Al Rouse was too weak to move and was left in his tent. Three of the five who left Camp IV died on the way down: only Diemberger and another Austrian, Willi Bauer, survived, exhausted, frostbitten, traumatized for life. The total death toll on K2 that summer was 13.

Horrified as Alison was, there was no sign she questioned her own devotion to pursuing the same goals that had held such appeal for Julie Tullis. Alison had not known any of those who died and the disaster seemed remote, as if mortality was something that happened to other people. Similarly, when her father suffered a heart attack in August 1984, she seemed simply to assume he would get better. To see the man who had sparked her love for the hills hitched to tubes and machines in a hospital intensive care unit was a shock. But the doctors promised that his chances of making a full recovery were good, and Alison accepted their prognosis—which, mercifully, was accurate. She was sure he would be out on the fells again before long, and as her mother remembers, on arriving at his bedside in Hereford, on the Welsh border, Alison's first question, after checking on her father's progress, was if anyone knew where she might buy some knickers.

The death of Catherine Freer was different: her passing shook Alison's own sense of invulnerability. "She was a wonderful person," Alison said years later, "a brilliant person. I felt that she was a gentle person in the wrong body. She looked so strong and aggressive and was so gentle and kind. She really wanted a husband and children." Catherine was also highly skilled as a climber, and her judgment was excellent. For the first time, Alison began to realize that the formula she had repeated at least since her first trip to the Alps, that all fatal accidents were the result of human error, might be a delusion.

Yet while Catherine's death made her pause, it did not stop her, and her preparations for Ama Dablam proceeded as before. It may seem callous to those who have never climbed that the depressingly regular fatalities on the world's more dangerous mountains do not seem to make any difference to those mountaineers who are left and carry on. In later years non-climbing journalists asked Alison how she could continue knowing that friends like Catherine Freer had died, and she usually answered by saying that climbing was simply what she did, and she would be more careful. It was an unsatisfactory answer, and as so often with Alison, concealed a complexity of feeling. But like Catherine, she climbed because she knew no other experience could be so intense, provide such a contrast between toil and sublime fulfilment; and like Catherine, Alison knew the price to be paid was risk, not just to life and limb but to personal finance, relationships, and conventional careers.

Catherine Freer understood the nature of the risks she was taking and would admit her equivocal feelings about climbing, would acknowledge that death frightened her and that she sometimes doubted the wisdom of what she was doing. For Alison, that kind of self-analysis was rare. In public she never discussed the possibility of dying, other than to say she had too much to live for, as if others who had died in the mountains had not. In fact, she was frightened of dying, just as she was frightened of admitting to herself that there were other ways of living, perhaps better than the one she had chosen.

A few weeks before leaving for Ama Dablam, Alison took a step toward wider recognition when she made a television documentary, which was eventually shown in the United States. The cameras followed her on the south face of the Aiguille du Midi, a sunny climb on golden granite above Chamonix. In the program, titled *The Games Climbers Play*, Alison portrayed herself as hard, professional, almost without emotion, dedicated single-mindedly to achieving her goals. "You have to put climbing first in your life, whether in relationships or whatever. If you don't put climbing first then you never achieve anything," she told the camera. She betrayed no sign that this pose was a carapace, grown to protect her vulnerabilities.

Underneath, she was as confused as ever, about both her relationship and her career. A few days before filming began she had written in her diary: "I feel I['ve] almost achieved recognition as a climber—I don't want to lose it before really proving it."

As often in her life, the person she was trying hardest to convince was herself.

Alison left for Nepal at the end of September, accompanied by Susan, her brother-in-law Steve, and Steve Aisthorpe, another of the Ama Dablam climbers. In Kathmandu they met Bill O'Connor, an old Nepal hand, who had arrived earlier to deal with the necessary government formalities. Steeped in the culture of the Himalayan peoples, he took Alison and the others to Boudha, a center of Tibetan Buddhism. The previous year Alison had been too excited to take in much. Now she began to appreciate a culture so different from her own. She felt an affinity with the Sherpas, members of a small tribe of Tibetan origin who live in the shadow of Everest and the surrounding hills. Alison admired their more measured lives, their calm approach to their children. At the same time, the otherness of being on an expedition and the absence of day-to-day problems allowed her to idealize her situation at home, to forget its difficulties, and she found herself creating a soft-focus vision in her mind of domestic bliss and security.

The trek to base camp was made much sweeter by the presence of her sister. Sharing the mountains with someone so close gave a new richness to Alison's experience. "We both need each other's friendship and it's wonderful to find and develop it," she wrote in her diary. When Sue and her husband left Alison at base camp to continue trekking round the Khumbu, the sisters cried. Then Alison and the rest of the team turned to concentrate on Ama Dablam.

The weather earlier in the season had been dreadful, with sudden storms and heavy snow. Another strong British team had been turned back in late September by illness and poor conditions, and most of the climbers were now heading home, leaving two members to make a final attempt. As they came down from the mountain, Alison and Steve Aisthorpe walked up to meet them. Andy Perkins and Henry Todd had done no better than in their previous attempts, struggling through heavy, loose snow, fatigued by weeks of effort. Their expedition was a shoestring affair in comparison to the one that had just arrived. The two climbers were filthy, and had spent weeks living on a diet of rice and lentils. Perkins recalls his astonishment when, as they talked in the mess tent about the challenges the new climbers would face, he was presented with fish cakes cut into heart shapes.

However enticing their victuals, Alison's expedition was no more fortunate with the weather. They were planning to climb Ama Dablam's southwest ridge, which in the mid-1980s was still a formidable challenge. More recently, lines of fixed ropes have been placed from low down on the mountain to the top, making it straightforward for even inexperienced climbers to reach the summit. But in 1987 climbers faced steep, awkward sections on both rock and ice.

Two days after setting up base camp, Alison and her team walked up easy slopes to the start of the real climbing at 16,500 feet. There they pitched their tents and spent an uncomfortable night as their bodies struggled to adjust to the altitude. In the morning it began to snow. There was no alternative but to descend. For three days more the weather was merely mediocre, with low cloud and flurries of snow. Then, in the evening of October 19, there was a terrific storm. By morning, three feet of new snow had fallen, causing havoc throughout the region. At the height of the busiest trekking and climbing season, when the weather is usually settled, hundreds of people had been caught out high in the mountains, and reports were circulating all over the Khumbu about casualties. After the storm had cleared, the climbers realized that without having the supplies that they'd planned on being brought up to base camp by yak, they would soon run short of food and the kerosene to cook it on. Despite the heavy snow, they struggled down to the village of Pangboche, where Sue was waiting for them, worried they might have been higher on the mountain when the tempest struck. She had been trying to cross a high pass into the neighboring valley and had been forced to turn back. Alison squeezed into the tent Sue was sharing with Steve, delighted to be reunited with her sister.

For the second time in a few months, Alison was about to be confronted with mortality. On the following day she wrote:

> I now realize just how lucky we have all been—climbers and trekkers too. This morning we woke up to see the funeral procession of a yak driver going up to the cremation—very sobering. A little girl was so frightened that she grabbed hold of my hand.

The team had been in Nepal for more than two weeks and had made no significant progress. Nor could they move back up the mountain until the new snow had cleared. Bill O'Connor and

Alison went for long walks, discussing their plans and hopes for the future. Part of the time she questioned him about subjects that might benefit her career, especially photography and raising her profile with potential business sponsors. But they also talked about more personal subjects, including her relationship with Jim. O'Connor had met her for the first time in the late 1970s, when she was still the Bivouac Saturday girl, before her relationship with Ballard began. "I never used to think of them as an entity, as a pair," he recalls. "Considering how young she was, their relationship wasn't physically close. It didn't appear to be very emotional. It was almost like an arrangement; she was getting out of it what she wanted and obviously Jim was as well."

Yet she was in an introspective mood, still affected by Freer's death and the aftermath of the storm. Even before leaving Kathmandu, she had sat late one night with Susan on the balcony of their hotel, discussing whether the time had come for her to become a mother. Eternally pragmatic, referring everything to mountaineering, Alison, Sue says, speculated that having a baby might make her a better climber, as it had made Ingrid Christianssen a better marathon runner.

One morning, as Bill and Alison idled at base camp, gazing at a mountain that remained effectively unclimbable, a runner arrived from Kathmandu with an urgent message from home: Bill's wife, Sally, was pregnant. He was delighted, but the news had as great a significance for Alison. Life, she now knew, was more fragile than she could have imagined. A baby, she believed, would resolve her problems with Jim, and give her life its missing sense of direction. It would also finally prove both to herself and her family that her decision to leave in 1980 had been the right one. On returning to England, she decided, she would try to conceive a child. But Bill O'Connor thought that, "she had children to try and make things work."

At the end of October the climbers finally managed to return to their camp on the mountain, only to find their tents and everything in them had been destroyed by avalanches. Without ever really starting, the expedition was over. Alison hardly seemed to mind, impatient to start on the new life she had mapped out:

> I'd like to go home, I'm missing all the benefits of love, good food, shopping for the best fruit, veg and bread available. I'm looking forward to preparing my study—finishing our bedrooms—and trying to have a family.

The cold shock of this moment would haunt Alison for some time, counterbalanced by the sudden warmth of a small hand taking hers. So often the risks she faced in the mountains seemed academic: stated but not fully understood. Now, in front of her eyes, was the physical evidence of just how easy it was to get caught out and how fragile her future might be.

She pursued her vision of a contented family life with her usual determination. By late December her mood had soared. The shops were enjoying a buoyant Christmas, and the house had been redecorated. When she came to reflect in her diary on the progress she had made in 1987, she had to acknowledge that her climbing had been indifferent. But for the business and her family, she thought, the future was stable and bright. Early the following year, Jim's divorce was made final, nine years after Jean had left. By the last week in February 1988, Alison was feeling nauseous in the mornings and took a pregnancy test. It was positive. She drove to see her parents to tell them that she and Jim were getting married, and that John and Joyce would soon be grandparents.

Like most brides Alison took considerable trouble over finding something to wear, finally choosing an expensive, smart pink suit. The ceremony, on April 23, was at Belper Register Office. There were few guests: Jim and Alison's business partners, Sue and Dick and their partners, together with John and Joyce. By mutual consent, Bev, Alison's oldest and dearest friend, was not invited, nor were any of her recent companions in the mountains. After the formalities, there was lunch in a local hotel, before the party drove to the Hargreaves' home in Belper for tea. They played cards until 10 p.m., and then Alison and Jim went home. Like much in Jim and Alison's relationship, their wedding was a matter-of-fact occasion.

Nevertheless, during the months of her pregnancy, Alison and Jim were closer than they had been since the first days after her departure from Belper. For the first time since she had started climbing in the Alps, they seemed to be working together toward the same ends.

Alison remained physically active. She went rock climbing in early May on a day-long honeymoon with Jim on the North Yorkshire moors, and walking for a week with her parents across Dartmoor and Exmoor. But she was starting to feel tired. She was working hard on the house, getting things right for the baby's arrival. She was heavier and bigger, and the baby was kicking vigorously. As spring turned to summer, she seemed ready to relax quietly into motherhood.

Yet even now she wanted one last big climb, one final achievement before the onset of feeding and sleepless nights; a route so significant that even if she were absent from mountaineering for a while, she would not be forgotten. Mindful of her responsibilities, she sought advice from Dr. Charles Clarke, a neurologist and world expert on high-altitude medicine, who had climbed in the Himalaya with Chris Bonington. What, she asked, would be the consequences on her unborn child of climbing at altitude? Privately Clarke considered the risks were slight, but he told Alison that an extended visit to high altitude in the second trimester of pregnancy would be "unseemly," prompting her to abandon a tentative plan to go to Alaska. At the same time, Clarke said, he could see no reason why she should not climb in the Alps. Alison leaped at the suggestion. In the Alps, there was only one route that would sate her desire for long enough: the north face of the Eiger.

Alison was well aware that Britain's most famous professional mountaineer, Chris Bonington, had partly made his name with the first British ascent in 1962 of the north face, the Eigerwand. The ascent had helped him earn a living from climbing; he had written the first of several successful books and given well-attended public lectures. Ultimately, it led to commercial sponsorship for future ventures, and a long and lasting high media profile. The intervening years had not dimmed the Eigerwand's notoriety. It had received less than a handful of female ascents, and none by a British woman.

Despite its dangers, the north wall of the Eiger, first climbed in 1938, is not the most difficult climb in the Alps. Other routes make greater technical demands, require more skill or strength, contain sections of steeper ice. But there are good reasons why it is one of the handful of mountains that are most often recognized by the non-climbing public, why its myth is even greater than its considerable reality.

To begin with, it is huge. The Eiger's North Face, shaped like a vast, black armchair, is more than 6,000 feet high. Part of the northern rampart of the Bernese Oberland, it towers over green meadows and lakes and is easily visible from the south German plain, more than a hundred miles away. The rock, a friable, dark gray limestone, has been shattered by frost; and for much of the face's great distance climbers are threatened by stones, which are glued to the upper face by ice at night and then freed by the sun's warmth. On the vast, tilted stadium known as the Second Ice Field, the bombardment starts soon after dawn. If they find themselves there at the wrong time, mountaineers are vulnerable to projectiles ranging in size from pebbles to blocks as big as a television. In bad weather the wall acts as a cauldron for fierce local storms, which often strike even when the surrounding peaks are clear. Then the skies will darken; the rock becomes unclimbable.

The Eigerwand is famous most of all because of its dramatic position above the tiny hamlet of Kleine Scheidegg. Sightseers can follow the progress of climbers through telescopes on the terraces of hotels, turning the mountain into a vast amphitheatre, where the spectacle can become macabre as quickly as the weather worsens. Long before it was climbed, the Eigerwand generated myths. When Max Sedlmayer and Karl Mehringer, two experienced climbers from Munich, set out in August 1934 to make the first attempt on the wall, their progress was monitored closely. Clouds obscured them from view as their initially rapid progress ground to a slow crawl. On the night of their third bivouac a terrible storm broke across the face, but when it cleared on the fifth day they were still climbing. All this was watched from Kleine Scheidegg, each twist provided fresh copy for the journalists who watched through the telescopes.

On the evening of the fifth day the clouds returned, and Sedlmayer and Mehringer were never seen alive again. Weeks later,

Ernst Udet, a celebrated German pilot from the Great War, flew close to the face and saw a figure frozen upright on a narrow ledge where the climbers must have spent their last, agonizing night. Of the other climber there was no sign, and the place became known as Death Bivouac. The north wall, the Nordwand, got a new name, Mordwand—the murder wall.

The mountain became a metaphor for Hitler and the Nazis, nature's toughest testing ground for German manhood. In 1936, the year of the Berlin Olympics, there was another attempt by four would-be heroes: the Bavarians, Toni Kurz and Andreas Hinterstoisser, and two Austrians, Willy Angerer and Edi Rainer. They made steady if slow progress, with Hinterstoisser leading a critical horizontal traverse across smooth limestone slabs to the base of an ice field. But Angerer was struck by a falling stone, and when the weather closed in they elected to descend. Now, however, the gathering storm had made the rock slippery, coating it with a thin film of ice. Hinterstoisser, who had led so brilliantly, could not find a way back across the traverse to easier ground, and fell to his death. Rainer froze to death, and Angerer was strangled by the rope when he fell. Only Kurz remained alive.

Inside the Eiger, a railway tunnel bores through the rock to a mountain restaurant at the nearby Jungfraujoch. Halfway up the wall a small window overlooks the north face, and rescuers rushed up to it on a special train, shouting encouragement to Toni Kurz, pleading with him to make it through the night. He hung from a piton in the frozen darkness, icicles forming on his crampons, and in the morning chopped spare rope from Angerer's body to lower a line down toward his rescuers, who watched from below, unable to reach him. Using the rope, he began to descend the sheer rocks. With his hands frozen, it took hours to perform this task, and just as it seemed he would make it, Kurz became stuck at a knot joining two lengths of rope. He struggled for a few more minutes, mumbling to himself, his face swollen purple from fatigue and the cold. *"Ich kann nicht mehr!"*—"I'm finished!"—he said, quite clearly, and he tipped forward and perished, still hanging from the rope. Those below could almost touch his feet.

Such a public death brought condemnation from the Swiss newspapers and the democratic parts of the climbing world, including the Alpine Club in London. A Swiss journalist, one of many critical commentators, wrote: "What is to become of a generation to which society offers no social existence and which has only one thing left to look to, a single day's glory? To be a bit of a hero, a bit of a soldier, sportsman or record-breaker, a gladiator, victorious one day, defeated the next." Two years later, in 1938, another team of Germans and Austrians finally succeeded where Kurz and his companions had died, and they were fêted by Hitler and the Nazi media. During the 1950s one of the victorious four, Heinrich Harrer, wrote *The White Spider*, an account of his own climb and of the disasters that had both preceded and followed it, with hardly any reference to its political context, nor his own membership of the Nazi SS. It was this book that Alison had read and reread in her bedroom at home in Belper as a teenage girl.

At the start of July, less than three and a half months before she gave birth, she left for the Alps with Steve Aisthorpe. As they got into the car, she felt the baby kicking vigorously. A few days earlier she had tried on her mountaineering clothes and they fitted, despite her swelling stomach, although, as she told her diary, only just.

They had tried to warm up with a route in the mountains around Chamonix but retreated from their climb before reaching the summit; the mountains were in poor condition. Aisthorpe phoned a friend in Interlaken, close to the Eiger, and discovered that the forecast in Switzerland was better. There was no time left for an introductory climb, and they drove to Grindelwald, the starting point for the Eiger. Alison had done nothing that approximated serious training for many weeks. On the eve of the climb she admitted in her diary that she was worried, about both the weather and her own physical condition. She decided not to telephone home: "Sorry I haven't yet rung, JB—wanted to ring you when I've something more of interest to tell you! I hope our sprog is OK, I'm trying to look after it."

On July 9 Steve and Alison caught an early train from Grindelwald to the halt known as Eigergletscher, a short walk across steeply sloping meadows from the bottom of the looming wall. Tucked inside the lid of her rucksack, wrapped in a plastic bag, were her pregnancy records. The face was enveloped in mist and they had to ask the stationmaster for directions to the base of the climb. Somewhat bemused but seeing their huge rucksacks and coils of rope, he directed them to the right path. For many climbers, the most popular time for attempts on the Eigerwand is autumn, when with luck the rock will be dry, and temperatures are low enough to keep the fusillades of stones frozen in place. In 1988, the one thing Alison could not do was wait until autumn. As they made their way up the loose but easy lower rocks of the face, the weather was warm and humid. There was a lot of snow lying on the ledges, melting rapidly and soaking the rock below, and Aisthorpe wondered whether they had a real chance of finishing the climb.

Alison was climbing slowly but steadily, and they wasted little time in finding the correct route. At Difficult Crack, the start of real climbing on the face, they dug out a ledge from the drifted snow to spend the night on. Alison had a troubled night; she was much more tired than usual, and felt overcome by nausea, vomiting several times. Despite her discomfort, they were away again at first light, across the Hinterstoisser Traverse, up the steep Ice Hose chimney, and then up and across the Second Ice Field, a 55-degree plaque of frozen snow suspended over the face, the size of 16 football pitches. All day Alison felt as if her energy were being sapped, a lethargy she had never experienced on a big climb before, and now she told Aisthorpe she didn't feel confident enough to lead. The ice was hard and brittle, and their axes and crampons hardly bit through its gray surface as they tried to hurry across. They listened nervously for the stonefall that rakes the ice field in warm weather, cracking the air like pistol shots, and they wanted to be across it before the sun hit the top of the face and unleashed a bombardment. They climbed slowly. Alison remained steady and psychologically strong despite the awkwardness of climbing while pregnant. As the evening shadows lengthened, they reached Death Bivouac, the ledge where Mehringer and Sedlmayer had perished. In her diary Alison made no comment on its reputation, stating only that there was enough room to lie down and so ease the pressure on her stomach, where her climbing harness was digging into her belly and her unborn child.

Perched on the ledge in the early hours of the following day, she held the stove between her knees and melted snow for drinks. The climbing above was relentless, and Aisthorpe climbed back down to the belay at one point, feeling too insecure on the flint-hard ice. Alison for once took over the lead and steadily worked her way up the pitch, allowing them to go on with the climb. On the steep, rocky corner called the Ramp, she felt heavy and ungainly, her balance disturbed by the baby pressing against her, and again Steve led for most of the day. Not once did she complain or suggest they retreat. At the top of the Ramp, they scrambled up a section of brittle rock and then worked their way back into the wall's center, along the broad line of ledges known as the Traverse of the Gods. Beyond lay another ice field, the White Spider, which sits at the heart of the upper face. By now it was misty and spindrift avalanches were pouring down the ice field, bringing stones with them. It was impossible to continue, so they dug themselves a ledge and waited for the cold night to freeze the face into silence and security. That night it snowed, and as they huddled on their ledge, Steve and Alison nervously watched the lightning of an electric storm playing over the foothills in the distance. Marooned near the top of the Eigerwand, with retreat unimaginable, they needed to get off the mountain as quickly as they could.

It was still misty next morning, but behind the cloud they sensed the warmth of the sun and felt sure it would clear. As they continued up the White Spider, the snow was crisp and firm and they made good progress. At last Alison began to allow herself the idea that she and Aisthorpe might finish the climb. In the final Exit Cracks, there was enough ice to allow rapid progress; but the rock was compact, and there were few pitons to be found and no other protection. A fall would have killed them both and they had to go cautiously, keeping their concentration until they were safe.

In the early afternoon they were on the ridge leading to the summit, but the knife-edge of snow was melting and had reached the consistency of granulated sugar. Somewhere on the lower part of the face, Aisthorpe's watch strap had broken and they had lost their only means of knowing the time. Both felt it was late and despite their compelling desire to escape the mountain, they chose to bivouac and wait for a full day's light to descend. As they sat in the snow, and the sky refused to get darker, they finally realized they could have made it down the mountain's west flank that day, but by then they were faced with another night out. Aisthorpe, without a sleeping bag, was half-frozen, and Alison shifted constantly to try to ease the discomfort of the baby pressing against her.

Moving down the following morning, anxiously testing each patch of snow, treading cautiously on slippery, verglased rocks, they reached the bottom of the mountain at midday. Alison sat in the toilet of the Eiffelgletscher station and stripped off her underwear, massaging her legs, which were swollen like balloons from the knee down. She was utterly spent.

Not once in her account of the climb written shortly afterward did she admit to misgivings about the wisdom of what she had done, but when she talked about the Eiger in later years, her pride was blunted with a certain hesitancy. She could remember too clearly those cramped nights with her child kicking against her as she struggled to sleep. Deep down she knew it had not been sensible. Aisthorpe recalls: "I suppose I was ignorant. I didn't have kids of my own then. Alison didn't look pregnant at the start of the climb, but she did at the end."

Alison had blocked out her doubts in order to go on the Eigerwand, and so became the first British woman to complete the most infamous climb in the Alps. Her success was widely reported by the national newspapers and television. Yet even as they celebrated her triumph, it was overshadowed by the fact that she had climbed the wall in an advanced state of pregnancy. Among non-mountaineers, Alison's climb was seen as a physiological curiosity, not the genuine sporting achievement it had been. Privately, other women climbers, especially those who had had children, wondered whether her ambition and desire for recognition had pushed her too far. As for Alison, she knew she would not be climbing anything so demanding for some time to come. But even as she claimed the prize of the Eigerwand, her need to prove herself was undiminished.

CHAPTER 6

A MOTHER ON THE MATTERHORN

When Alison felt the first contractions of labor, she was wearing her rock-climbing shoes and harness, paying out a rope at the bottom of her nearest crag, the gritstone towers of Cromford Black Rocks. Although she knew the birth was imminent, she had gone with Jim to snatch just one more route before motherhood began. Nine months pregnant, she was for once content to let him lead. She bore the sudden pain without complaining, paying out the rope until he reached the top. Then she suggested they might go home and call the hospital. Thomas John Ballard was delivered safely at 5:35 a.m. on October 16, 1988, weighing seven pounds nine ounces, at Babbington Hospital, Belper. He took a lot of pushing out. As Jim told the visitors who came to Alison's hospital bedside, she had strained so hard she had sustained conjunctival hemorrhages. With anyone else, the doctors would have had to resort to forceps or a Caesarian section, but Alison's pelvic muscles were so strong she had managed the job on her own.

Alison had an instinctive rapport with children, and even during those periods when she felt most unsure about her relationship with Jim, she had longed for the chance to bring up her own. A few weeks before the birth, she spent a week at the seaside with Julianne Dickens, whose husband, Phil, had recently begun to work for Ballard, and their three offspring: "She was absolutely brilliant with them. She knew exactly how to talk to them. She threw herself into the holiday body and soul. There she was, 36 weeks pregnant, digging sand castles and making boats on the beach." Her fitness and energy gave her advantages in looking after children, as well as climbing mountains. When Phil and Julianne had moved house a few months earlier, Alison looked after their toddler son all day. As evening fell, Julianne was surprised to discover that Alison had somehow managed to clean their new kitchen, unpack and store all its contents, and wash and dry their pots, plate and cutlery, all while carrying the boy around on her back.

Nevertheless, Alison found the demands and absolute dependence of a newborn baby something of a shock. Well before Tom's birth, Alison and Jim had decided that she would give up full-time work, although she would remain a partner in the business. Their roles would be split on traditional gender lines. He expected her to cope on her own, and although he slept in a separate room, he blamed Alison if his night was disturbed. On October 28 Alison's diary records: "We were up until 1:30 this morning what with wind, hiccups, feeds, changing etc. Jim was woken by the screaming and came and told me off — so I was upset too. At 5:00 T J was hungry again." The following day she wanted to go out into the garden, leaving Tom with his father, but according to the diary he insisted on her waiting until the baby was asleep. Alison wondered, "Why do I let him intimidate me?" Stuck in her house on the hill, she was lonely. Alison and Jim had always led an insular life, and now her social isolation bore on her heavily. She had not joined an antenatal group, and knew no other mothers with children the same age; for her there was no support system of advice shared over coffee, no nearby friends to break up the monotony of feeding, bathing, and changing nappies. "Her life with Jim and Tom surrounded her like a little cocoon," says Julianne Dickens. "She just didn't live in the ordinary world of mothers and babies."

One compensation was the profound love she felt for Tom. "How come I'm happy to sit and watch my child for hour after hour?" she asked on December 12. "It's so lovely to see him discovering things for himself." Another was the renewed closeness she felt for her parents. When she wanted adult company, it was most often to her parents that she turned. Increasingly since the mid-1980s, but especially following John's retirement in 1989, she found freedom from the problems she faced in the walks and holidays she shared with her parents. In 1990 she put Tom in a backpack and joined them on a wintry ascent of Glyder Fach in Snowdonia. Her typically infectious enthusiasm for the hills is what John remembers of that ascent; she kept the pressure she was under to herself. John and Joyce delighted in their first grandchild, and before long they were looking after him regularly.

If Jim was sometimes bad tempered, there were good reasons. For years the business had been steadily expanding. There was the Faces factory, and in addition to the two Bivouac shops, Jim and his partners, Alison, Ian Parsons, and Ian Brown, had also bought a small outdoor store in Sheffield, Don Morrison's.

In order to do so they had mortgaged themselves to the hilt. Unusually their business was a partnership, not a limited company. If it began to fail they would be personally liable for its losses. For years Jim had assumed he would always be successful, and boasted of his own skill in business in much the same way as he bragged about Alison's climbing. Now, however, the bubble was beginning to burst.

Part of the problem was the worsening state of the British economy. The late 1980s were a time of inflation and high interest rates, followed by a deep recession at the start of the following decade. In these conditions, thousands of small businesses, that had once seemed buoyant were squeezed to the point of collapse. As unemployment rose, demand for climbing equipment and other outdoor sporting luxuries faltered. By the beginning of 1989, takings at Don Morrison's were less than the cost of keeping it open, and it began to drain resources from the other parts of Jim's business empire. Alison and Jim had been praying for a snowy winter to boost sales of expensive and profitable ski gear. Instead, the weather in the Alps was dry and mild, and they found themselves sitting on a mountain of stock, which no one wanted to buy.

At the same time, Jim's approach to doing business over many years meant that when he hit hard times, his suppliers were less inclined to tolerate late payments than might otherwise have been the case. In September 1984 Andrew Spencer, known to one and all as "Spanner," had joined his staff, working mainly in the shops. He rapidly discovered Jim's approach to paperwork was less than meticulous: "For the first four months, it was all cash-in-hand, no tax, no national insurance, no questions asked," he says. "I'd just left school, and I knew no better. Alison was struggling to keep things in order. But with hindsight, it was turning to chaos." More damagingly, Jim was becoming known to manufacturers of both finished goods for the shops and raw materials for the factory as a slow payer, and they were becoming reluctant to supply him without being paid in advance. "The range on offer in the shops was gradually getting smaller," says Spanner. Again, this made it harder to survive the recession. At the end of the 1970s, the Bivouac had had a local monopoly. Ten years later, it had several aggressive rivals.

Long before Tom's birth, Alison had largely lost interest in helping to run the business, and had little idea of how serious the situation was becoming. One day in April 1989 Alison took Tom to the Faces factory in Matlock to pick up Jim. To her horror, representatives from the Inland Revenue turned up with bailiffs, demanding immediate payment, and threatened to seize their goods if this could not be made. Seeing Alison's shock, Jim told her there was a new government policy to demand payments on time, and wrote out a check. But for the first time, she realized that the affluence and comfort she had taken for granted for nearly ten years might one day come to an end.

Jim hoped the answer lay in a range of innovative climbing protection devices he had been developing with Phil Dickens, an engineering lecturer at Nottingham University. In the summer of 1988 the Faces partners, including Alison, had formed a limited company with him, New Dawn Engineering, and rented a factory in Rotherham, on the far side of Sheffield. They acquired cheap loans from British Coal and British Steel, part of a scheme designed to regenerate an area devastated by the closure of mines and steelworks. Phil Dickens resigned from his university job and came to work for the new firm. However, in February 1989, just as the New

Dawn factory began production, the authoritative *Mountain* magazine published a devastating review, claiming Cads, as they were called, were difficult to place in cracks and prone to slipping. To this day, Phil Dickens believes the article was unfair, and that Cads were an excellent product, which could have made big profits. But the damage was done.

The financial stress did little for the quality of life at home. As Jim worked harder to bail out the business, he was less inclined than ever to help Alison with the baby, or with other chores around the house. Both of them were exhausted, and as she complained to her diary, they were arguing constantly, "like cat and dog." Next day, for the first time since Tom's birth, he assaulted her. As the pressure on the business mounted during 1989, the violence in Alison's marriage became more frequent than at any other time. After an assault in August he was filled with remorse, and for many months the physical abuse ceased.

Many women would have found her situation intolerable. If not for Tom, she declared, they would be heading for the divorce courts, barely a year after their marriage. But familiar patterns were not so easily broken, and as so often before, she suffered from a debilitating ambivalence. Difficult as life with Jim could be, Alison was already thinking longingly about having their second child.

As so often in the past, climbing was her outlet and escape. On the day after Tom first slept in his own room in a proper cot, she drove up to Harborough Rocks. It was still winter, and the crags were deserted. But there was no wind, and the temperature was mild. The baby was with her mother, but Alison was still breastfeeding: she didn't have much time. Nervous, excited, she pulled on her rock shoes, lacing them tightly, and tied her bag of magnesium chalk around her waist before grasping the rock with her hands. At first she felt ungainly and stiff, warming up with a few easy routes, savoring the texture of the pitted limestone. Soon, however, the familiar moves began to fall into place, and she eased up the rock with renewed confidence. To climb solo well is the most liberating of all climbing experiences. There is no encumbering paraphernalia; no ropes, carabiners and harnesses, no partner whose plans or abilities may differ from one's own. Of course, it is also more dangerous. Even at Harborough, nowhere more than 25 feet high, a slip may mean a broken leg or worse. But as Alison climbed alone that day, and on many such days to come, she felt exultant, confident, absorbed. After an hour she was sweating, ready to face her life's uncertainties once again.

By late spring Tom was weaned and able to crawl, and she felt able to leave him with her parents for several hours or a whole day. For the time being there could be no question of a lengthy mountaineering trip, and Alison made determined efforts to get back to a standard of roped rock climbing she had not reached for several years. Often her partner was Julianne Dickens: "We started with easier routes, but pretty quickly Alison was leading me up Extremely Severes. She had a fierce confidence, a fearlessness; and although she was small, her hands were like steel claws. Pretty soon I realized I couldn't keep up." The two women climbed together regularly throughout the summer. Julianne made no secret of the fact that her own marriage, under the pressure of the long hours for low wages that Phil was enduring at New Dawn Engineering, was under strain. But she had not the merest inkling that Alison too was unhappy. Julianne saw only the public Alison, the dauntingly efficient businesswoman, mother and climber.

Alison was devoted to Tom, and the pages of her diary are filled with delight at the progress of her "darling little chap." When he sat up, crawled, and walked for the first time, and when he said his first words, she was filled with pride. But after a year in which much of her existence had been devoted to nurturing Tom's, and in which she had received little support from her partner, she wanted to put herself first again, to reassert her independent, adult identity. Other women feel an urge to go back to work as teachers, doctors, or lawyers, to involve themselves in a career again. Alison saw her career as mountaineering and she longed to fulfill herself in the only way she knew. "She always said, she had to be happy to be a good mother," says Susan. "And she could only be happy if she climbed. And she still had ambition. It burned."

At the same time, while Catherine Freer's death had shaken Alison's confidence, forcing her to accept the intellectual proposition that mountaineering might eventually kill her, at a deeper, emotional level, she did not believe that it would. The philosophy she had begun to formulate after first climbing in the Alps with Ian Parsons in 1983, that mountain accidents could always be avoided, had taken deep roots. Alison believed people usually got hurt only when they lacked sufficient skills or the judgment to read conditions and the weather. This belief meant that to go on mountaineering after becoming a mother posed no dilemma; she had a strategy for overcoming the thought that one day she might not come back. Many mountaineering fathers share the same belief. It is not without some justification, since climbers who know when rocks and ice are more likely to fall out of the sky are less likely to be hit by them. It was not that Alison believed herself infallible. But she thought herself cautious, and thus unlikely to get into really serious trouble. What she forgot was that there had been times when she had been incautious, too pushy. Through

September, she begged Jim to give her the chance to go to the Alps. Steve Aisthorpe, her partner from the Eigerwand, was free in October. Surely, she argued, after nearly 12 months of meeting her family's every need, at last she was due a break? Jim agreed to look after Tom while she was away. On October 6 Alison and Steve set off down the motorway, bound for Chamonix.

At first the weather was poor. The Mont Blanc massif was beset by storms, the peaks laden with fresh snow. After almost a week they had managed only the Chèré Couloir on Mont Blanc du Tacul, a short route of no great significance that she had done before. Finally the last of the storms passed away. On a blue, frosty evening they reached the deserted mountain hut on the Argentière glacier, alone beneath the north walls that surround it. There was no sound, no wind to break the stillness. Alison and Steve had their sights set on the north face of Les Droites, 3,500 feet of unrelenting ice.

The mountain was in far from ideal condition. The ice in the first gullies and on the ice field above was flint-hard, and the points of their crampons and axes barely scratched its surface. And on Les Droites there is nowhere to hide, no cosy chimneys in which to seek refuge, no ledges to give relief from the exposure: only the vastness of the icefield, a huge, sloping rink that steepens to verticality in the headwall beneath the summit. Looking at the face from the bottom, Steve had wanted to turn back. Alison, suppressing her own admitted doubts, urged him on, promising they would spend a comfortable night on a bivouac ledge. By nightfall, they had found only a tiny rocky outcrop sticking out from the ice, and after an hour's chopping with their axes, they had cleared only enough space to squat. They had climbed barely half the distance, and the main difficulties were still to come. Alison spent the evening making drinks by melting chips of ice. It was not a comfortable night, and they roused themselves at dawn. Chilled and cramped, it took two hours to get moving. Alison told her diary she had a sense of dread. Now she feared rather than savored the commitment and exposure of being on a big route. Perhaps, she confided, now that she had a child, she should scale down her ambitions after all.

Above lay a maze of vertical rock, seamed with icy ramps and runnels that offered several alternatives. They chose the most direct way to the top, but also the steepest, a corridor of ice that falls straight as an arrow from the rocky gap between the mountain's two summits. Their progress was painfully slow. All day the autumn sun was hidden by the mountain, and as they took turns to wait while the other climbed, they shivered inside their anoraks. Alison's arms ached from the effort of grasping her axes, her calves from the strain of balancing on crampon points, hour after hour. Darkness caught them still 650 feet from the top, on steep ground, with no proper bivouac in sight. They drove ice screws into the mountain and hung from their harnesses, dangling helplessly over the void. They had no way of getting inside their sleeping bags and the cold was like a heavy weight. There was nowhere to balance the stove, nothing to do but shiver, huddled against the mountain. All night, Alison obsessively checked her watch, on each occasion incredulous that so little time had passed.

There was more steep climbing to come. The last pitch, a vertical stream of ice, took Steve an hour and a half to lead. Beyond were the easier slopes of the final couloir, where the sun beckoned through the gap between the summits, coaxing them to make a final effort. They made it just before noon. But there was no easy way off, no stroll to a waiting cable car. On the south side of the

TOP: Alison beams at the summit of Bunster Hill, above Dovedale in Derbyshire, December 1965. BOTTOM: Alison, left, and Sue pose at Marske beach, near Saltburn, North Yorkshire, July 1964.

Photos: John Hargreaves (both)

TOP: Joyce Hargreaves with, left to right, Sue, Alison, and Dick, walks along the Mawddach estuary railway bridge, Barmouth, Mid-Wales, August 1970. BOTTOM: Alison on Bird Rock looks across the Afon Cadair valley to Mynydd Pennant, Mid-Wales, July 1970. RIGHT: Alison climbs the route Debauchery on High Tor above Matlock, Derbyshire, 1982, age twenty.

TOP: Alison crawls along the icefield at the start of the north face of the Matterhorn, Swiss Alps. BOTTOM: Alison reaches for a new hold on the south face of the Aiguille du Midi above Chamonix, French Alps.

TOP, LEFT: John and Alison Hargreaves set off to climb the Welsh 3,000-foot mountains, 1983. TOP, RIGHT: Alison and Jim Ballard celebrate their wedding day in 1988. BOTTOM: Alison, Tom, and Kate vacation at Keppoch beach, Arisaig, West Highlands.

Photos: Dave Collier (top), Gill Round (bottom)

TOP: Alison, Kate, and Tom relax at base camp on the south side of Everest in Nepal in 1994. BOTTOM: Alison is interviewed by Alison Osius after returning from Everest from her first attempt. RIGHT, TOP: The north face of Everest glares at base camp in the Rongbuk Valley. RIGHT, BOTTOM: Alison chats with George Mallory II shortly before her unsupported ascent of the north ridge of Everest; Mallory also climbed the mountain in 1995.

Photos: Ed Douglas (top), Mallory Collection (bottom)

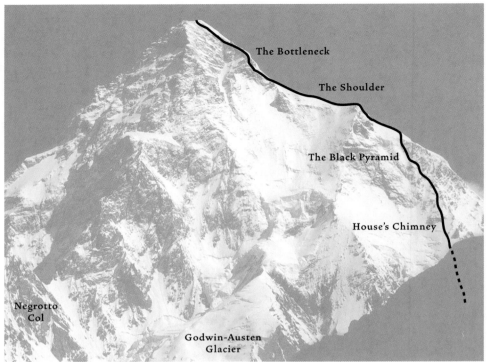

The Bottleneck

The Shoulder

The Black Pyramid

House's Chimney

Negrotto
Col

Godwin-Austen
Glacier

Photos: Roger Payne (top), Alan Hinkes (bottom)

TOP: The Abruzzi Spur forms a line on the south side of K2, in the Karakoram, Pakistan. BOTTOM: Alison climbs fixed ropes on the lower section of K2's Abruzzi Spur.

mountain they followed a gully, rappelling from pitons fixed in its flanks. At the bottom clouds were brewing, obscuring the route. The glacier was a mess, Alison wrote, a tottering jumble of icy towers and crevasses. At last they reached an easy path, where Alison allowed herself "to cry a little—holding back sobs that really wanted to come out."

They should have been on their way back to England. Alison was fearful, not only for their safety but of the likely reactions of those who waited at home. Yet her hopes of reaching the valley that night were dashed. As they passed the Couvercle Hut, a primitive shed in the lee of an overhanging boulder, the storm that had been brewing all day broke with gales and lightning. They took shelter but lacked food, and spent a long night in the cloud-wreathed hut. The mist was still down when they awoke but, exhausted as she was, Alison had no choice but to leave immediately. The following day was Tom's first birthday. After four hours of tough walking to the Montenvers station, a train ride to Chamonix, and then a quick shower and the long drive home, she made it in the early hours of the morning, just before her son woke up.

She was used to sudden contrasts between the two facets of her life, and she made the switch instantly. On October 16, the day of Tom's birthday, she visited her family in Belper; a few days later, she threw a party for him and made a huge iced cake in the shape of a mushroom. The climb on Les Droites—another first British female ascent—had sated her.

Alison and her family saw in the new decade at Grindelwald in Switzerland, on a skiing holiday frustrated by an absence of snow. As she drank toasts with Jim and her parents to a prosperous 1990, the comfortable life that she had enjoyed for ten years was about to come under sustained attack. The losses in the shops continued to mount, absorbing any profits from the Faces factory. Meanwhile, serving the debts Jim and his partners had incurred in buying Don Morrison's and the New Dawn factory was becoming more and more expensive. "We kept waiting for the end of the tunnel, but it never seemed to come," Ian Parsons says. "It got to the stage where we were working for the bank." In hindsight, perhaps Jim should have sold or closed his loss-making enterprises, and then he might have withstood the deepening economic storm. Instead, he began to adopt questionable tactics, which harmed not only his reputation but his ability to stay in business at all.

At first the man who bore the brunt of them was Phil Dickens, who was still trying to make the new rock-climbing protection firm, New Dawn Engineering, a success. "Jim has this inbuilt thing about owing people money," he says. "For him, it's no stigma. In fact, quite the reverse. The way he ran the business was that if you could avoid paying bills, you would." Applied to the makers of rucksacks, ropes, and anoraks, this was awkward enough, but at least these manufacturers understood their market and knew it was under pressure. Jim Ballard was not the only retailer who had to be chased up. The suppliers of New Dawn were in a rather different category. The gear the firm was making relied on components made of high-specification extruded aluminium, available only from a few specialized outlets used to dealing with vast orders from the aircraft industry. Dickens had had to beg them to go to the trouble of filling New Dawn's tiny orders at all. These firms were used to being paid on time, without fail. When Jim began to procrastinate, they simply refused to have anything more to do with him.

Dickens said: "If you lose your supplier, you can't make anything. I could understand why Jim operated the way he did; it was like having an extra overdraft facility. We lost our suppliers twice. Each time, I had to scour the country, trying to find a new one. It wasn't easy. Word gets around." Finally, in June 1990, Phil Dickens told Jim he was leaving New Dawn to return to academia. On the money he was making, he could barely feed his children, but Jim did not take his resignation well. Phil Dickens says: "We'd been pretty good friends. We'd been in and out of each other's houses. Our kids had started growing up together. But he really turned on me." Alison backed her husband. Phil might well want more money and more time with his family, she noted tartly, but so did everyone else.

Notwithstanding the rising debt, Alison was longing for another child. Jim was reluctant, but she put her case persistently: Tom needed a playmate before he became too old; there would be few extra costs because the second child could inherit most of Tom's baby clothes and furniture; it would even increase their income by the government child benefit of £7.25 a week. Having failed to persuade him orally, she set out her argument in the form of a letter: "Dear Jim, I should love to have another baby," she began. "There are many reasons, some of which I have written down, as you are not prepared to listen to me . . . I know pressures on you are greater than ever before. But please don't ignore me and put it off until another better time — cos it won't be." By the middle of July, she was pregnant.

At the end of that month Alison took Tom for a holiday in Braemar with her parents and Susan, who had recently separated from her husband. After years of concealing her troubles and doubts, she began to disclose them to her immediate family for the first time. Susan says: "There's one conversation that always sticks in my mind, when Ali told me she didn't know if she'd still have a house to go to when she got home. Since moving in with Jim, she'd always had this impenetrable veneer. Now it was starting to crack. I began to realize how shaky things were."

The new year, 1991, brought little sign of improvement. Alison was in the final weeks of her pregnancy, planning to have her baby at home. At the same time, she was uncertain how long that home would be hers. Their mortgage payments were three months in arrears. Jim's moods were unpredictable; a good day in the shops could make him unexpectedly cheerful, ready to socialize and charm. More often, he was grumpy and withdrawn.

Katherine Marjorie Ballard, Alison's second child, was born at home on March 28, more than ten days late. From an early age, her physical resemblance to her mother was unusually close. Alison's joy at her healthy baby was soon tempered by Jim's continuing depression and anxiety. He and the other partners were trying to reduce their losses by selling Don Morrison's to the staff who worked there, but the deal was not going well. Within a few weeks, it collapsed. Under the strain of impending ruin, Ballard and Ian Brown were starting to fall out. Brown began to make plans for an exit.

Day after day Alison complained in her diary of exhaustion and loneliness. One spring morning she went out for a walk with her children, carrying Kate in a papoose sling and pushing Tom in his buggy. By chance, she met Dawn Hopkinson, her old friend and climbing partner from the Derwent Mountaineering Club. Dawn saw the strain etched in Alison's face, and at first found it hard to believe that this was the carefree girl she had known a decade earlier. In the following months the two met often. "She was devoted to her children. That was obvious," Dawn says. "But she said it was hard, having to do everything." Little by little,

Alison was becoming readier to shed her emotional shell. She was drawing closer again to Bev England, by now a chain store executive, married to a policeman. In the pages of Alison's diaries, the childlike, naive tone of earlier years had vanished. At 29, and a mother of two, Alison was an increasingly depressive adult. On June 5 she wondered:

> *Why do I get myself into such a state — it can only be a combination of tiredness and lack of self-confidence/depression. Whatever happened to that young, self-confident "I can do it" teenager? I now seem to be able to "turn away" from anything and take the easiest option — failed climber/businesswoman/wife and now mother.*
>
> *I think I do my best — it's obviously not good enough.*

In these moods of depressed reflection Alison often compared herself to other, apparently more fulfilled, female mountaineers. One of them was Catherine Destivelle, the Frenchwoman she had climbed with years earlier on the international meet in the Verdon gorge. Like Alison, Catherine had become inspired by bigger mountains. She also had a new partner and mentor, Alison's old Himalayan comrade, Jeff Lowe. The pair had met at an international climbing competition in Utah in 1988, two years after the expedition to Kangtega. They had fallen in love, and under Lowe's experienced tutelage, Destivelle had been learning new skills and techniques. Lowe lived with Destivelle at her home near Chamonix, and in the summer of 1990 she joined him on an expedition to climb the Nameless Tower, a huge granite needle in Pakistan, close to K2. David Breashears, a mountain climber and filmmaker, made a documentary about the climb. In the Alps, Catherine used the skills she had acquired from Jeff Lowe to spend ten days making a new route on the west face of the Petit Dru, an "artificial" or "aid" climb, where she made progress up an almost featureless granite wall by hammering scores of knife-blade pitons into almost invisible cracks. All the way up, she was followed by television cameramen in helicopters, and afterward she was featured in a ten-page spread in *Paris-Match*.

Alison found her apparently effortless progress difficult to bear. Catherine's life seemed devoid of struggle; she had only to smile, so it seemed to Alison, and commercial sponsors came running. Yet it was Alison who had met Lowe first, she who had won his friendship and respect through her determination and ability. Now, she noted bitterly, he had turned up to speak with Destivelle at a mountaineering festival in Buxton, a few miles up the road from Alison's home, where the couple were fêted by the specialist climbing press as stars. Alison's friends noticed her feeling of rivalry, a resentment borne of her belief that Catherine was claiming a monopoly of recognition, some of which should rightfully be Alison's. "You could sense it, this intense feeling of competitiveness she had with Destivelle," Ian Brown says. "She tried to keep it hidden, but sometimes it would show."

At the same time she began to consider whether there might be ways to emulate her rival's success. Try as Jim might, she had little faith in his ability to rescue the business and their former way of life. She still longed for the freedom to climb. For the first time she began to consider whether pursuing her passion might reestablish her family's security.

Meanwhile, just as after the birth of Tom, she returned to the rocks, seeking solace in short, intense bouts of solo climbing. Usually she would drop the children at her parents', before setting off alone for one of the local crags. In one seven-day period in August, she climbed 27 routes in this fashion at Burbage North, 40 at Birchen Edge, 17 at Stanage, and 20 at Ramshaw Rocks. Slowly, the routes she was prepared to tackle in this fashion were getting more difficult. Two years earlier, she would rarely attempt to solo a Very Severe. Now, she was venturing on to Hard Very Severes, and even routes graded Extreme. Where once she had confined her solo climbs to Derbyshire, where the exposure is never very great, now, when she had the opportunity, she would solo on the mountain cliffs of Wales, hundreds of feet above the ground: here a slip would mean not a broken bone, but almost certain death. The next step was obvious, and it was already emerging in her mind: a solo of a long and difficult route in the Alps. Then, she believed, she might begin to challenge Catherine Destivelle's media dominance.

She knew the risks. Even on a cliff of solid gritstone, usually one of the strongest and most reliable of rocks, a hold may break unexpectedly, and really skilled performers, like the late Paul Williams, who fell from the top of a climb he had soloed many times before, have been killed as a result. But as she tried to expunge her unhappiness with this lonely activity, Alison thought herself safe. In an unpublished interview with the *Observer* newspaper she said: "I don't fall. When I rock climb, I don't fall off. You climb better soloing because you have to. You have to control the fear." And as she pushed herself closer toward the limits she might have contemplated with a rope, her troubles receded further, as her adrenalin-charged focus increased.

Thus the year 1991 wore on toward its dismal end. Jim found it almost impossible to discuss the impending catastrophe. There were orders from climbing shops that wanted Faces gear, but no money to pay for materials in order to fulfill them. The house was on the market, but as the national recession deepened, no one wanted to buy it. The children, sensing their parents' anxiety, were fractious and difficult. On October 16 Tom was three, and in her diary Alison wrote that she had achieved nothing of value throughout his life. Jim had become an "island," she added, marooned in a sea of despair.

For twelve months and more Jim had juggled funds between accounts and the various arms of the business in an attempt to stay solvent, but Alison knew that eventually, this exercise would become impossible to sustain. If Jim could no longer provide, then it would be she who would somehow take over as family bread-winner. With no professional skills or qualifications, there was only one way Alison knew how to make money. But if she were to launch herself as a serious professional mountaineer, capable of attracting lucrative sponsorship, book deals, and lecture tours, she would have to do something spectacular. On January 14, 1992, Alison told Jim she wanted to go to the Alps that winter and attempt a major face on her own. Somehow, he said, he would find a way to pay for the venture from the firm's depleted coffers. He would look after the children in her absence, or if she preferred them to accompany her, he would send one of the staff to mind them while she was actually climbing.

Alison was apprehensive. She craved success and escape to the mountains, but equally she feared failure and the likely recrimi-nations from Jim if she used up some of their diminishing resources without coming home in triumph. But when she weighed her decision, she remembered the sensual pleasures of dazzling summits and cobalt skies, of wielding an ice ax high above glaciers, crampons biting on thick white ice. However unpleasant the consequences of failure, and as much as she craved the rewards of success, above all she wanted the experience of making the attempt. When the days got just a little longer, she decided, she would leave Tom and Kate with Jim and travel to Zermatt. There she would try to make the first female solo ascent of the north face of the Matterhorn. If she succeeded, she would be the first woman to climb any of the great north faces on her own, let alone in the harsh conditions of winter. Her career would be relaunched, and recognition assured.

On February 26 Alison left her children with Jim, and at five in the morning set off on the long, familiar drive to Chamonix. For the first time, however, she was alone. That night she checked into a cheap hotel in Les Praz, a mile out of town. Dazed by the enormity of what she was planning to attempt, she found it impossible to sleep.

Solo climbing in the Alps in winter is a lonely experience. There are none of the queues found at the foot of popular routes in summer, and the hordes thronging the ski pistes lie far below. Alison's near penury intensified her solitude. In the valley, she ate alone, dining off bread and cheese or slices of takeaway pizza. One night in a Chamonix bar, she met some British climbers, including Nigel Shepherd, her boyfriend from years earlier, and they invited her to join them for dinner. Unable to afford the menu, Alison stuck to water and cheap wine, claiming she didn't "feel that hungry."

Alison decided to acclimatize by making some training climbs around the Mont Blanc Range, heading off across the untracked snow on skis, dependent on her own reserves. After a week she had climbed four routes of steadily increasing difficulty. At first she had felt intimidated by the solitude and scale, but as she gained confidence, she began to love the autonomy of climbing alone and being utterly responsible for her own safety. "I find when I'm on my own it's very simple to make clearcut decisions and feel no external influences," she wrote. "Only me to 'please,' weigh up facts and decide." The contrast with the lack of control she exercised over her life in Derbyshire was absolute. And in winter, when the snow cover reaches into the valleys, and the vistas extend for a hundred miles in the cold clear air, the Alps regain the trackless purity of the world's greatest ranges.

Nevertheless, she felt the absence of her children. "I've got back some of my old self-confidence and have really enjoyed my days in the mountains, but every time I see children I think of mine," she wrote one evening. "At breakfast I found it very hard to hold back tears when two lovely sprogs appeared." Tom and Kate would have enjoyed coming with her, she reflected, but that would have made it difficult for her to concentrate on climbing.

Alison would have liked to see Jeff Lowe, and telephoned Catherine Destivelle's number when she came down to the valley between climbs. On the first occasion, she reached Lothar, Catherine's former partner and business manager, but neither Destivelle nor Jeff was in. Then, on March 4, Catherine answered: Jeff was on his way back from a trade show in Munich and was planning to go climbing as soon as he arrived. Alison was disappointed. She told both Lothar and Catherine what she was planning, and both wished her luck. Later that day she drove to Zermatt and checked into her old haunt from the days of her partnership with Ian Parsons, Frau Biner's Bahnhof Hotel.

On the following day Alison trudged up from Zermatt to the Hörnli refuge beneath the Matterhorn. The weather forecast was excellent, but there the weather broke. For two days the mountain was invisible, beset by wind and swirling snow. There were several parties in the hut, some planning to try the north face, others the easier Hörnli Ridge, and they passed the time easily. At such times and in such places, as they steady themselves before a big route, there is a natural, unforced camaraderie among mountaineers, a generosity and intimacy born of facing a common risk. They passed the time discussing the mountains and drinking tea. A German made Welsh rarebits for everyone.

On the second evening the sky began to clear. The route looked hard, but possible. Alison remembered that when she had climbed it with Ian Parsons eight years earlier, she had been struck by the lack of good protection or belays; by the lack of security, even with a rope. Soloing, she told herself, would make little difference. She slept soundly and rose at 1:30 a.m. It was cold but still, and after forcing down some instant strawberry porridge, she ventured into the night. The face loomed in the starlight, faintly luminescent. She had hoped to leave later, but four Swiss had designs on the same route. The consequences of being hit by ice or stones dislodged by climbers above are more likely to be fatal for those climbing alone and unroped. She had to get on the face first.

Alison had hoped to find the ice field that makes up the first third of the face an easy slope of frozen snow. Instead, scoured clean by the wind, it was in the worst possible condition. Instead of white frozen snow, as easy to climb as compacted polystyrene, there was only gray, brittle ice. She was faced with a struggle for every step, with footholds only millimeters deep, and the phenomenon known as "dinnerplating," when a blow from an ice axe shears the ice from the surface in big, round chunks, and the axe must be swung again and again until the climber feels secure. She climbed a little way and wondered what to do, gazing fearfully at the 1,200 feet of ice field that still stretched out above her. Soon the four Swiss climbers caught her up, then decided to descend. Teetering on her front points, Alison tried to rest, waiting for daylight to illuminate the way ahead. When it came, her decision was made easily. The face was out of condition, and she turned to descend. She had no doubts. Far better to return when conditions were safer. The mountain would always be there.

Safely back on the glacier, Alison remembered Jim's reaction to her expedition to Nepal in 1987. Why, he had asked her, had she not "grabbed another peak" after being defeated by Ama Dablam? The day was already well advanced, but the sun was shining and the wind was still. "I felt I should make an effort and at least get something to show on this beautiful summit day," Alison wrote. Even here, she was less autonomous than she believed. Above the hut, the Hörnli Ridge, the route of the mountain's first ascent, snaked up invitingly, a switchback of rock and ice. Beside the north face, it looked relatively easy, and Alison set off for the summit. After climbing for six hours, she reached the top at five past two in the afternoon, still in plenty of time to descend. Beyond a wooden Madonna, the shining mountains stretched out in all directions. Delighted with her aerie, Alison peered down into Italy and across to the squat bulk of distant Mont Blanc. Climbing could still offer her moments of perfect joy.

Not far from the top she met two Germans and a Canadian; one of them was the man who made her toast the evening before. They had been too slow to reach the summit, and now, as they tried to retreat, it was clear they were poorly equipped. They had only a short length of rope, too short to use for rappels, which in the icy conditions of winter, were the only practical way to get down. On the way up, the Hörnli Ridge had been a pleasant, sunny scramble.

Now, as the shadows lengthened and the temperature fell, its steep steps seemed fearsome, and the route, so easy to find on the ascent, obscure. To the left, sweeping down uninterrupted for 4,000 feet, was the gaping drop of the Matterhorn's east face. It is one of the most dangerous places in all the Alps. Alison knew that since four men plunged its length after taking part in the mountain's first ascent in 1865, the face had claimed more than 400 victims, most of them caught after slipping or losing their way on the Hörnli ridge.

For Alison there was no choice to be made. The other climbers had put themselves in peril, but her duty was to help them down. She took out her full-length 50-meter rope from her rucksack, and promised to accompany them, at least as far as the Solvay Hut—a tiny emergency shelter perched on a ledge about 13,000 feet up.

With four on the rope, the descent seemed to take for ever. As a schoolgirl, Alison had taken hours to descend from Grooved Arête on Tryfan. Now she was using the same techniques on a fiercely cold Alpine winter's night, in temperatures far below freezing. Again and again she repeated the familiar process. She would find a flake of rock, or perhaps an iron stanchion fixed by the Zermatt guides, double the rope around it, probe the darkness with her head lamp, then descend. Then came the wait for the others, so slow, so slow. But the rope was new, and as she pulled one end to release it, it kept getting tangled in dense, spaghetti-like knots. Sometimes she had to climb back up to loosen it: each tangle was more time lost, a longer exposure to the biting cold. Beneath thick layers of fleece clothing, Alison began to shiver uncontrollably, fighting to maintain her concentration. Before long, she had lost all sensation in her feet.

At ten o'clock, eight hours after Alison left the summit, the party made it to the hut. They had moved so slowly, but Alison never thought of going it alone. The hut, a bare cabin with a rough bunk and blankets, provided little warmth or comfort. Inside, her worst fears were realized. As she took off her boots, she discovered her toes were encased in ice. In the warmth of the sunny morning, her feet had become soaked with condensation and sweat; and during the slow descent, with its long periods of immobility as she waited for the others to make their rappels, this moisture had frozen solid. Desperate to restore circulation, she tried to melt the ice beneath layers of blankets, but her right big toe remained white and numb. She was suffering from frostbite.

Alison knew that without speedy medical treatment, she might face amputation: she had lost all sensation. She tried massage in an attempt to restore circulation, but to no avail. Terrified, she was up at first light, eager to leave. But Alison had no thought of putting herself first, of abandoning her new companions; what was right was automatic. There was still a long way to the bottom of the ridge; it would take more rappels and delicate climbing down, all of which might damage her toe further. Fighting tears, she continued to shepherd the others down to safety. They moved jerkily, dazed by dehydration, and Alison, by far the most capable of the ad hoc team, felt responsible for them all. After a final rappel, Alison rushed ahead to the Hörnli refuge; then, after a hurried drink, on down the snowy path to the cable car at Schwarsee.

In Zermatt, cold, wet, and exhausted, she changed her clothes and got into her car. By nine in the evening she was back in Chamonix. She knew Jim was away on business and she tried to phone Jeff Lowe, but there was no reply. She was still on her own. At the local hospital, famous the world over for its success in treating frostbite, she sat in the foyer, where a nurse noticed her wet sock through her sandal: "She gets me to sit down. I cry. *Nobody* speaks a word of English." A doctor came and admitted her, hooking her up to a drip and placing her feet in an oxygen bath. At last she could relax and eat: hot soup, bread, and cheese. It was the first thing she had consumed since leaving the Solvay Hut at dawn, and, as she told her diary, the first proper meal she had eaten since leaving Derbyshire. The hospital food, she noted grimly, was free of charge.

In one sense, Alison was lucky; her injuries could have been much worse. For six days she rested. But the doctors said it would be many months before she could contemplate serious mountaineering, and weeks before she would be free of pain. On March 10, her fourth day in hospital, the surgeons cut away the dead tissue from Alison's toes, and to her relief, told her she would escape the loss of any digits. During the afternoon she read French climbing magazines, and noted with some bitterness a glamorous picture spread featuring Catherine Destivelle. Alison had finished her diary for the day, and dined well on vegetables and fish. Tired and bored, she was getting ready for sleep. Then, at 7:45 p.m., in a state of terrible anguish, she began to write again:

> *I'm devastated. I've just had some of the worst news I could ever have had. Catherine Destivelle's soloed the Eiger ... I want to go outside and scream ... I want to hide away for ever ... I feel terrible, shallow, useless. There's no point in me climbing, in doing anything. I just fail at everything.*

Alison believed, in her bitter disappointment, that Catherine had been prompted to climb on hearing Alison's intention. In fact,

Destivelle had been planning to solo the north face of the Eiger for several weeks, and Alison's messages for Jeff Lowe were of no relevance. But Alison, having begun to rebuild her confidence and self-esteem, was now in free-fall, in no mood to consider the situation rationally. She had built up her trip to the Matterhorn as her shining opportunity. Now she was returning wounded and unsuccessful, while Catherine was triumphant.

She turned to the subject again and again. On March 12, a few days after returning to England, she reflected in her diary on how she had wasted her chance to become the first woman to solo a big north face in winter, if only by a few days. "Can I ever regain my self-confidence and do anything again—or do I just have no fire left in my belly?"

On that day, not only Alison but four experienced Swiss mountaineers had turned back. Soloing the Matterhorn ice field in the prevailing conditions would have been a risk too great. But in her depression, Alison saw her own prudence and good judgment as a weakness. Along with her plummeting self-esteem, Alison felt a deep and disproportionate sense of rivalry with Catherine. "She started really running her down," says Bev England. "She said she'd only got where she had because she'd latched on to various men, while Ali had to do it all by herself." Alison had acquired a new, dangerous ambition: to beat Destivelle at her own game, to demonstrate that she was the superior athlete.

During Alison's absence, the crisis afflicting the business and her family's own finances had, if anything, got worse. Jim was talking about giving up altogether, but seemed unable to make decisions. Once again he was showing classic signs of depression: irritable and withdrawn, he often seemed unable to rouse himself to tackle his many problems, preferring to lounge around the house or watch daytime TV. Alison was hobbling, unable to put her toe on the ground, and ordinary domestic duties caused her pain.

Four days later, after another rumbling row, Alison visited the Faces factory, finding it messy and disorganized. "I really do wonder if this is the end for Jim and I.... I came with nothing—maybe after 12 years I shall go with nothing—except two healthy children and some climbing experience."

Jim's financial juggling act was nearing the end. His creditors were beginning to resort to legal action in an attempt to recover the money he and his partners owed. In the spring of 1992, the local county courts recorded the first of a series of judgments against him. One by one the Faces workers, whose pay checks had bounced, were handing in their notice.

Nick Morely, the Bivouac's last manager, remembers the dying months of Ballard's business with bemused wonder. He had started work there in 1989, and even then he found that this was a job with unusual challenges: "When I started, the books were in chaos and there was almost no stock. I tried to get everything on a proper footing. But suppliers wouldn't even send round price lists once they heard where I was from, our reputation was so bad." After years of decline and the rise of local competition, custom had slowed to a trickle: "There were a lot of days when only one person would come into the shop, and some with none at all. Eventually we didn't even stock the most basic items." By the end of 1990, Morely was often not getting paid and, without another job to go for, he would simply pocket the cash from the rare items he did manage to sell and leave a scribbled note in the till. By late spring 1992, it was hardly worth going in at all. He had draped a cloth screen across the back of the shop to hide the empty shelves and, little by little, he moved it forward. The phone was cut off, the bill unpaid. Jim was seldom seen.

Alison's frostbite was still not perfectly healed, and in the middle of June she opened up a nasty wound when she banged her toe. It says much for her fevered mental state that a few days later, on a trip to her parents' Welsh cottage, she forced her injured foot into tight rock-climbing shoes and spent two days in a furious blur of solo climbing.

Superficially, she seemed to be coping. She trained, she mothered, she took part in various mountaineering committees. But the stress she was under was affecting her health. Toward the end of June, she began to suffer mysterious attacks. Sometimes they occurred when she went out for a run, but also when she was relaxing. Her skin turned red and blotchy, she felt unable to breathe and was immensely weary, close to collapse. Her general practitioner was baffled and referred her to a specialist in Derby. He concluded that her nervous system was in revolt, unable to withstand the pressure. The attacks might be psychosomatic in origin, but they were serious enough to warrant physical treatment. At the beginning of July, Alison began a three-month course of steroids.

Sick, depressed, and beset by a sense of failure, Alison's life was in disarray. The bailiffs were circling, her husband apparently helpless. With or without him, she had to find an exit.

CHAPTER 7

MOUNTAINEERING GYPSIES

One chilly evening toward the end of February 1993, Alison and Jim sat in their kitchen with their neighbors from the farm, Ted and Jackie Johnson. The last dinner they were to eat at Meerbrook Lea was on the table, and behind them, filling half the room, was a clump of blue plastic barrels. Jim gestured toward them. There, he said grimly, were all the family's worldly goods. The following morning, they would be loading the barrels and the children into an ancient Land Rover and leaving forever the house where Alison had lived for 13 years.

There had been no easy solution to their dismal circumstances. As Alison told her sister in a letter the previous August, the plan she and Jim developed in the summer of 1992 followed "four months in a terrible, drifting state," and might well turn out to "take us down a blind alley." But after another of her mysterious attacks, which left her terrified and gasping for air, Alison believed she had no other option. At the beginning of the following year she wrote: "We're going away—all of us, to Europe, for me to climb and JB to mind the sprogs." Their home let and the business abandoned, the family would live in tents, moving around the mountains, stowing their few possessions in the Land Rover. For income, they would rely on sponsorship and a book that Alison planned to write about her climbs.

None of the sponsorship had yet been raised, and there was no contract to write the book. But it was, in essence, the life of a professional mountaineer. "I hope to make a go of it," Alison wrote.

> If we don't go now we never will—JB will find something else to attract his attention in business, and I shall never know if I can make it as a climber. Soon the kids will be settled at school; so here we go. I feel a lot happier.

It meant hardship and more uncertainty. But for Alison, the attempt to transform herself into a professional mountaineer offered a new direction and a release from the pent-up frustrations that near bankruptcy and a failing relationship had created within her. They would simply drive away from the chaos of the past.

Her first goal, which she hoped to accomplish in the spring and summer of 1993, was to climb the six most famous north faces in the Alps. These routes had first been labeled in the 1940s by the French guide Gaston Rébuffat in his book *Starlight and Storm*. According to Rébuffat, these were the hardest and most beautiful routes in the Alps, and the few mountaineers who had climbed them all could number themselves among the greats. The list was full of the romance and history of mountain climbing, and while none of the faces was any longer at the leading edge of alpinism, they took commitment, were often dangerous, and few had been climbed solo by a woman.

The Alps, though, would be only the start. Alison had written to a British medical expedition planning to climb Everest in the autumn of 1994 to conduct research into high-altitude physiology, but all the places on it were taken. But in August 1992, as she sat at home working at her sewing machine, Tom heard the postman and rushed to fetch the mail for his mother. There was a letter postmarked Argyll, home of one of the Everest expedition's leaders. A team member had dropped out, he wrote, and would Alison like to join them? "I could have jumped higher than the ceiling," she wrote in her diary. Bursting with joy but with the phone cut off, she was forced to keep the news to herself. She added: "I know it doesn't guarantee success but it does guarantee an attempt." Amid the ruins of her life with Jim, a childhood dream had been realized. She was going to Everest.

Alison knew that the first part of their plan, her climbing solo in the Alps, had plenty of pitfalls. She and Jim would be forced to live in claustrophobic proximity to each other, just the two of them and the children for long stretches of time on campsites, being together constantly when she wasn't climbing or training. The idea made her uneasy. "Can we really survive months of close confinement?" Alison asked herself in her diary. "Jim wouldn't be able to handle my failures . . . he likes to be the one pulling the strings, but he won't be able to all the time." She understood that their plan would also impose heavy burdens on her partner. He would be abandoning the business ambitions that had motivated him for 20 years, and would be forced to undertake a heavier share of caring for the children. It would require him to make substantial changes to his self-image and to his very traditional attitude to parenting and gender roles. This only added to Alison's sense of responsibility, and made her anxious that by becoming the family's sole breadwinner, she might feel a dangerous pressure to succeed.

Alison was trying to get fit for her new way of life, and followed a grueling program of long runs and plenty of easy solo climbing. She had never been very scientific in her training, but she understood that she would have to keep going for long periods. She could climb at the standard required, but she needed to do it for hours on end. With an aim in sight, she began to focus on the goal she had set herself. Still, they would not be ready to leave for months, and the stresses of the life she planned to abandon continued to mount. The last of the Faces workers in the Matlock factory had resigned, and in an attempt to maintain any kind of income, Alison had brought one of the industrial sewing machines back to the house so she could start work at home. She was making up climbers' chalk bags and gaiters again, returning to a means of subsistence she had left behind ten years earlier. The mortgage was becoming further and further in arrears, and her credit card had reached its limit. One morning Jim asked for the last ten pounds in Alison's bank account to buy petrol. She had been saving the money to pay for Tom's play group, she said. When she demurred, he hurled a basket of logs across the floor.

Alison's isolation at home deepened. The telephone was disconnected, her car, bought in a moment of recklessness a few months earlier, was repossessed. She wrote in her diary that she was trapped in the house with the children, unable to take them shopping or to play in one of the local parks. The days grew colder, and there was no money to pay for coal or heating fuel. Alison was forced to accept her neighbours' generosity and gather logs in their woods for the fire.

Even worse, their plans for escape hit an immediate hurdle. Alison discovered that Rebecca Stephens, a British financial journalist with only minimal climbing experience, was to join an expedition to Everest the following spring, the 40th anniversary of the mountain's first ascent by Edmund Hillary and Tenzing Norgay. Stephens had climbed only a handful of big mountains, including Denali, the highest peak in North America, and she had stuck to the easiest routes, helped and encouraged by her partner John Barry, the former head of the national mountain training center at Plas y Brenin in Wales. Yet while Stephens might lack climbing pedigree, helped by Sherpas and supplementary oxygen, her chances of success on Everest were reasonably good. Stephens and Barry were planning to attempt the South Col route, which Hillary and Tenzing climbed in 1953. When Nepal opened its borders after the Second World War, mountaineers quickly realized that the best chance of success on Everest was from the south. A long, hanging valley called the Western Cwm climbs from a tumbling icefall at 20,000 feet to the start of a 45-degree slope at 22,500 feet in three long but easy-angled miles. At the top of the slope, at 26,000 feet, is the South Col, from where climbers go in one long day to the summit on Everest's Southeast Ridge. For most of its distance, climbing Everest is straightforward, a comfortably angled climb on snow and ice that in good weather even novice climbers can manage, since it involves little more than walking in crampons. Because of its height and the chance of bad weather, climbing Everest will never be a negligible achievement, but Stephens could expect its few difficult sections to be equipped with ropes, making the ascent more a test of determination and stamina than climbing ability.

Among the mountaineering cognoscenti, Alison believed solo climbs of the Alpine north faces would constitute the greater achievement. But if Stephens got up Everest, it would be she who would benefit from mainstream media acclaim. "She spoke of throwing up all her plans to get herself on an earlier Everest expedition," Sue recalls. "She wanted to pay whatever it took to get herself out there. But there was no money, and Jim wouldn't agree. He said they'd made their plans and they were going to stick to them. They were not going to Everest until 1994."

Jim now saw himself as Alison's manager, and he spent much of the autumn on the telephone in the old Faces factory, using the one line that still worked, in an attempt to attract commercial sponsors. He had little success. Many of the firms he approached for support were the same companies that had become frustrated over the years by his way of doing business. Jim and Alison's approach was naive and unambitious, with no clear indication of how or what potential sponsors might gain. Alison was a famous climber trying something exciting, they argued, so companies had a duty to support her. In reality, there was little to distinguish her from the hundreds of would-be explorers who send out begging letters every day. Most were simply thrown away.

One of the companies they approached was Sprayway, a waterproof clothing manufacturer based in Manchester. It had begun as a small concern, much like Jim Ballard's, making garments for sailors. Over the years it had prospered and extended its range, and by the early 1990s it was expanding rapidly to include the general outdoor market. When Alison's letter landed on the desk of the managing director, John Hunt, he ignored it. But for once it was Alison, rather than her husband, who followed up the letter with a telephone call. Hunt was intrigued and asked to see her.

They met in December, and Hunt warmed to her confidence and determination. The company had never before sponsored anyone, but were looking to raise their profile in the quickly growing outdoor market. Hunt agreed to pay her a retainer of £600 per month for three years and to provide her with the equipment she needed. There would also be bonuses if she succeeded. In return she would assist in promoting the company and help to develop its products. Compared to the sums other professional sportswomen earn, it was not much; but by living frugally, Alison could keep her family fed. The deal proved a turning point, and in the absence of any other family income, her ambition of becoming the breadwinner was being fulfilled. When Alison told her parents, her mother recalls, she was "chuffed to bits."

Toward the end of the year she sold the idea of a book about her six Alpine climbs to Maggie Body, an editor at Hodder & Stoughton, who has worked with many of the best-known mountaineering authors. They met for lunch near Hodder's offices in Bedford Square in London, and like John Hunt, Body was impressed by Alison's confident shell. Body did not foresee a large potential market, and could offer an advance of only £3,000. To Alison, whose home was on the verge of repossession, it must have seemed like much more. The nomadic climbing life she was planning would be financially straitened, but it was at last beginning to seem possible.

Alison researched the six north faces carefully. She had climbed three of them before: those of the Eiger, Matterhorn, and Grandes Jorasses. For information about the others, she turned to Bill O'Connor, leader of the abortive attempt on Ama Dablam in 1987. He thought she would have little difficulty on the Piz Badile, a spade-shaped wedge of granite on the Swiss-Italian border;

rarely very steep, the climbing was well within her capabilities. But climbing delicate granite slabs with no rope 3,000 feet above the ground would require a strong mind. The Badile also has a reputation for sudden bad weather. On the first ascent, in 1937, the climbers were caught in a storm and had to fight their way down, two of them dying from cold and exhaustion before they reached safety. O'Connor had also climbed the north face of the Cima Grande, a precipitous limestone tooth in the Italian Dolomites. Again, Alison was technically capable of finishing the climb; the only question was whether the exposure and frightening steepness of the Cima Grande would put her off. The Cima Grande is 2,000 feet high and mostly vertical. Every time Alison looked down at her feet to place them on holds, she would see the ground beneath her. Could she cope with the moments of doubt she might feel on such a steep face? The final north face, that of the Petit Dru above Chamonix, was in the heart of the French Alps, psychologically Alison's home from home. It posed more varied problems, with its share of ice and loose rock, and a long, awkward descent.

Alison, Jim, and the children drove steadily to the French Alps and spent a week around Chamonix, living at first in a rented caravan and watching the indifferent weather. Alison took the children sledging and managed a little rock climbing to keep herself fit; but with heavy snow lying on the mountains, it would be some time before she could start on the climbs that had brought them all out there. On March 28 they had a party for Kate's second birthday, but a few days later their time in the caravan expired. They were forced to start camping, the ground soaked and muddy. They covered the floor of the children's tent with insulating mats and Tom spread his toys across the groundcloth. Kate usually slept with her parents after waking in the night, crying until they stumbled across the cold, dark campsite from their own tent to fetch her.

Back in Derbyshire, what was left of Alison's former life was rapidly unraveling. She and Jim had left her parents' house in Belper as a forwarding address, and a few days after their departure, bailiffs called on John and Joyce, demanding Jim's arrears of council tax. There was worse to come. On the morning Jim and Alison had gone to the Alps, Jim had told them that unless the mortgage lenders were given £10,000 immediately, they were likely to repossess the house and sell it, the hapless tenant notwithstanding. John and Joyce had been making occasional contributions toward the mortgage for some time, but this was a sum they were not prepared to lend: "We could see our money disappearing into a black hole," Joyce says. Their only contact with their daughter and her husband was through intermittent telephone calls. Alison, aware of their problems, at least seemed appropriately concerned.

The long-delayed inevitable fell on April 13, when the building society began court proceedings to repossess Meerbrook Lea. Informed of the impending loss of his house, Jim took no action. It was left to John and Joyce to organize a removal van and rescue what they could of Jim and Alison's possessions—including their furniture and all Alison's personal diaries stretching back to 1973.

Adrift in Europe, Alison and her children were now homeless. "We were so proud of her and what she was doing," Joyce says. "But she was having to achieve it in such difficult conditions." For a few months Ian Parsons raked over the embers of their business, trying to get something going again, but as the debts and creditors' court judgments mounted, he gave up the struggle. He had remained a true friend, paying for the removal van to take

Alison and Jim's things from Meerbrook Lea and paying off her credit card until his house was also repossessed. To those who knew him, he seemed to have aged years in a few months. The entire business went into liquidation.

By the beginning of May, after six weeks of rain, wind, and snow, Alison still hadn't tried any of the six north faces on her list. The tent had been ransacked one day while she was out rock climbing, and some of her limited supply of money stolen. The Land Rover had needed expensive new tires, and then developed a gearbox fault that threatened to keep it off the road altogether. Local villagers told her that it was one of the worst springs on record, but that was no consolation to Alison, desperately needing to get something done to keep sponsors and her publisher happy. The whole project was teetering on the edge of disaster, and if she failed then her plan to be a professional mountaineer would be over before it had really begun. To escape the depression, the family drove to the coast near Marseilles, where Alison could spend a few days climbing on the limestone sea cliffs to keep in shape, while Tom and Kate built sand castles on the beach. But she was in France to climb mountains, not relax at the seaside, and as soon as possible they returned to the Alps.

In the Massif des Ecrins, a remote area 70 miles south of Mont Blanc, the weather was a little better, and she actually managed to climb some easy peaks. But there they suffered a second theft when an English conman carefully chose the two most valuable barrels to steal, those packed with climbing gear. If she had not removed her ice axes and crampons to dry them in the Land Rover, Alison could not have continued at all. A few days after the theft, she managed to reach the top of the area's highest peak, the Barre des Ecrins. Given the weather and conditions, it was a creditable achievement, but set against the two or three north faces she hoped to have completed, it was little more than training, a steep snow slope at altitude with no difficult climbing. Alison, Jim, and the children returned to Chamonix to wait for settled weather, and to replace the stolen gear. They had no choice except to sit it out and hope for a change in fortune.

Instead, things got worse. In Chamonix Alison discovered that Rebecca Stephens had become the first British woman to climb Mount Everest. Every British newspaper on the Chamonix newsstands had her face on the front page, and she had been on every television news program. As far as the British public was concerned, Stephens was now the most famous female mountaineer in the world, and the fact that she had climbed only a handful of peaks before Everest was completely irrelevant. She had picked the challenge that was certain to have the widest impact, attaching herself to a team that gave her an excellent chance of success. Stephens overcame considerable problems; her first summit bid had ended in failure and she had shown real courage and determination in going back up for another try. She had used a number of Sherpas to support her successful climb, and relied heavily on bottles of supplementary oxygen to boost her effort, but none of that mattered to the non-climbing public. To Alison it mattered acutely.

She felt cheated again, much as she had at the success of Catherine Destivelle. Her immediate reactions, as she struggled with her children on sodden campsites, can only be imagined, but later she told both Susan and Bev England that try as she might, she could not avoid a sense of bitterness and envy. Had Jim not vetoed the idea, she might have been on Everest herself that spring, and given her fitness and experience, she would have had a strong chance of beating Stephens to the record. It was in her nature to brood on disappointments like this, and, immaturely, Alison often saw the success of others as personally demeaning. While her insecurity over the talent she nurtured had undermined her perspective, the desire to prove herself remained undimmed.

Early in June the weather eased long enough for Alison to try her first north-face solo: the Matterhorn. At first, all went well, but 1,000 feet up, at the top of the First Ice Field, she was forced to turn back. The rocks above were plastered in wet snow, and to continue would have been too hazardous. It was the right decision, but disheartening none the less. She still hadn't climbed one of the six north faces after months of waiting. While Alison was thus engaged on the Matterhorn, a middle-aged Englishman called Richard Allen arrived at the campsite in Täsch at the start of a walking holiday. A long-standing member of the Alpine Club, Allen had worked for the construction group Kier and had recently returned to Europe after working at a very senior level on the project to build the new Hong Kong airport. Alison couldn't know it, but Richard Allen's management skills would eventually be of great help to her career as a friendship built up between them.

Allen had seen an older man looking after two young children and thought it unusual. He was further intrigued when a young woman appeared, obviously down from the mountains, who began making dinner and getting the children ready for bed, reading them stories, and settling them down. It was only later that he discovered she had been a third of the way up the Matterhorn's North Face in awful conditions that morning. They ate dinner together and Allen, whose path would cross Alison and her family's several times over the next few weeks, was struck by the tough enthusiasm the children showed for camping, playing outside even in bad weather, and Alison's determination.

After her return to the valley, the family left Switzerland and drove back once more to Chamonix, where the more favorable French exchange rate made food and campsites cheaper. Still the clouds stayed low, the mountains unclimbable. Most mornings Alison ran from Chamonix to the railway station at Montenvers, a height gain up a rough forest path of nearly 3,000 feet. The rest of the day she would try to keep the children amused while bickering with her husband. Jim is the only adult witness to most of those miserable weeks of inactivity, but later Alison told her friends and family that the trip had been fraught with tension. All their futures seemed to rest on Alison's mountaineering success, and every time she came down from the hills without having climbed a major face, she felt herself confronted by their needs and expectations. On previous forays to the Alps, Jim had sometimes been woundingly critical of her failures. This time, Alison said later, there had been huge rows about her lack of progress. Alison was caught again in a wretched situation but committed to seeing it through. She could think of no other way.

At some point during these weeks of frustration, Alison decided to alter her plans. In *Starlight and Storm*, Rébuffat wrote that there were two routes on the broad north wall of the Grandes Jorasses that were worthy of his list: the Croz and Walker Spurs. When Alison had climbed the Croz with Ian Parsons, it had taken them four days, and they found it their hardest Alpine climb. They had failed on the Walker nine years earlier in exactly the conditions that Alison was trying to deal with in 1993: too much fresh, wet snow lying over the rock. However, to the left of the two spurs, on the far left side of the face, is a more amenable proposition, the line of gullies and ice fields known as the Shroud, the route she had once contemplated climbing with Jim. Unlike the Croz and Walker, the Shroud involves no long sections of difficult rock; and after a few steep pitches near the start, the angle lies back to a more comfortable 55 degrees. With modern ice axes and crampons, and given good conditions, it is straightforward; it has even been descended by snowboard. Alison knew the climb did not rate as one of the six great north faces, but it had never been climbed solo by a woman. Stifling her misgivings, on June 16 she left the campsite, heading for the Shroud.

Most climbers contemplating a major solo climb would have spent a few francs on the mountain railway up to Montenvers at the foot of the Mer de Glace to conserve their energy, but Alison couldn't afford to waste money and she wound slowly up through the pine forests above Chamonix on foot. In her account of these climbs, *A Hard Day's Summer*, she wrote: "At Montenvers I experienced a slight apprehension! Was the plan wise? Yes!" Public admissions of doubt from Alison, even ones as breathless and throwaway as this, were very rare, and it's easy to imagine her alongside the tourists eating ice creams and looking at the view, weighing up her situation, thinking about her children in the valley and the future they faced. She felt she had little choice but to go on.

After the long hike up to the hut at the foot of the Grandes Jorasses, she set out early the following morning. The climb went well and conditions were generally good. Once through the early difficulties she worked steadily up the ice field above, slowing as she neared the top as the altitude began to affect her. A fierce wind developed and clouds boiled up, seemingly from nowhere. The forecast had been wrong. On the descent she caught two French guides who had started ahead of her, and she waited to one side as the snow they dislodged buffeted her. Once they were clear, Alison continued to the ridge above and then joined them, abseiling back to the glacier she had stepped from that morning.

The descent was long and wearying, and she could find nothing to drink when she reached the station at Montenvers, but finally, as she stumbled toward camp, a figure emerged from the shadows ambling slowly toward her. It was Jim, and she was delighted to see him. It was a poignant moment and one they both dwelt on later. "He hugged me, pleased to see me whether I had climbed the face or not," she wrote. "It was me back safe that mattered. Bursting with pride I told him." Suddenly, the antagonism and failure were gone. Alison was now shivering, her sweat-soaked clothes clammy against her skin. By that time of night, the campsite showers were closed and Jim was forced to fill buckets from the washbasins with hot water. Alison stood naked outside her tent as he poured the water over her head and then allowed herself to be dressed by him and put into a sleeping bag. "She was the young girl," he wrote afterward , "tired and needing to be looked after."

Next came a second attempt at the Matterhorn, which finished even lower than the first. The wind blew snow and stones against her as she climbed tentatively up and down the start of the ice field, wanting to go on but doubting the weather. She scanned the clouds racing past the summit, but despite her need to continue, retreated to the Hörnli Hut. Alison waited there until the following morning, but the weather was worse and she decided to go back to the valley. At Zermatt, Tom and Kate were playing on the swings in a local park, but despite her exhaustion, Alison took them for a walk around town, looking in toy shop windows at things they could not possibly afford. The mountain nagged at the back of her mind, and she contemplated returning to the Matterhorn that very afternoon, but Jim dissuaded her. Instead, Alison spent the following morning in the park with the children before shouldering her rucksack. She was back at the Hörnli refuge close to the bottom of the face by midafternoon.

This time her efforts were rewarded. Reaching the bottom of the north face at 5 a.m., Alison found conditions on the First Ice Field more nerve-racking than before, and she climbed cautiously as her ice axes splintered the brittle, unfriendly ice and she teetered on her crampon points. As the sun slowly rose behind the mountains at her back, she moved right on to an awkward ramp a third of the way up the face that mixed ice and rock climbing. Scratching at the rock with her crampons, touching handholds slippery with ice, it would have been insecure and intimidating for two, but Alison was alone, relying on her own mental strength to keep going, with no rope to stop her if she fell. She told herself that at the top of the ramp, she would have finished two-thirds of the climb and be on easier ground, but when Alison got there, she discovered the rock was covered with powder snow, which had to be swept clear from every handhold before she could grasp it and move up. The wind strengthened and clouds swirled in around her. Never before had she been so committed; to slip was to die, but retreat was just as unthinkable. Slowly she neared the mountain's apex and a final snowy gully before standing on the summit. There was no time to waste, and no view to see at the top. A storm was sweeping in across the mountain. She had to get down as quickly as possible. Using the experience of her two previous ascents, she made rapid progress down the easier Hörnli Ridge. "As the lightning flashed around me and spots of rain turned into heavier bursts," she wrote, "I smiled at the fact that yet again

I was not to take things for granted." Finally, after 14 hours, she reached the base of the mountain and was safe.

Alison had made the first solo by a woman of the Matterhorn's North Face, a stunning piece of climbing in marginal conditions. The route may have been climbed more than 60 years before, but its dangers hadn't altered at all. Facing them alone had required complete self-control and a great deal of courage. When she stopped at the Hotel Bahnhof, her old friend Frau Biner was amazed and also a little alarmed that Alison should have soloed such a demanding route in the indifferent weather that squatted over the Alps that summer.

With money scarcer than ever, it now made sense to go to the nearby Bernese Oberland, so Alison could climb the Eiger, but for almost a month the weather was unremittingly bad. For three drenched and muddy weeks, Alison, Jim, and the children camped at Grindelwald while the tourists came and quickly went to escape the dreary conditions. The mountains were white, plastered with a quantity of snow that was usually long gone by July. "There were a lot of times I thought, 'Let's just give up and go home,'" Alison said later in an interview with the authors. "But I had committed myself. There are times when people don't feel like going to the office. I had to treat this as my work. Families kept arriving on our campsite, and after two days in the mud, they were giving up in despair. That was when I got depressed. I'd only done two routes and already it was the end of July." Alison, who had seen the mountains as a magical place, the landscape of her childhood and her happiest days as an adult, now equated them with the daily commute and the tedium of the regular job she had fought to avoid. Her blessed escape had become a necessary chore. Expectation compressed her spirit; she had a book to deliver and sponsors to impress. Alison felt herself on the professional climber's treadmill, forced to launch herself at objectives she might otherwise have left alone and all of it compounded by the yawning void she faced if her plan failed.

Climbing the north face of the Eiger plastered with snow in uneven weather was a daunting proposition. Alison had found the route hard going when pregnant with Tom, and she must have balked at the idea of the long, cold nights threatened with storms, and the days dodging stonefall. Luckily, as she and Jim saw it, there was an alternative to the true Eiger Nordwand. To its left, beyond a wide, broken spur, is a route climbed in 1932 by four Swiss mountaineers led by Dr. Hans Lauper, a Zürich dentist and classical scholar. For several years in the 1930s, a number of more traditional climbers, including the committee that ran the Alpine Club in London, denounced the Nordwand itself as a mere variation, an unnecessary addition to Lauper's climb which did not merit the appalling risks and mounting loss of life. It was a doubtful opinion even then, and no serious Alpinist still believes it to be true.

By choosing the Lauper route instead of the real north face, Alison was backing away from her original plan, just as she had done by climbing the Shroud on the Grandes Jorasses. Given the dreadful weather, the long wait at Grindelwald, her lack of resources, and the pressure on her to finish the other three climbs, her decision was understandable. But the Lauper route is much easier and safer, and, like the Shroud, it consists mainly of a snow and ice slope. It has none of the Nordwand's historical resonance; for Hans Lauper and his friends, there were no Death Bivouacs, no nightmare struggles in the teeth of storms.

As it happened, the Lauper was in poor condition and the crux section, a usually icy ramp known as the Hoheneis, ran with water.

The line described in her guidebook proved difficult to follow, and she chose an alternative that looked easier but was nevertheless tenuous and demanding. With the temperature rising, softening the snow and increasing the risk of a slide, she had to move fast. She cut straight up to the ridge at the top of the face, thinking that there she could relax, but with the heavy snow and strong winds, a cornice of snow curled off the ridge above the 6,000-foot void below. She had little idea how robust the cornice would be; if it collapsed she would go with it, plunging down the north face. Carefully, she edged toward the summit, still keeping a tight grip on her concentration even as she reached the top.

The sun had been beating down for hours, turning the snow on the easy west flank into slush. As she descended from the summit, she had to focus hard as her crampons cut through the snow to the loose rocks beneath, threatening to trip her. She discovered some footprints and felt reassured that someone else had been on the mountain that day. Soon after, she came across a blue anorak lying abandoned in the snow, then more equipment: a head lamp, a wallet stuffed with Spanish pesetas, a new harness, a single crampon, and an ice ax with an empty glove still forced through its leash. She thought these finds bizarre, but close to safety, she was beginning to celebrate her ascent. Suddenly, turning a corner and preparing to climb down a steeper section of rock, she saw a red rucksack. Alison traversed toward it and realized that there was a body still attached to it. The rucksack had split on the rocks as the man fell, throwing its contents out. "There was no need to check if he was still alive," she wrote. "I knew instantly that he was dead; the way he lay, the color of his body, his half-naked chest, lightly clad, his clothes ripped and shredded. There was no movement, no sound." She imagined the body tumbling down the mountainside and dared not approach in case the dead man's eyes should haunt her for ever. Instead, she sat down and wept.

If in her early 20s she had tricked herself into a state of denial over the risks she was exposed to as a mountaineer, the simple poignancy of her description of this incident shines out. Faced with the horror of a brutal death, she responds with the deep emotions that she often kept hidden, her refusal to look into the man's eyes an acknowledgment of her own fears. It was a signal of how her emotional personality would mature in the last two years of her life. A rescue helicopter had already been summoned; when it reached her, the winchman shook her hand and congratulated her on her solo of the Lauper. But, she wrote, "All that mattered to me was the contorted wreck of a man I had been standing guard over for the past half hour. All I wanted was for him and me to get out of there." That evening, she walked into the campsite at Grindelwald. Dumping her rucksack by the tent, she went to look for her children in the nearby playground. They were playing on a roundabout and didn't see her at first. She sat there watching them, thinking about the life that had ended on the mountain that day. Then, finally, Tom caught sight of his mother sitting alone and rushed over to give her a hug.

Despite the trauma of Alison's discovery, the Eiger was the turning point in her summer's fortunes. At last the weather improved, and remained comparatively settled throughout August. When they returned to Chamonix a few days later, they met Ian Sykes, a friend from Scotland. He bought the children ice cream and chips, the first time they had enjoyed either in five months. The psychological boost of company other than their own brought Jim and Alison's optimism flooding back. They picked wild bilberries and raspberries in the woods above the campsite, and took the children camping in the Aiguilles Rouges, the mountains facing Mont Blanc on the other side of the valley. In the morning, bivouacking beside Lac Blanc, their sleeping-bags rimed with ice, they watched the sun hit the upper slopes of the mountain.

On the following day, they drove through Italy to the Bregaglia range in Switzerland, where Alison climbed the north face of the Piz Badile, the fourth on her list. This time there was no waiting or frustration, and she reveled in the warm, sunny rock, overtaking several roped parties as she climbed quickly, barely pausing when she found sections high on the mountain running with water. Her confidence was flooding back. A week later she was again in Chamonix for her fifth major climb, the north face of the Petit Dru. At the bottom cable-car section she met Mark Twight, her old friend from Kangtega, and they shared the awkward descent to the glacier below her route. Then she was on her own, struggling up wet, rubble-strewn slopes at the bottom of the face. Later, as she gained momentum, she felt exhilarated and confident, poised above the abyss, climbing with speed and grace on firm granite. All around her, as the exposure grew, the vista of peaks and glaciers unfolded beneath a clear blue sky. At one point, wriggling through a strange horizontal crack, she became stuck and had to fight the urge to laugh as her feet lost contact with the rock. Without a rope, above thousands of feet of empty air, she felt no tinge of fear. The Dru is a spectacular mountain, an almost perfect spire. Very few men had climbed its north face alone, and certainly no women. After the doubt and depression of the spring, when nothing seemed possible, Alison was suddenly doing everything she said she would.

A week later, following Ian Sykes's advice, she snuck under the looming north face of the Cima Grande in the Dolomites and started climbing before fear could overcome her. To begin with, she climbed nervously on the vertical limestone, retreating from a difficult pitch as she struggled to find momentum. Again, her mental strength saw her through; and despite gathering bad weather, she launched herself up the vast cliff. Alison finished the top section in a rainstorm and, as she hurried down the other side, recalled stories of electric storms in the Dolomites, of climbers being struck on the exposed faces. The clouds, however, remained silent. Jim saw her drenched figure emerge from the downpour, she was holding up all the fingers of one hand and the thumb of the other: the six faces were, after a fashion, completed. If she was ecstatic to have completed her task, at the back of her mind were doubts about how her achievement would be judged.

The family stayed in France, at first camping and then renting a cheap chalet in Chamonix, where Alison began work on her book. At the end of September she flew home for the annual outdoor trade fair at Harrogate, where she would be helping to publicize the products of her new sponsor, Sprayway. It should have been an enjoyable week. Alison's parents had rented a cottage nearby, and she stayed with them during the show. She had done something that no female climber, British or foreign, had accomplished before, and can be forgiven for having expected to spend part of her time soaking up some much needed praise. Instead, Alison began to understand that the climbing world was filled with suspicion about her north-face solos. Few doubted that she had climbed the routes, but there were real objections about the way she and Jim were presenting them.

The total time she had spent climbing on the six routes, she stated, was less than 24 hours. The Shroud, she claimed, took two and a quarter hours, possibly the fastest ascent ever, the

Cima Grande less than three and a half hours, the Piz Badile only two. The feat even gave her the name of her book, *A Hard Day's Summer*. There is no evidence that Alison did not climb the six routes at a blistering pace. But a total time of less than 24 hours seemed unlikely, and needlessly artificial. Perhaps, spurred by the brouhaha over Rebecca Stephens's ascent of Everest, Alison and Jim were simply trying to emphasize the magnitude of her achievements.

There were complaints, too, that she had counted her climb on the Eiger as the north face. Even worse, there was also Jim's suggestion that the route Alison followed up the Eiger was somehow a major new variation. It is possible that there were very short stretches on Alison's line that had not been climbed before, but the triumphalism of his note in her book was damaging: "We were seeing history in the making. Alison was writing her talent on the greatest of the Alpine faces. She was creating a new climb, cutting up and left from the Lauper."

To a non-climber, getting up the Eiger by any route is impressive enough, but to the cognoscenti, this kind of embroidery was judged embarrassing. Taken together with the idea that the Shroud was somehow worthy of inclusion in Rébuffat's list of the six north faces, it amounted to confusion of the most dubious kind. To Bill O'Connor, who had the greatest admiration for Alison as a climber, it was perplexing: "Surely she knew that people out there would know that [her claim] wasn't straight or not honest and would call into question all the other things she had done?" Alison's climbs needed no embellishment at all; they were impressive, courageous, and better than almost anything achieved by a British woman before. But Jim's hyperbole and Alison's acquiescence injured her reputation. The "scene," that narrow core of climbers who had made the sport their lives, turned its back on her. "I think she felt she had been rejected by the climbing community," O'Connor says. The world she had wanted to feel part of had doubted her integrity, and it must have hurt badly.

Back in France she carried on working on her book, living frugally and keeping fit, but the doubts raised at Harrogate began to prey on her mind. Climbing alone during the summer meant there were no outstanding photographs to accompany any lectures or magazine articles, handicapping her new career as a professional climber. Jim had styled himself a photographer, but the pictures he got of her scrambling on the Bossons Glacier near the Chamonix main road were poor. The French climbing magazines Alison picked up in Chamonix were full of extraordinary photographs, saturated with color, taken from dizzying perspectives. Pictures like that of her would be difficult to ignore. The cloud hanging over her grew as she sat in her cheap chalet, struggling to write. Had she compromised with the Shroud when she knew she should have tried the Croz or Walker Spurs? She had made a commitment and she doubted that she had fulfilled it. It was intolerable.

The first winter snows had fallen across the mountains, and Chamonix was gearing up for the ski season. Alison had wanted her Alpine solos to launch her professional climbing career, but the response had been muted. If the climbing itself had thrilled her, she now needed recognition as well, both for money and for her own self-confidence. Alison decided to do a climb so extraordinary that even her harshest critics would find it difficult to ignore. In 1985 she had climbed the Croz with Ian Parsons. Now she would solo it in winter conditions.

Not far from her chalet was a bar-cum-climbers' dormitory, Le Vagabond. Its British owner, David Sharrock, was a talented mountain photographer, and he agreed to photograph Alison's progress from a helicopter. On November 10 Alison left her children sleeping in their beds and met Sharrock on the Chamonix helipad just before dawn. They flew up out of the valley, straight toward the Grandes Jorasses. Hovering above the deep black *bergschrund*, the crevasse formed in the angle between the mountain face and the glacier below, the pilot dropped her safely on the far side. Then she began climbing, her face tucked into the hood of her jacket against the spindrift pouring down the mountain. Soon she found two new ice screws buried in the ice. She took them out and clipped them to her harness. It was only later that she learned they had been left behind by three Koreans who had fallen to their deaths while retreating from the mountain some days earlier.

The route she had followed with Ian in the autumn of 1985 was layered with thick snow. Clearing it away from the rocks beneath would have taken too much time, so instead she climbed a thin runnel of ice. As she inched her way up it, the ice became so narrow that she had to place her axes one above the other with no room to use them side by side. Teetering in a desperate position, she tried to bring her right foot up: "I kicked a placement, the ice shattered," she wrote later. "It all fell off, taking my left foot with it. Helpless, I was left suspended from my two delicate ax placements, and, just as I thought things couldn't get any worse, the spindrift reappeared." The powder snow poured over her, insinuating itself through every opening in her waterproof clothing as she clung to the shafts of her axes, poised above the drop. At last the avalanche began to ease. Awash with adrenalin, aware that her axes could rip out at any time, she brought a foot higher and kicked it gently into the little ice remaining. It held. Closing her eyes, she stood gingerly on her new foothold and took out one of the axes, swiftly and neatly burying it in good ice above. She climbed out of trouble and the angle eased. She had come as close as she ever wanted to the edge of the abyss.

Her pace increased a little, but the route was in poor condition. In some places, climbing rock was unavoidable, and she had to brush the snow from every hold. Alison needed no reminder of the seriousness of her position, but it came when she found a buried ice ax, with other equipment clipped to it. Its owner, she assumed, was now lying in the bergschrund at the foot of the face, thousands of feet below. For the second time in four months, she had made a macabre discovery, but this time, in contrast with the Eiger, she was in peril herself.

With most of the huge face now beneath her, within 500 feet of the summit and comparative safety, she was faced with another desperate section, a horizontal rocky traverse on tiny, freezing fingerholds, with her crampons just balancing on granite edges the width of a matchstick. All the time the weather was worsening, the wind freshening, and the cloud sweeping round from Mont Blanc. The wind buffeted her body, throwing Alison off balance. There was no room for fear, just concentration as she struggled up the final awkward groove and on to the summit. There was no time for celebration: the weather might soon trap her on the mountain for the night, and she had no bivouac gear to protect her praise. The helicopter pilot dropped a cable for her to attach to her climbing harness, but as she reached out, it swung away from her fingertips and she nearly lost her balance. The wind was now almost too strong for the pilot to wait, but on the second attempt the cable plopped safely onto the snow and she clipped it into her harness. Immediately the pilot climbed and banked away from the mountain, lifting Alison into space. She hung there, thousands of feet above the ground, as she was winched on board, the pilot's face a picture of relief and congratulation.

There could be no doubt about this ascent, performed unroped in poor conditions on a difficult route in front of a photographer, and her climb was reported by the climbing media all around Europe and North America, alongside Sharrock's pictures. Far more than her efforts in the summer, Alison's solo of the Croz Spur had put her center-stage all over the climbing world. In Europe her ascent was met with unequivocal praise, and even in Britain the boldness of her climb went some way to rescuing her image. The scale of her achievement had answered her critics, and the judgmental British climbing scene couldn't begrudge her praise. With the Croz, and the promise of a book to come on her extraordinary summer, her career was at last building momentum. For the moment at least she had acted independently of Jim and used Sharrock's skill to capture her undoubted courage. She had found a route to success.

The expense of the climb had exhausted her funds, but after so many months of frustration and disappointment, Alison could feel entitled to a sense of unalloyed pride. Four days after climbing the Croz Spur, she flew back to Britain with her family, abandoning the now-ruined Land Rover in Chamonix. At the airport they hired a car, and drove to Alison's parents in Derbyshire. She had nowhere else left to go.

After nine months spent so closely in each other's company, Alison and Jim were near to breaking point. Soon after they arrived in Derbyshire, Alison renewed her friendship with Bev England. In a series of talks over coffee and long country walks, Alison began to disclose some of her real feelings for the first time, and the distance built up between the two women during her years with Jim fell away. Before their departure, Bev had suspected that things were far from well; Alison had told her that they had been reduced to "subsistence living." On their return, Alison hid nothing, saying that her time with Jim in the Alps had often been a nightmare. "I saw no future for them. I told her: 'Go on girl, get him out of your system,'" Bev says.

Jim's presence soon became onerous at the Hargreaves' home in Belper. With no job, house, or business, he had nothing to do but spend his days alternately watching television and berating potential sponsors on the telephone for their failure to back his "genius" wife's forthcoming trip to Everest. "He was telling them how brilliant Ali was," Joyce recalls, "that they simply had to sponsor her." Sue adds: "We were all very aware that things between them hadn't been very good. Finally Mum took Ali aside and said, 'Do you mind if I blow up at him?' Ali said: 'Fine, go ahead.'"

On November 25 there was an explosive row. Joyce tore into Jim for his attitude to the repossession of Meerbrook Lea and for what she saw as his inability to face the mess left behind. Then she told Jim to get out. He replied that Alison would never see him again, but the following morning, after an awkward breakfast, Alison left with him and the children to drive to Penmaenmawr to stay in the Hargreaves' holiday cottage. Alison was back later that day, without Jim or the kids. For the next month she shuttled awkwardly back and forth, over a miserable Christmas. Sometimes the children stayed with her in Derbyshire; at other times, while she worked on her book and tried to prepare for Everest, they stayed in Wales with Jim. She had no clear plan. Without a proper home of her own, she felt rootless and insecure. "She'd got this tremendous sense of achievement," Bev says. "But she was wretched.

Between expeditions, she loved domesticity." More than once Alison told her friends and family she believed her marriage was over. At the same time, she found the practical consequences of separation almost impossible to bear. After her visit to Wales for Christmas, she tried to bring her children back to Belper. She rang her mother in tears, explaining that Tom refused to get in the car, wanting to stay with his father. Joyce told her to leave Tom and just bring Kate. Alison arrived with her later that day.

As the new year began, Alison resolved to take back control. "Jim seemed a busted flush," says Susan. "She was making the decisions." The first step was to find a house to rent, and soon she located a property in Eyam, a few miles north of Belper, close to the gritstone edges of Froggatt and Curbar. Once again, she decided to try to make her marriage work. Susan thought it unlikely she would succeed. "The phone calls we had, the conversations, seeing them together, how they reacted—it seemed it could only go one way." Behind her continued indecisiveness, Alison was already worried how the courts might view the risks she took to make a living, and her absences in the mountains. "She was frightened," Sue says, "of losing the children."

At the same time, she needed a settled home life to carry on mountaineering. How, she wondered, could she try to climb Mount Everest if she became a single parent? But how else could she make a living for her family? Alison found Tom a place at the school in Eyam, concentrated on the coming expedition, and tried to reestablish a semblance of domestic harmony. As had always been planned, Jim and the children would accompany her to base camp.

The articles Alison wrote about the Croz Spur helped maintain her tenuous finances and raised her media profile, but as she talked to potential sponsors, she knew that merely to reach the top of Everest would no longer be enough. Meanwhile, Catherine Destivelle was already diminishing the scale of Alison's triumphs in the Alps. In 1992 she had soloed the "proper" route on the Eiger while Alison lay in Chamonix hospital. Now she had done the same on the Jorasses' Walker Spur. Both were winter solos of routes that Alison, because of the weather, had avoided in summer.

While Rebecca Stephens prospered on the back of her Everest climb, Alison continued to struggle. She knew that to achieve a similar level of recognition, she would have to do something even more remarkable. Since Everest had already been climbed by a British female, then she would do it completely alone, without bottles of oxygen. The plucky mum, solo on the world's highest mountain—at last she had an objective to excite the mainstream media. At the end of July 1994 Alison, Jim, and the children left Derbyshire for Heathrow airport, their departure heralded in the national press. John and Joyce, who had accompanied the children on the train, watched them disappear into the lounge. Jim, at least, seemed to be under no illusions about what Alison was planning. "Let's face it," he told reporters, "I have to accept there's a fair chance she won't be coming back."

CHAPTER 8

EVEREST ALONE

Focused on Everest, Alison Hargreaves lived at high speed and intensely. Between leaving for Nepal at the end of July 1994 and the expedition to K2 a year later, she moved house four times, gave lectures both in Britain and abroad, had a book published and signed a contract for another, was fêted by media all over the world, and went on three Himalayan expeditions. Most difficult of all, she also began planning an independent life for herself and her children away from Jim. The speed of these events, the contrast between blissful weeks in the mountains and the relentless demands of a suddenly successful career, cannot have failed to confuse and disorient her at times; some who knew Alison have said they were concerned by the frenetic pace of her life, that she had put too much pressure on herself to succeed. There was some truth in this view, although given the state of her marriage it is not surprising that she was under pressure. But for much of this period she was happy. While she felt isolated in her marriage, her relationship with her parents and her sister grew stronger and stronger. Moreover, Alison was finally achieving the things she had dreamed of, and being recognized, in most quarters, as one of the greatest female mountaineers ever.

Her first expedition to Everest was in the late summer of 1994. She joined a medical expedition led by Simon Currin, a general practitioner from mid-Wales. The team of more than 30 doctors, physiologists, and environmental scientists were planning to climb the mountain, but also to conduct research into the effect of altitude on humans and the impact that climbers and trekkers were having in the region of Nepal immediately around Everest. Alison was an independent member, contributing to the team's scientific purpose as someone to be tested and measured, but climbing at her own pace and carrying her own gear. Climbing the mountain entirely on her own was not, however, feasible. The route up Everest from the southern, Nepalese, side starts through a tumbling glacial cascade of ice cliffs and crevasses. Each season a route is found through this obstacle and ropes fixed to safeguard climbers and Sherpas passing through it. Not using this line of ropes would have been foolish, but it had been placed there by others. Later, at the top camp placed at the South Col at 26,000 feet, a day's climb from the summit, she would also use the team's summit tents.

Much more importantly, Alison chose not to use bottles of oxygen throughout her attempt, relying only on what little air there is at such high altitudes. As with so many aspects of climbing on Everest, it is the rules imposed by individuals on themselves that give the sport its compelling purpose. Alison saw climbing Everest unsupported and "without gas" as the purest and most satisfactory method and preferable because it was harder. She would feel a greater sense of achievement and create a much greater impact in the media. But making an ascent without supplementary oxygen makes Everest a much tougher proposition, with a far greater risk of frostbite and physical collapse. Most climbers, not strong enough to do it on their own, are only too grateful for Sherpas to carry their equipment and supply them with oxygen. This is how Rebecca Stephens had reached the summit the year before. What Alison was proposing takes a lung-bursting effort, struggling up steep snow slopes at 26,000 feet and above, a triumph of desire over the physiological reality that the body is dying.

The process of acclimatization that Alison had come to understand on Kangtega effectively ceases at about 16,000 feet. This is the highest altitude at which people live and work on a permanent basis, where the level of oxygen is half that at sea level. Above 16,000 feet the biochemistry of the blood can no longer adjust to the reduced level of oxygen and increased breathing—the hyperventilatory response—cannot compensate enough. Above 26,000 feet the process of physical deterioration accelerates, and climbers who stay at such extreme altitude will inevitably die, probably in a matter of days, as their bodies simply fail from hypoxia.

Near the summit of Everest, where there is only a third of the level of oxygen found at sea level, the body's functions are horrendously impaired. Everything takes longer as the brain struggles with hypoxia. Making a cup of tea or putting on boots become trials of will; even thought itself is dulled and reduced. Climbers often report hallucinations as they climb, of meeting non-existent companions or imagining conversations. After Doug Scott reached the summit in 1975 on the expedition to the Southwest Face that had so inspired Alison, his oxygen ran out, and he and his partner Dougal Haston were forced to dig a snow cave and shelter for the night.

Scott described experiencing a presence who offered him advice; Haston held conversations with people who weren't there. Both men fought off sleep, convinced they would die should they fail to stay awake. Many climbers not using bottled oxygen suffer permanent short-term memory loss after returning; frostbite is common. Heart failure and collapse from exhaustion are well documented. It's not surprising that the short list of those who have stood on top of the world without bottled gas includes many of the best high-altitude climbers in history, and despite knowing the possible consequences, Alison was desperate to join them.

The mountain had been climbed by several women since Junko Tabei made the first female ascent in 1975, but only a New Zealander, Lydia Bradey, had climbed it without bottled oxygen. Her ascent had been hotly disputed by the rest of her team, but, as Alison came to believe after being initially sceptical, those doubts were unjustified. A Sherpa called Ang Rita who had met Bradey just below the summit found her delirious and crawling on all fours. He tried to convince her to come down but she refused. Ang Rita looked her in the eye and said: "You are going to die!" Bradey, however, persevered, and her ascent is now widely accepted. Even so, she had relied on the support of her team in placing camps and supplies high on the mountain before they left her behind to climb alongside a Spanish team to the summit. Only two Britons, a friend and climbing partner of Alison's called Stephen Venables, and Harry Taylor, a former SAS officer, had reached the top without bottled oxygen. Both men had suffered terribly, Venables later having several toes amputated after suffering from frostbite. The chances of Alison succeeding on her own seemed minimal.

The 1994 expedition's progress was hampered by the weather, first by clouds swirling through the Western Cwm below the South

Col, and then by strong winds heralding the approach of winter. The children reveled in the adventure and were largely healthy. Only once, while lodging at Gorak Shep just before Base Camp at an altitude of more than 16,000 feet, were there doubts about them being physically capable of remaining with Alison. Kate, after being irritable all day, began complaining of a headache and may have been suffering from slight altitude sickness. The safest option for a victim of altitude sickness is to descend. Alison did not hesitate, lifting Kate onto her back and, with a small group that included Tom, hurrying to a lower altitude through the night, to the health post at Pheriche, where they were last sure that Kate had been in perfect health. She recovered strongly and neither of the children was ill again.

Having Tom and Kate with her was an immense encouragement to Alison, and expedition members recall how much the children enjoyed the adventure. Jim's presence was more complicated. The Nepalese government had recently raised the peak royalty, which all expeditions to Everest have to pay for permission to climb, from a few thousand dollars for a whole expedition to $10,000 per climber. Given the failure of their business, it is not surprising that this extra burden was beyond Jim and Alison's resources, and it was not finally paid until they reached Nepal with money given to her by a new Italian sponsor, Ferrino. The expedition, made up of amateurs despite its scientific purpose, could ill afford to do without the money, and Currin told Jim and Alison that unless the fee was forthcoming she would be off the team. With the mountain so close, his frustration was understandable, but Jim took the demand personally and made his feelings about Currin obvious. He also criticized the expedition for using oxygen, denigrating their mountaineering skill and contrasting them unfavorably with his "genius" wife. Expedition members recall that Alison was embarrassed by his attitude and that he became the butt of expedition jokes. She was generally popular with the other climbers and built a number of close friendships, and Jim's forthright opinions, in an arena of which he had no direct experience, visibly upset her.

Despite the difficult weather, Alison made determined attempts to reach the summit, and in doing so proved to herself and others that she could climb strongly over 26,000 feet, the first time she had been to such high altitudes. Gradually she acclimatized to the thin air and built up stamina, climbing progressively higher on the mountain before returning to Base Camp to rest. On her first bid to go all the way to the summit, she climbed through the ice-fall and up the Western Cwm and reached the South Col. But fierce winds drove her back to a lower camp before she could climb the last 3,100 feet to the top. Later, in October, she went back, and, leaving her tent on the South Col at 1 a.m., struggled through the frozen night to reach nearly 28,000 feet. The summit loomed barely 1,000 feet above her, encouraging her to take a chance, starting a battle within her between ambition and prudence. Some climbers call it summit fever, when rational decision-making gets lost in the irresistible urge to go on. The winds froze Alison's body, increasing the risk of frostbite in her fingers and toes. She always carried in her mind the memory of the trade fair in 1983 where Jean-Marc Boivin introduced her to the climber whose hands had been ruined by frostbite, and had made a rule that if she felt the onset of frostbite she would descend. She spoke often of her fears of bringing up children without the fingers to hold them. Worse still, her eyesight was failing, making her imagine, in the predawn half-light, that she had cerebral edema, that fluid was building up on her brain, squeezing the light from her eyes. Doubt comes easily high on a mountain, and Simon Currin believes her eyesight problems were transient and not the early symptoms of edema. But her decision to descend and wait for warmer weather showed intelligence and caution.

Most climbers, after weeks on the mountain, are thinner, weaker, and less healthy, often suffering from a persistent hacking cough from the dry, thin air. Alison suffered too, but she still wasn't prepared to give up. Despite her fatigue, she made the colossal effort of returning to the South Col again, just as two other expedition members, both using bottled oxygen, were planning their attempt. When they radioed down the following morning that Alison had remained behind, Jim was furious: "I could not believe the string of expletives he came out with about her," recalls one team member who was at Base Camp when the message came through. "He was angry at her for staying in bed." Jim, living vicariously through Alison's achievements and plotting her career, took her decision very personally. His overriding emotion, as it often had been throughout their relationship when she failed on a big climb, was anger. Alison had wondered in her diary how he would cope with the failures. Now she knew. She needed no encouragement to feel miserable at not reaching the summit. She later wrote that on leaving the mountain she felt empty, "as if someone had ripped out my stomach," a particularly brutal image. Jim's pressure only made things worse.

Others on the expedition recognized that their relationship was breaking apart. When she returned to Britain, Alison told Susan and Bev England that she had fallen in love with one of the other team members. It was, according to Bev, an intense though doomed relationship, which had irrevocably and positively altered the way Alison saw her life. "I felt I had got the old Ali back," Bev says, "the carefree girl I'd known back in the 1970s. She hadn't been the same person for years. There had been a long period when I felt you couldn't reach her. I think that was because she'd been covering so much up." As they walked through the meadows in Belper where they had grown up together dreaming of the climbs they would do, Alison described a depth of affection Bev had not seen before. "She really loved him. He paid her compliments and attention, all the things she wasn't getting from Jim. The relationship was important in allowing her to get a new handle on life." Bev believes that Alison's biggest mistake was to stay with Jim after they returned from the Alps at the end of 1993. "He pushed her terribly. Whatever she did was never enough. Ali's exact words were: 'Jim blamed me' for the failure on Everest. She was very hurt by that. It hurt her terribly. All he could think of was getting the money for a second go."

When Alison and Jim returned from Everest in late October, they moved immediately to a holiday cottage near Fort William, the first of two short-term lets they would occupy before securing longer-term accommodation. Tom began school in the town. (His teacher, wishing to integrate him into his class, asked him where he had been living before. "Everest Base Camp," he replied.) There were several reasons why the family decamped to Scotland. Certainly, Alison and Jim wanted to bring their children up in a wild and adventurous setting and the hills around Fort William offered that. Alison would also have instant access to the mountains she loved. But Scotland was also a fresh start, away from the creditors and bad feeling that had built up in Derbyshire with the collapse of the business.

She barely had time to settle in their new home before flying to Canada for a mountain film and book festival in the Rockies ski resort of Banff to speak on her solo climbs in the Alps. The organizers had taken a risk, giving her a prominent slot on the opening night when few climbers in North America knew who she was. Despite this, the theater's main auditorium, seating almost 1,000 people, sold out and her lecture had to be broadcast simultaneously to two smaller theaters. Her performance was tentative and understated but well received; Alison was only beginning to understand that lecturing and writing were difficult skills that had to be learned, rather than an automatic qualification that came with being a good climber. But she was happy in Canada, pleased to be in a climbing scene that accepted her willingly and did not instinctively undermine her achievements.

During her week in Banff, she also participated in a panel discussion with several well-known female climbers on the role of women in adventure, including the subject of risk and motherhood. It was the first time she'd had to face the issue among women who shared her knowledge and love of the mountains. Sharon Wood, the first North American to climb Everest, was doubtful that the risks were justified and recalls finding Alison alternately defensive and brash when responding to questions about her decision, as a mother, to carry on climbing big mountains like Everest and K2. Few at the festival had any idea of the pressures she was now under, and why she had to be so determined to succeed; only her ambition shone through.

In the evening she drank with other visiting British climbers, including Sir Chris Bonington and Joe Simpson. Alison felt at the heart of things at Banff after years of feeling isolated and underrated in her own country. It seemed that everything she had been through that year had been worth it. After the festival finished, she stayed on for a ski trip into the mountains, staying in a hut at Lake O'Hara. Bernadette McDonald, the festival organizer, remembers her as being very happy, delighting in the mountains and asking questions about the climbing but also admitting that her personal life was in difficulty and needed resolving. She told other organizers that she wanted people to know she was now separated from Jim.

Back in Britain, her book on the Alpine solos, *A Hard Day's Summer*, was published. It was not well received. Alison had tried to repay those sponsors who had backed her climbs by frequent references to their products in the text. "I refuelled with a litre of Isostar," she wrote, adding in brackets, "never known anything like it for rehydration!" This apparently shameless plugging, coupled with the book's brevity, damaged its reputation. Days after it was published, she told Alison Osius, an American journalist who had flown to England to interview her at a mountain literature festival near Wakefield, that the book had disappointed her. "I absolutely hate it. I'm a very unconfident writer. If I wrote it again, I'd do it in a different style. I'd be more open."

Her interview with Osius was unusually frank. Admitting a lack of confidence or uncertainty was something she had done only within the confines of her diary or to her sister and closest friends. Osius is a direct but sympathetic person and her credibility as a climber—she later became the first woman to be president of the American Alpine Club—probably persuaded Alison, who was still confused and anxious about what to do, to be unguarded. She deliberately told Osius that she wanted a divorce from Jim, a fact that Osius later double-checked by telephone, weeks after the interview took place. Telling strangers what she was planning made her decision more real, as though it might actually happen. "We've just sort of grown apart," she explained to Osius. "We have totally different opinions. There's no animosity at all. I want to change things. I've got an awful lot of years left." It was a curiously defensive admission, but she knew that it would anger Jim.

Alison was not as certain about seeking a final split from Jim as she made out to Alison Osius. Susan had invited Alison and Jim to her wedding in early December, but Alison said she wanted to come without him. In late November she and Alison discussed whether she could bring the children to the wedding—Jim was against it—and simply not go home. There were "many furtive phone calls" in which this "escape plan" was discussed between the two sisters, but by the time the wedding took place, Alison seemed to have changed her mind again and was staying. Her courage to act had gone.

The relationship, however, was effectively over. Alison and Jim led separate lives at Rowan Cottage; Alison consulted solicitors about her legal options in a future divorce. Her overriding worry was losing custody of the children, and she told Bev that this was why she had decided not to leave Jim when she went to Susan's wedding: She was worried it would affect any future decision of the court over who would have care of Tom and Kate. Bev and Alison talked again over Christmas. "She was desperate, sobbing down the phone. I wish I'd been 20 minutes away and could have gone round. But she was in Scotland. There was nothing I could do."

Alison's dilemma was simple but inescapable. She had to provide for her family and in order to do that she had to carry on climbing and making headlines. But that required her to go away. In fact, so far she had hardly been separated at all from the children; they had been with her in the Alps, when she had spent relatively few nights away, and they had gone with her to Everest. It was the future that concerned her. Tom and Kate would not be able to come on the expeditions she was planning, and she needed someone to care for them. She could hardly leave her husband and then immediately hand her children over to someone else before going off to the Himalaya for six months; that would not impress a judge either. It left her in an agony of indecision, and in early December she wrote a long letter to Susan about her confusion and unhappiness. She complained that she felt she was carrying too much of the burden domestically as well as trying to earn a living, and recalled how she had managed single-handedly with the children and running Meerbrook Lea, chopping wood for the fire when the money ran out for coal, as Jim spent most of his waking hours propping up the business. Now in Scotland, once the children were in bed, she would work, writing letters and sorting out pictures, organizing her expeditions and chasing sponsors, baking, and cleaning. She was bitter at herself as well as Jim, and told Susan she was being pursued over the debts left behind by the collapse of Faces and the shops. She knew she could be happy, and with her children or in the mountains she often was, but, she told Susan, the rest of it seemed uncertain. She sensed her climbing could flourish but only if she left her children to go back to Everest. "There are," she concluded to Sue, "far more mountains out there to climb than just the physical ones."

If her personal life seemed impossible to resolve, at least she could take active steps to remove Jim from her professional life. She had been profoundly embarrassed by his reaction to her failure on Everest and resolved to put her career in the hands of others. While she had been away, Sprayway, as her main sponsor, had been deluged with press inquiries about her climb, but with no information available from Nepal, was not able to capitalize on her progress. There was a residual tension between the company and Alison, and she needed to come up with a dramatic plan to keep interest in her career alive and Sprayway involved. Returning to Everest with an effective support team would resolve that problem.

Alison was invited to speak at the Alpine Club's general meeting about her recent climbs. She had been a full member of the oldest mountaineering club in the world since 1985, but the idea of speaking in front of so many of her heroes left her feeling scared. The hall was packed and her lecture well received, a mark of approval, which, coming from peers rather than the media, meant a great deal to her. Afterward she had dinner with Richard Allen, and they renewed their friendship from their meeting at Täsch the year before. She mentioned to him a plan she was formulating of a series of Himalayan climbs that she would attempt alone.

The idea had been put to her by George Band two weeks earlier, after a committee meeting at the Alpine Club. Band had been on the successful Everest expedition of 1953 and in 1955 made the first ascent of the world's third-highest peak, Kangchenjunga. He told Alison he thought it a shame that no British climbers would try the mountain during next year's anniversary, as Rebecca Stephens and Harry Taylor had done on Everest in 1993. Band was planning to lead a party to the foot of the mountain during the spring and suggested she come with them to attempt to repeat their climb. Since, he continued, she was already thinking of going back to Everest, why not connect the two expeditions in some way and then continue on to K2, the world's second highest mountain? It was a startling prospect. Nobody, man or woman, had climbed the three highest mountains on earth in the same year, and Kangchenjunga had not been climbed by a woman at all.

Coming from someone like George Band, a highly regarded figure within the Alpine Club, the plan had an added luster. Also, at a deeper level, it appealed to her love of lists, which she had made about every aspect of her life since she started keeping a diary as a young girl. To her ordered mind, there was something innately satisfying about a list of climbs. "I like to have targets," she told Alison Osius. "I like to have lists of things to do. Climbing on a wall just for the sake of it doesn't really appeal. I like to have goals." She spoke often of the real fear she felt if, should she climb Everest, she was left without something for which to aim. A list of peaks that big would fill the gap completely. When she arrived back in Scotland after catching the sleeper north, she found a letter from an American friend, Richard Celsi, whom she had met in Nepal that autumn. He was offering her a place on an expedition to K2 next summer. After her conversation with George Band, it seemed fate was giving Alison a prompt she could not ignore. She accepted.

It was one thing to agree to join an expedition, but quite another to pay for it—let alone three. Alison was still relying on her small retainer from Sprayway and on what she could make from lectures and articles. What she needed was someone who could capitalize on her appeal. A mother of two attempting to climb the three highest mountains in the world was a marketable idea, but she no longer trusted Jim to run her affairs. "The people she mixed with," he later told the *Sunday Times*, "felt my abrasive style of northern honesty was not the way to bring on a glittering career. They still believed you needed lots of contacts and smooth talking, which turned out to be complete garbage—but she felt that too."

In fact, Alison did not need persuading to seek help elsewhere. Before her Alpine Club lecture she had talked of her need to find an agent, and during her dinner with Richard Allen she was clearly thinking of him as a likely candidate. Allen, for his part, wanted to explore ways that he could visit the Himalaya. Alison probably had little idea of the scale of the operation he had been running in Hong Kong, but her ignorance gave her the courage to ask him, late in the year, to consider acting as her manager. She said she would pay him, although she had no money. Allen was wealthy and gently refused her offer. He suggested they go climbing together; if they found they got on, he would consider it. They met in January, climbing together on Ben Alder in the Highlands of Scotland. Allen remembers her intense pleasure at being outside in the mountains and, like John Hunt and many others, was charmed by her. He was also impressed by her self-possession on steep ground. "All her gear was in the right place at the right instant," he recalls. "The efficiency was incredible." Allen's climbing career had largely been confined to the Alps and now, in retirement, he thought helping Alison would be the perfect opportunity to see the Himalaya.

He helped her produce a small color brochure outlining her plans and he went to work looking for a corporate sponsor; given the short time scale it was, not surprisingly, a search in vain. He had more success finding a publisher. Through a contact of George Band's at Random House, he negotiated a book deal with the prestigious London firm of Jonathan Cape. Tony Colwell, her editor at Cape, thought her proposal thin, but was also taken by her openness. "She had a lovely, quiet sense of humor. She seemed a robust, wise, entertaining, charming, Derbyshire girl." Cape offered her an advance of £15,000, a considerable step up from her previous book deal, and Alison was on her way. The "contacts and smooth talking" that Jim disparaged were beginning to have an effect, although ultimately Allen subsidized Alison's expedition to Everest from his own pocket.

Alison had initially wanted to try Everest from the south side again. It is generally considered the easiest route, and if she was going to continue to Kangchenjunga afterward by helicopter, then it made logistical sense. But she struggled to find an expedition going there with a place still available on its permit. With only weeks before the spring season on the mountain began, she contacted Russell Brice, a Chamonix-based New Zealander who had organized a number of expeditions to the north side of Everest in Tibet, and was planning to return that spring. "Russell was just brilliant," Allen recalls. "We did a deal there, and then with only two or three weeks before he was due to fly." The usual route from the north of Everest is longer and considered harder than that from the south, and far fewer climbers have reached the summit from that direction. While the route via the South Col is almost entirely on snow and ice, the North Ridge is rockier and climbers spend longer at high altitude. The top camp is at more than 27,250 feet, more than 1,000 feet higher than the top camp on the south side, a potentially critical difference for someone climbing without bottled oxygen. The advantage for Alison in choosing to climb from Tibet was in being able to climb more independently, with no icefall to breach as there was in Nepal.

Most of these arrangements were made without Jim's participation or even his knowledge. The British mountaineer Alan Hinkes had also joined the expedition to K2, and over the winter he visited Alison in Scotland to sort out arrangements and shoot footage for a television program he was making about his climb.

Alison told him what she was planning and tried to interest him in joining the expedition to Kangchenjunga. She also asked him not to mention these plans to Jim. Ultimately, however, with her decision to climb from Tibet, it proved impossible to go to Kangchenjunga after climbing Everest, and she decided to reconsider an attempt later in 1995 or early 1996.

During early January, Joyce and John stayed at Rowan Cottage, walking in the hills with Alison as she trained for her return to Everest. They bought her a car, a Volkswagen Polo, to get around in as she planned the trilogy. Bill O'Connor also dropped by, and during dinner, as Jim spoke breathlessly and erroneously about Alison's prospects, he intervened to contradict him. It was the first time that Alison's parents had seen Jim made to look foolish, and the incident gave them the impression that his influence on their daughter was fading fast. Yet Jim's contacts could still prove helpful to Alison. Their friend Ian Sykes offered Alison free public relations support from the ski station at Nevis Range. While she was on the mountain, Sykes's press relations managers Cally Fleming and Alison Hood would issue bulletins on her progress from information supplied via Russell Brice's satellite fax at base camp. With the flow of information catered for, the problems Sprayway had encountered would be overcome.

On February 17, Alison's 33rd birthday, Bev spoke to her and found her just as confused as ever about what to do. She talked about putting the children into a nursery school and going back to college, even of becoming a doctor. "If I can get all three [mountains] in the bag, it would give me some financial security," she told Bev. "I can settle down to life with the children, do some lectures."

In mid-March, Richard Allen arranged for her equipment to be freighted to Tibet. He told her that she should do two things before leaving for Everest: make a statement about her marital status and draw up a will. "She did neither of those," he recalls wryly. "She could tackle all sorts of obstacles but not problems like that."

Two weeks later she stayed with her parents in Derbyshire before leaving for Tibet. She also saw Bev, and they talked about the relationship she had had on Everest the previous autumn and how things had not worked out. It had, Bev believes, only strengthened Alison's conviction that her long-term future would be apart from Jim. "It's made me realize," she told her, "there will be other people for me." Bev gave her a gold chain to take with her to go with a teddy bear from Susan, gifts that touched her deeply. In their last phone call before she left, Bev told Alison to make sure she got up this time. Alison said: "I'll make sure I do, I'm not going back there, because it's horrible!" Then she caught the train to Euston where she met her parents. She asked them to sort out some remaining personal financial arrangements to keep Jim from becoming involved in her affairs again, and they helped her with her luggage to Heathrow, where Richard Allen was waiting. After less than five months at home, Alison was on her way back to Everest.

After two days in Kathmandu sorting out Chinese visas, they flew north over Everest on their way to Lhasa, but their plane was diverted because of severe turbulence and they were forced to spend two nights in Chengdu. While waiting for their flight, Allen spotted the soldier, diplomat, and politician Sir Fitzroy Maclean, author of *Eastern Approaches* and a man often rumored to be Ian Fleming's role model for James Bond. He was taking a group of tourists around Tibet, and Allen suggested they speak with him. Alison, suddenly shy, demurred, but with a book to write, Allen knew good copy when he saw it. They talked with the old man for an hour and a half before flying to Lhasa. "Instantly I fell in love with Tibet," Alison wrote. "Its stark barrenness filled me with excitement. There was something about the Tibetan Plateau that made me feel alive."

And as they toured Lhasa, visiting the Potala Palace and the heart of Tibetan Buddhism, the Jokhang, Allen took pleasure in watching the various members of the expedition becoming familiar with each other. Brice would not be leading the expedition in the conventional sense; rather, he would provide logistical support, organizing camps and Sherpas and running Base Camp with its communications center. All the climbers were geared up for the intense effort of reaching the summit of Everest, judging and watching each other like fighters in the ring before the bell sounds. Among the others using Brice's services was a one-legged climber named Tom Whittaker, a Welsh-born American who was trying to become the first disabled person to climb the mountain. He was supported by Greg Child, an Australian living in Seattle who had a string of impressive Himalayan climbs to his credit as well as being an excellent rock climber. His laconic style contrasted with Alison's generous and less reflective personality, but they developed a strong mutual respect. "She never had a bad word for anyone," he said. "She was supportive, kind, a good sport—a sweetheart, really. She could be entertaining and funny." It was a side of Alison's character that few saw, often because she felt defensive about her record among other good climbers. It had earned her a reputation for being intense and ambitious, but those immediately around her at Everest Base Camp that year all remark on her easy manner and pleasure at being where she was.

Also climbing with Whittaker and Child were the British filmmaker Leo Dickinson, his wife, Mandy, and his assistant Eric Jones, the soft-spoken Welshman who had soloed the north face of the Eiger and later sky-dived from Angel Falls in South America at the age of 60, whom Alison had known since 1978 from his café beneath the cliffs at Tremadog in Wales. It delighted Alison to be in such well-traveled and interesting company, where she was far removed from the nightmare of her personal life and could concentrate on the job in hand. "Within two days [of reaching base camp]," she wrote in the *Alpine Club Journal*, "I was active—and happy!" The practical difficulties of climbing Everest, being on the move, working physically hard, resting in the evening, and talking with other climbers made her contented and relaxed.

Although the first ascent of Everest was made from Nepal to the south, the north side of the mountain is soaked in climbing history. It was from Tibet that the first attempts were made on the mountain in the 1920s, and it was on the North Ridge that George Mallory and Andrew Irvine disappeared, still struggling toward the summit. In those days of Empire, the climbers wore tweed coats and had rudimentary equipment, suffering terrible deprivations and looking, in George Bernard Shaw's phrase, like "a picnic in Connemara [Ireland] surprised by a snowstorm." Despite this, several climbers came close to reaching the summit, and Mallory* and Irvine may have done so. An army officer named Edward Norton reached 28,126 feet in 1924, the same year Mallory and Irvine disappeared, without bottled oxygen. Only 900 feet from the top but exhausted and hypoxic, Norton turned around at one o'clock in the afternoon, sure that if he continued he would die. After the invasion of Tibet by China in late 1950, access to the north side of the mountain was restricted to non-Chinese climbers until the 1980s. When

---

*Mallory's body was found in 1999.

the border reopened, Reinhold Messner made what many still regard as the finest ascent of Everest ever, climbing alone, with no other climber on the mountain, in the monsoon and without bottled oxygen to the summit.

In 1995 the Base Camp area, supplied by a road built by the Chinese in the late 1950s, was full of climbers of varying skill and experience, with over ten expeditions attempting the mountain. They had brought satellite phones and truckloads of high-tech equipment, with enough tents to form a small village. It would prove to be a highly successful season, with 66 climbers reaching the top during an unprecedented period of good weather. One veteran Everester commented afterward that if bad weather had suddenly hit the mountain, there would have been a number of fatalities as inexperienced climbers got caught out. The following year this exact scenario occurred, and eight climbers died, including two mountain guides, Rob Hall and Scott Fischer, taking care of inexperienced clients.

Alison benefited from the good conditions in 1995 as much as anyone. The rest of the climbers were relying on each other and the scores of Sherpas, ferrying loads of equipment and supplies and setting up and supplying camps. But Alison carried all her own gear, including tent, sleeping bag, clothing, and food, 15 miles up the East Rongbuk Glacier to Advanced Base, a long day's march for the fittest climber. Advanced Base Camp is at 21,000 feet, but after hiking around Base Camp up to similar altitudes, she felt well acclimatized. From Advanced Base she would systematically ferry her equipment up the mountain on her own back. It could never be a solo ascent; there were too many others on the mountain for that, and she never claimed it was. Yet to climb unsupported as she did required more effort than almost anyone else made that spring, and she climbed in as pure a style as was possible. On her first morning at Advanced Base, she woke early. Most climbers would have switched on a personal stereo or dozed. Alison got up and started cleaning the mess tent to make it more comfortable, adding her familiar touch of domesticity to the harsh surroundings.

Slowly she made progress, making three trips up the glacier and steep snow slopes to the North Col at 23,000 feet and spending one night there to acclimatize. Leaving early in the morning, before the warm sun could slow her down in soft snow, she shouldered a pack of around 20 pounds and started the 2,000 foot ascent. She carried a special high-altitude tent, light but incredibly strong to cope with the ferocious winds of an Everest storm. Just as important was her stove, specially modified to burn in the thinner air and essential for melting snow to rehydrate and keep her blood, syrupy with extra red blood cells, pumping round her veins. She needed plenty of extra fuel to keep it burning throughout her attempt. Food was always a struggle, the high altitude blunting her appetite so that even the sweetest foods seemed dull and cloying. Inside her tent was a thick foam sleeping mat to insulate her from the cold ground, a down-filled sleeping bag, and the few odds and ends—balaclavas, spare gloves, socks, and batteries for the head lamp—that she would need in the coming weeks. By the late morning, she had delivered that day's load and was on her way back to Advanced Base. It was hard and monotonous work, slogging up the long white slope, breaking each hour into manageable sections of a few steps then a rest, but she did it all joyfully, pleased that things were going as planned. Alison's next step would be to carry a tent, stove, fuel, and supplies, two loads more in all, to the next campsite at 24,930 feet at the top of a long, easy-angled snow slope. From here she would climb to a final campsite at 27,230 feet, close to the rock crest of the North Ridge. Then she would be in a position to try for the summit, still three-quarters of a mile away and almost 2,000 feet higher. While the first part of the route, up to Camp II at 24,930 feet, is on snow and ice slopes, which are simply hard work to climb, the north ridge itself is rocky, with downward pointing tiles of rock like those on a roof. It is easy-angled and at sea level would be trivial, but at such high altitudes and especially without bottled oxygen, it would require absolute concentration not to slip. At the top of the ridge, just below the summit, are two steps of vertical rock, the second of which has some awkward climbing, but Alison knew that an aluminium ladder had been lashed against it years before, making her passage straightforward. The climbing was far easier than routes she tackled in the Alps, or even on Kangtega, but the leaden weight of altitude made it all seem so hard.

With all her equipment needed for the higher camps now at the North Col, she decided to descend and rest in the greater comfort and lower altitude of Russell Brice's base camp, where Richard Allen, with nothing much to do except cheer her on, was managing the communications center. Those around Alison during her time off at Base Camp all attest to her complete control and focus. In filmed interviews with Leo Dickinson she appears composed and remarkably healthy, and although she describes the odds of succeeding as long as 50 to 1, there is a quiet assurance about her, as if she seemed to know she would get to the top. She would sit in Russell Brice's mess tent drinking tea and joining in the banter among the other climbers or visitors who dropped in. "One of the advantages [or] disadvantages," she wrote in the *Alpine Club Journal*, "of coming down from a higher to a lower altitude is the amount of energy it seems to give you. Long evenings of drinking and discussions crushed my good intentions of rest and relaxation." Child's cuttingly funny observations about the less competent climbers at base camp would make her laugh even as she recoiled at his cynicism. She became close to Mandy Dickinson, who was working with her husband on the film about Tom Whittaker. Talking and being with such contrasting personalities, seeing the way they dealt with their lives, gave her confidence to open up and find a perspective on her problems at home that she could never manage when she was embroiled in it.

But her other life, apparently left at home thousands of miles away, intervened as public interest in the climb grew. With his staff stretched to the limit in handling press inquiries, Ian Sykes asked Jim to help out. Alison was furious that Jim was now back helping run her career, and she said so to Richard Allen. "She didn't want him to have anything to do with it," Allen recalls, "and she was not one to mince words." He now found himself caught between them. Alison, of course, could have made her views known directly. "I'm sure she wanted to get away and become independent," Allen says. But her indecision in ending her relationship with Jim had been a feature of her life for years. There was nothing she could do from a remote corner of Tibet to change that now.

In early May she returned to the mountain, making the day-long trek up the East Rongbuk to Advanced Base, then climbing the snow and ice slopes up to the North Col. She continued with a rucksack of equipment to about 24,300 feet, but still short of the next campsite where she planned to pitch a tent at 24,930 feet. Alison felt exhausted, short of breath and energy. There was no way she could continue, and she dropped back to Camp I at the North Col, disappointed and suddenly shaken by the possibility of failure. The following day she carried the second rucksack of equipment she needed for Camp II to where she had dropped the first load the day before. At first she contemplated pushing on to Camp II immediately and coming back later that day for the equipment she left in the snow. But she knew there would not be enough time to make it back up to Camp II to spend the night there, which was vital to her program of gradual acclimatization. Cramming the second pile of gear into her rucksack, she shouldered her double load, as much as 40 pounds, and carried it with gritty determination for the last 600 feet to Camp II. This kind of bravura performance irritated those men she passed as they slogged up the mountain, dragging themselves up fixed rope she did not need. The Sherpas, on the other hand, recognized her strength and joked with her as they passed. "*Didi!* Sister! You strong man!" Respect from men who took more risks and performed better than most of the western climbers touched her deeply.

The weight of her abnormally heavy rucksack was almost too much for her, but she ground out the remaining steps to Camp II and set about establishing herself. Using large flat stones, she built a platform for the tent, her breath rasping in the dry thin air. She covered this base with abandoned tent fabric strewn around the campsite, and then set up her own tent, tying it down with some found rope to protect it from the winds blasting up from the North Col. All these tasks would be done by Sherpas on other expeditions, but Alison was alone, doing everything for herself. Shoveling snow into a nylon bag, she settled into her tent to start the long process of making drinks to ward off the dangers of dehydration. She arranged her tent carefully, showing the skills of organization that Richard Allen had noticed on their day together in the Scottish Highlands. Food went on one side, together with fuel for the stove and snow for melting. On the other side of the tent she laid out the clothes she would need higher on the mountain: gloves, balaclavas, and her battery-heated boots to ward off frostbite, her greatest fear. Then she turned the stove on and crawled into her sleeping bag. Alone at Camp II, high on the mountain, she became convinced that someone or something was pacing round her tent but she was too frightened to open the door and have a look. "I knew there couldn't be anyone there, but at least it felt friendly," she wrote. "I consoled myself that they [or] it was checking everything was okay." Then she fell into a deep sleep.

In the morning she descended the snow ridge to the North Col at 23,000 feet and then continued down the steep slopes to Advanced Base to rest for a few days. She was now in a position to try for the summit, and the weather seemed settled. She needed low winds and high pressure, which meant warmer temperatures and more oxygen in the extreme high altitude around Everest's Summit. As she chatted with her friends and calmed her mind, playing cards or Monopoly, sleeping in her tent or eating as much as she could take, the barometer sat rock steady. She had been moving toward this moment for most of her life, and her whole being became focused on the next few days.

On May 11 she left Advanced Base early in the morning and climbed quickly to the North Col. Collecting a spare tent for Camp III, she climbed on to Camp II and stopped for the night early to rehydrate as fully as she could. Her body would perform far better if she could keep drinking. That night she slept well, giving her an even better chance of success, but climbing above Camp II in the early morning, she slowed as she reached 26,000 feet, the threshold of the so-called Death Zone, where the body's deterioration from hypoxia becomes alarmingly fast. "Every few steps I needed much longer to recover, and I felt as if I would never reach my destination," she wrote. In the late afternoon the agony seemed over as she reached the tiny group of tents already established at 27,230 feet—Camp III. But to her horror, she could find no unoccupied platforms and ambled round the tents in a daze of hypoxia, looking for somewhere—anywhere—she could lie down and wait for morning. Finally, with no other option available, she found a promising 45-degree slope of ice and rubble and started scraping out a narrow platform—on all fours at over 27,000 feet, shifting stones with her hands and chopping at the ice with her ax. After an hour's effort, she had a narrow, two-feet-wide ledge on which to erect her tent. Half of it flopped over the slope, an area she used to store gear so she could stretch out on her frozen bed to begin making drinks.

On the radio to Leo Dickinson at advanced base, she seemed amazingly lucid, chatting almost normally about how she felt physically and what she planned for the following day. In a nearby tent, two Italian climbers, Marco Bianchi and Christian Kuntner, were also preparing to climb to the summit. "The Italians," Alison told Dickinson with a giggle, "are waving at me to go over." Then the long night began. In an effort to cut down the weight she would have to carry to Camp III, Alison had left her sleeping bag at the camp below, relying on her down suit to keep her alive. She put on every piece of clothing she had with her, but she barely dozed through the hours of cold and darkness, checking her watch as she had on previous bivouacs, waiting for the time to depart. At around 3 a.m., she came out of her tent to begin climbing, but it was bitterly cold and she went back inside for an hour, sleeping deeply for the first time that night. Refreshed, she was awake again at 4:20 a.m. and began climbing soon after, enough light leaking from the predawn sky for her to switch off her head lamp. In her pack were two cameras, a radio, a water bottle, and fresh batteries for her heated socks.

At first, fresh snow on some of the shattered black rocks she scrambled over slowed her progress; but as she picked her way up toward the crest of the North Ridge, it became more consolidated and she increased her pace. As the morning wore on, the temperature rose and she felt much more comfortable than she had high on the Southeast Ridge the year before. It looked as though she would make it, and the probability spurred her on. The Italians were ahead of her, firming up the trail and moving strongly, but Alison kept up with their pace, often managing as many as 20 steps before she was forced to stop and suck at the thin air to slow her wildly beating heart. Even close to the summit, she managed eight or ten steps at a time.

By midmorning, she had crossed a rocky buttress called the first step, confusing it with the larger second step behind it, where the ladder had been fixed to make passing it more straightforward. She thought the absence of the ladder strange, but soon discovered her mistake as she climbed higher up the ridge. To her left she had constant views of the steep west flank of Makalu, the summit ridge of Lhotse ahead of her, both giant mountains and both now slipping below her line of sight. The astonishing landscape around her raised her morale, so that her slightly dreamy mental state was suffused with happiness. On the final stretch a patch of sugary, loose snow brought her to an almost complete standstill as she struggled to wade through it, her heart hammering against her chest and her head reeling from the effort. But she persevered and a few minutes below the summit she stopped and spoke again with Dickinson. Listening to their recorded exchange, the encouragement from her supporters below at Advanced Base and Base Camp is warm and palpable. Later she said: "There was so much enthusiasm from down below. It's something I've never had before. So many people wanted me to get there." Alison, isolated for so many years from other climbers, suddenly felt part of their world, and that people cared about what she was doing.

It had taken almost eight hours of agonizing effort, each step painful, the summit often seeming beyond her reach. But then she was there, in a moment of intense release. The desire, the ambition that had been within her since she started climbing would never be so strong again. She wept and said through her tears: "Tell my children I'm on the summit of the world and I love them dearly." Her words were indistinct and mumbled, and Dickinson chided her for being so brief. She repeated more slowly: "To Tom and Kate, my two children, I am on top of the world and I love them dearly." This was the quotation issued to the press, and it seemed rather formal and stilted. In fact, Alison was in terrific form, crying and laughing at the same time, extremely lucid despite the lack of oxygen, and very much in control. Greg Child said to her, his voice laced with irony: "Alison, you're my new hero!" She replied: "You are so sarcastic!" Mandy Dickinson, in tears herself, congratulated her and the style in which she had achieved the summit. Alison sent messages to her parents and thanked Russell Brice for his unerring organization and support, dedicating the climb to him. She was radiantly, burstingly happy as she watched the Italians, sharing the narrow summit, shoot video footage and take countless stills. "How long will you stay on the summit?" Dickinson asked. "It depends what the Italians offer," she came back, impressively lucid despite the lack of oxygen. In her pack were red silk flowers, which she placed by the wind-torn prayer flags tied to an aluminium surveying mast planted in the snow.

Inevitably, she had to return, and the first step she took on the long descent was the first step back to the chaos she had left at home. But as she plodded along the North Ridge, perched above the mountains around her, the only doubt in her mind was her own safety. "For me," she had told Greg Child, "the summit is getting back down to Base Camp." Climbers descending Everest are in real peril, the adrenalin driving them to the summit now gone. There are several instances of climbers giving up, both mentally and physically, as the desire that kept them moving is taken away. Fran Arsentiev, who became the first American woman to climb Everest without bottled oxygen three years after Alison's ascent, collapsed from exhaustion and died as she struggled down from the summit after spending three nights at over 26,000 feet. Now, as Alison turned to climb back down the ladder on the second step, her radio flipped out of her jacket pocket and bounced off down the North Face. She had promised to keep regular radio contact with her supporters at Advance Base, but that was now impossible. Russell Brice had been to Camp III that day, leaving a sleeping bag for Alison to use when she returned, an act of generosity that was typical, and one that made little difference to her claim to be unsupported on the mountain. When he arrived back at Advance Base and found Alison had been silent for hours, he kept a long vigil by the radio, the concern on his face visible despite his assurances to others on the mountain that he wasn't worried.

Finally, Ang Babu, lead Sherpa with another British-led team, passed a message on that she was safe. Reaching Camp III at 4 p.m., she found Brice's sleeping bag but decided to continue down, to get as low as possible that day in case of bad weather. Dismantling her tent and shouldering her pack, she set off down to Camp

II and relative safety. When Child saw her next day after she had descended to Advance Base, he was impressed by her physical condition. "She looked like she'd been out for a stroll," he said. "She didn't seem to have been ravaged by the altitude. She still had the chubby little cheeks she always had and appeared to be very well adapted to the whole high-altitude game. She struck me as someone who was well under control." Marco Bianchi, one of Europe's strongest high-altitude climbers, told a journalist in Kathmandu: "She is a new star of the Himalaya—of women for sure, but also of men. She climbs like a man. She is very strong. And very kind." The compliment may have been clumsy, but Alison had left a deep impression.

That night the Sherpas steamed a cake in her honor and, her face glowing with pleasure, she sat down with the others on Brice's expedition to celebrate. Dickinson filmed the small party, crowded in the mess tent at Advance Base, the others congratulating Alison not so much for the scale of her achievement, which was great, but as much because she was their friend and deserved to have climbed the mountain. She appears relaxed, fit, and still surfing on a wave of exultation; now all she had to do was go home.

The media's intense interest in Alison's success on Everest caught her and most other climbers by surprise. The story appeared on several front pages and led the television and radio news. A leading article in *The Times*, entitled "Alison of Everest," argued that the tired image of Everest had been refreshed by her achievement. "Miss Hargreaves is indefatigable," it concluded. "After a few weeks of rest in Scotland, she proposes to attempt K2. Only two years ago, she climbed the six classic north faces of the Alps in a single season. We salute the spirit, courage, and, yes, chutzpah shown by Alison of Everest." But Alison was not indefatigable, and the explosion of media interest, which she had been trying to ignite for years, overtook her in a particularly cruel way.

After resting for two days at base camp, Alison and Richard Allen took a truck north to the Friendship Highway, which links Lhasa with Kathmandu. They drove west and then south until a landslide at the head of the long gorge into Nepal forced them to abandon their vehicle. Another landslide had blocked the road farther on, and they were forced to hike 20 miles, stopping the night in a roadside shack. When they finally reached Nepal, the BBC was waiting with a camera crew, and Alison had her first intimation of the scale of interest in her climb in Britain.

Jim was now running the media operation at home and was telling the press of his delight at Alison's success. He also issued a statement saying that her ascent "was the most important climb ever undertaken by a woman in the history of mountaineering." The quotation was used by Sprayway in their advertising material, although it was attributed to Cally Fleming and not Jim Ballard. Alison Osius, in a final interview with Alison before she left for K2, asked about the claim made on her behalf. Alison laughed nervously and said she did not know where it had come from, despite it appearing on an official press release. Even now she could not bring herself to criticize Jim in public. Were such comments necessary, Osius asked? "No," Alison said. "I don't think they are necessary."

By now, however, the means of communicating her success were out of her hands. "Jim had taken complete control of it," Allen recalls. When she got to Kathmandu, Alison called Sue; she was in tears after Jim had criticized her for talking to the *Independent* without agreeing to a fee. "She was distraught," Sue says, "and at the same time, she had no idea of what she was coming back to."

When she arrived at Heathrow, an official boarded the plane and asked her to put on a baseball hat and dark glasses. It was, Richard Allen thought, bizarre, but there was a scrum of reporters and television crews and photographers waiting for her, and they had to be thwarted. Ian Sykes, Ian Sutherland, and Jim had formed an informal committee, which Jim had termed the "three wise men," to manage the media's interest in Alison, thus bypassing Allen's role. Sykes, who had given over his public relations team for free, wanted the press conference held not in London but at the Nevis Range ski station in the north of Scotland, and wanted Alison's first public comments on British soil to be made from there.

With Ian Sutherland and John Hunt of Sprayway, Alison flew to Glasgow, where she met her parents. The following day she gave a press conference at Nevis Range to a considerably smaller number of journalists than had waited for her the day before. Alison was also delighted to see Bev, who had driven up the day before. With Kate clinging to her arm, she answered questions from the press in Nevis Range's large cafeteria. In the opposite corner of the room, far from his wife's side, Jim did the same. It was the start of a strange and frenetic period that left Alison feeling confused and emotionally exhausted. That evening, in tears, she left her parents to return home with Jim. She was angry at his overbearing attitude to the press, still desperate to end the marriage, but she had nowhere else to go. She must have wished that she was back on the summit of Everest, her life unclouded by misery.

Meanwhile, Richard Allen went back to work on her behalf, despite Jim's sudden intervention. He renegotiated Alison's book contract with Cape from £15,000 to £30,000, with a further, smaller sum to be paid if she made a substantial effort on K2. With the extra funds, Alison was able to clear her debt on the

Everest trip and could go on to K2, a much cheaper mountain in terms of financial cost, without worrying how to pay for it. He also collected her gear and had it freighted to Pakistan, but he could no longer act as a buffer between her and Jim. She had wanted Allen to go with her to Everest so she had a supporter, someone in her camp. On K2 she would be on her own.

There were moments of joy and calm, as well as the avalanche of attention. Three days after the press conference, Alison had dinner with her parents and gave her father a small stone she had picked up near the summit of Everest. "Please look after it," she told him. "I won't be going back for another." Later she took Tom and Kate to stay in Cally Fleming's caravan on the coast near Oban. They collected shells from the beach and scrambled up the small hills above the sea. But the fortnight before she left for K2 was a fraught and difficult time. Jim and the children had been living in a small holiday cabin near Spean Bridge, and Alison wanted to find her first permanent home since Meerbrook Lea had been repossessed. Here she planned to start a new life without her husband. She looked for a house and found Stone Cottage, in the Great Glen beneath the dark north face of Ben Nevis. Without anyone to care for her children while she was in Pakistan, Jim would have to move in to look after them, at least until the start of August when she came home. Alison was determined to continue with her plan to climb K2 even though her friends and family could see that she did not need to go. "She was in turmoil," Sue says, "and she had no chance to think rationally, take stock of what she'd done and what it meant. If she'd made getting rid of Jim her top priority, she would have done it. But ambition was still driving her as well."

The days passed in a whirlwind, a mad scramble to get ready to leave, give interviews, and meet sponsors. Wherever she went there were people wanting to talk to her, but after the initial fanfare that greeted her climb, journalists who were less impressed wrote negatively about her. Alison was shocked at the level of attention, although it must have thrilled her as well, and was deeply hurt by columnists who used her new public persona to exercise their own prejudices. Emma Brooker of the *Guardian* asked her how she felt when Nigella Lawson of *The Times* wrote that her mountaineering was a neurosis that showed "a reality-denying self-centerdness." Alison had no frame of reference to consider such things; she did not intellectualize her life in the way that these journalists were doing. In all the years she had been climbing, it had not occurred to her that there might be people who thought climbing not just odd, but *wrong*. It made her feel she was being attacked for no other reason than being who she was. It was profoundly painful to her that she should be criticized for leaving her children, as if she were failing as a mother. Like many who achieve fame suddenly, she could not see that so much of what was written about her was meaningless and would quickly be forgotten.

But the round of interviews and meetings continued regardless, and she had no chance to adjust to the difference climbing Everest had made to her life. She flew to Italy to meet with Ferrino, one of her main sponsors. She spoke with old friends like Bill O'Connor, telling him her marriage was over. He was struck by her confusion about the future, and feared for how things would go on K2. On June 10, she took possession of Stone Cottage and settled Tom and Kate there before heading back to Nevis Range for another television interview. There she said goodbye to the children, holding them close. "Be good for Daddy," she told them as they clung to her. "Have lots of adventures to tell me about when I come home." Then their father drove them away to the new home Alison had found.

By late evening she was in London, staying with Susan, before appearing on television again in the morning. She told Susan she was more determined than ever to leave Jim. She regretted she had not spent more time with her parents and that she could not explain how complex her life had become. "She had no idea what she'd done getting up Everest without oxygen," Susan says. "She didn't know she didn't have to go to K2." But Alison was committed. She had told her sponsors, her publisher, her friends, the whole world that she was going to Pakistan. When she came back, she reasoned, there would be time to sort things out. The following morning, after her television interview in London, she flew north to Manchester for another, posed for a newspaper photographer, and then returned to Manchester airport where her parents were waiting with John Hunt and Richard Allen. At 7:25 p.m. exactly, Alison kissed her parents goodbye and walked into the departure lounge.

CHAPTER 9

NEMESIS

K2's South Face is more than two miles high, rising as a squat, foreshortened pyramid from the glacier below it, the final third capped with red-brown rocks sitting on cotton-white snow and framed, when it's clear, by an indigo sky. These are the only colors on the mountain except for the bright specks of people or tents. In bad weather all colors merge into different shades of gray, to crumple the soul and bleed enthusiasm. Spread around in all directions are the other peaks of the Karakoram, some of them even steeper. But K2 is the centerpiece, separate and unrivaled.

At the foot of the face is a shrine, a cairn of rust-colored rocks topped by a crude wooden cross, bleached bone-white by the sun. It commemorates the death in 1953 of an American mountaineer named Art Gilkey, who suffered a blood clot in his leg at 25,000 feet. His blood, turned to the consistency of treacle from dehydration and altitude, was too sluggish for his heart to cope, and the clot spread, to his lungs and his other leg. Outside his tent a storm raged, pinning Gilkey's expedition down, and every hour he weakened. His companions were sure he would die, but while he lived, they would help him. In freezing winds and spindrift, they dragged and lowered Gilkey foot by foot down the mountain; whenever they asked him how he was, he would smile and say: "Just fine." At one point, one of the climbers slipped, dragging four others with him on the ropes. The last man held them all, as well as Gilkey, and they struggled back up the slope, frozen, exhausted, and in shock, to reorganize and put up a tent to shelter in. When they finished and looked around for Gilkey, strapped up inside his sleeping bag, he was gone, swept away in an avalanche. Their release from responsibility probably saved their lives, and they built this cairn to his memory. Forty years later, shreds of clothing and part of Gilkey's jawbone were found on the glacier near the cairn itself, the Gilkey Memorial.

Fixed to the cairn just below the wooden cross is an aluminium plate with an inscription in honor of a British climber Nick Estcourt, who died in an avalanche in 1978 on K2's West Ridge. There are other memorials too. Some are formal, professionally made, carried to K2 from home by grieving relatives, but most of them have been extemporized at Base Camp from aluminium mess plates. The names of Americans, Austrians, Italians, Japanese, and Poles oxidize atom by atom in the thin air. Above the cairn stands K2, the world's second-highest mountain; below are the stones and ice of the Godwin Austen Glacier. Roughly speaking, for every three or four climbers who reach the summit of K2, one will have a plate or memorial added here.

A quarter of a mile from the cairn is a curved band of medial moraine, a wedge of stones that collects above the ice where two glaciers meet. It is here, at 16,500 feet above sea level, that those attempting K2 set up home. In the summer of 1986, during another tragic climbing season on K2, someone thought up a nickname for the little group of tent villages that had sprung up along this narrow band of loose stones. He called it "The Strip," because the straggling line of brightly colored tents looked like Main Street in a frontier town somewhere in the Wild West. Not surprisingly, with Base Camp full of desperadoes living wild and sometimes short lives on the fringes of society, the name stuck.

On July 1, 1995, Matt Comeskey and other members of a New Zealand expedition to K2 led by Peter Hillary, the son of Sir Edmund Hillary, arrived and walked down the Strip, greeting old friends and introducing themselves to the other climbers on the mountain that summer. With Hillary was his old friend Kim Logan, a self-effacing man who took great pleasure from just being in the mountains. Bruce Grant was a champion skier who, as Logan's protegé, had shown equal enthusiasm for mountaineering. Comeskey, then 31, had attempted K2 before, in 1993, and already knew Alan Hinkes, one of the two Britons at base camp. The first time he'd heard about Alison Hargreaves was on television at home in Wellington. News of her success on Everest had reached the other side of the world, but when he met her a few weeks later, Comeskey was surprised:

My first impression was that she looked so small, skinny legs in black tights sticking out of the bottom of an over-inflated bright green down jacket, like a puffed-up duckling. I guess one of Alison's charms, and perhaps part of the reason for the British media's fascination with her, was the fact that she was by appearance such an unlikely high-altitude climber. I wouldn't have picked her from a crowd and guessed that she was a high-performance athlete.

Alison had been at base camp for a week and was still unwinding from the long and difficult journey. She had arrived in Islamabad on June 12 in the middle of a heatwave, and made the short journey to the old colonial city of Rawalpindi with Alan Hinkes, where they checked into the Shalimar Hotel. Hinkes, a professional mountaineer from North Yorkshire, had been on many more expeditions than Alison, and to him the heat and dust of Pakistan were familiar. He had already climbed one of the 26,000-foot giants in the Karakoram, a mountain near K2 called Broad Peak, and he had also tried the route up K2, which he and Alison would attempt. He kept a cache of equipment in Islamabad and knew many of the Pakistani officials and agents who control and support climbing expeditions. Alison was disoriented and jet-lagged, exhausted by two weeks of emotional torment and almost constant media attention. Half an hour after collapsing into bed, she was woken by a reporter determined to get the first interview with her on Pakistani soil.

Alison's fatigue only added to the confusion she felt about leaving Tom and Kate and the direction her life was taking, but the pace was relentless. She spent her first afternoon in Pakistan at the British High Commission, meeting guests and diplomats at a reception in her honor and talking about her plans. That evening she was invited back for a party, and rushed out to buy shoes and a dress. On her previous trips Alison had had time to adjust to the different demands and pace of expedition life. This time her experience was condensed. Rob Slater, the leader of the team she and Hinkes were joining, had organized almost every aspect of their trip to K2; permits, supplies, and equipment were all in place, so there was little to delay them in Rawalpindi. Most of the expedition had left for K2 a fortnight before, planning to have set up two or even three camps on the route before Alison, Hinkes, and an American teammate, Kevin Cooney, expected to arrive. They were anxious to catch up.

Alison and Al Hinkes were in Rawalpindi for less than 48 hours before taking an internal flight north to the town of Skardu, at the foot of the Karakoram. The pilot recognized Alison from an item about her on the BBC and invited her to sit in the cockpit as the plane flew up the Indus valley toward the Karakoram. Now she could begin to contemplate the expedition and adjust to a more measured pace of life. She found the K2 Motel in Skardu, the hotel used and known by climbers and trekkers all over the world, to be "a lovely place, quiet and peaceful. Beautiful gardens and views over the Indus river. It is great to be here. Pakistan is a far nicer place than I expected. The people are kind and helpful and Skardu, particularly this place, is a delight." They spent a day and two nights in this oasis, resting from the journey and the noise of Rawalpindi, and adjusting to the higher altitude.

Hours before dawn on June 16, Alison was disturbed by someone tapping on the window of the room next door. She was awake instantly and showered, taking the chance to wash her hair in comfort one last time. She had been carrying a blow-dryer, a valued luxury, but now she packed it away because it was, as she told her diary, "the last time it would be used for a few weeks." At 5:30 a.m. two jeeps carrying the three climbers and their gear pulled out of the K2 Motel and headed for Askole, the roadhead at the start of the trail to K2 itself. During the first part of the journey, the arid brown valley was punctuated by the green of irrigated fields and villages. "This time last week I was on the Underground from Heathrow to Euston—tired as ever," she wrote. "Now I'm still tired as ever but in hot, dry, and dusty Pakistan." An hour later they started on the trek to Base Camp.

Alison's three expeditions to Nepal had involved short and generally pleasant treks to the foot of the mountains she was planning to climb, and while the Tibetan side of Everest is harsh, it can be reached by road. K2, however, is much more remote, and a substantial part of the approach follows the bleak and stony Baltoro Glacier. Here the fierce midsummer heat gave way to gloomy skies, with rain and snow squalls hiding the mountains, leaving a view of gray rocks and banks of crumbling moraine. The weather on June 19 was so bad they stayed in their tents for the whole day. The ache of being away from Tom and Kate returned. While she was moving, with an objective to reach, Alison's doubts about her future and what she was doing were suppressed. Sitting in a leaky tent with nothing to do but think of home was torture. For the next few days the weather stayed grim. As they trudged up the dreary glacier, there were heavy falls of snow, which Alison knew could delay their progress on the mountain. Al Hinkes remembers Alison walking alone during their trek to base camp. No one thought this unusual; climbers often like to move at their own pace on easy ground. But on K2 Alison had no confidant, no older and wiser friend, as Richard Allen had been on Everest, to whom she could express doubts and who would give her advice.

On June 24 she woke at Concordia, a confluence of glaciers in the shadow of a number of the earth's highest mountains. The evening before clouds had once again hidden the mountains, and when Alison checked her watch and realized it was still early, she contemplated having a lie-in. But her restless energy made her unzip her tent and there, framed in the doorway and lit by the pure light of early morning, was the vast pyramid of K2. She called out in a singing voice: "I can see K2!" Standing in her sleeping bag, Alison hopped around outside, taking photographs before the clouds returned.

K2 lies 12 miles and a final day's trek to the north from Concordia, with the mountain's Southeast Ridge, the upper section of their intended ascent, in stark profile. The peak is so remote from human habitation that when it was first measured in the 19th century, no local name for it could be found, and K2 kept its Survey of India tag—K for Karakoram and 2 for the second mountain in the group to be identified. Filippo de Filippi, an Italian who traveled to the area with the Duke of Abruzzi in 1909 and was one of the first westerners to see K2 close up, wrote afterward: "Down at the end, alone, detached from all the other mountains soared up K2, the indisputable sovereign of the region, gigantic and solitary, jealously defended by a vast throng of vassal peaks, protected from invasion by miles and miles of glacier. Even to get within sight of it demands so much contrivance." Alison was rarely so effusive. Nevertheless, her first sight of the mountain made a deep impact.

At the press conference she gave after Everest, barely three weeks earlier, she had been asked how she faced up to K2's reputation. Alison replied: "To be absolutely honest, I know almost nothing about it." Steeped as she was in mountaineering history, she was being disingenuous. Though K2 was first climbed in 1954 by an Italian expedition, it was another 23 years before the second ascent, and by the start of the 1980s, only 15 people had reached the top. Two of the four women who had climbed K2 before Alison, Liliane Barrard and Julie Tullis, had died during the descent, as had a number of men. By the time Alison saw K2 in 1995, there had been 113 successful ascents and 33 deaths. In 1986 alone, when Tullis, Al Rouse, and three others died in a week-long storm, there were 27 ascents and 12 deaths. From almost the beginning of its climbing history, K2 earned its epithet, the "savage mountain." In 1939 an expedition led by the Austrian-American Fritz Wiessner saw near triumph turn to disaster, when Wiessner, returning from his summit bid, was forced to abandon the inexperienced and half delirious Dudley Wolfe at 25,000 feet. Wolfe died days later, along with three high-altitude porters who had made a heroic attempt to rescue him.

The success rate on Everest was more than six times as high, and the death toll proportionately much lower. Plenty of those who have reached the summit of the world have relied on will-power rather than ability; Everest is a mountain where that is possible because it has easy-angled routes to the summit, where Sherpas can do much of the back-breaking work. On Everest, bottled oxygen is commonly used. K2 is different. "You get all sorts on Everest," Al Hinkes says. "Most people on K2 are bloody good climbers."

Alison knew that while K2 at 28,253 feet is 775 feet lower than Everest, the northerly latitude of the Karakoram means K2 is colder and its weather patterns are less stable. Climbers have often found themselves unable to leave Base Camp for days on end, and many of the deaths on K2 have been caused by a sudden change in weather, trapping climbers high on the mountain. Few novices have reached the top, and the roll-call of the dead reveals a long string of talented and famous mountaineers. Alison couldn't have been unaware of the nature of what she was taking on.

Her attitude to the possibility of injury or death had come under greater scrutiny as her fame increased. Emma Brooker, writing in the *Guardian*, was baffled by Alison's apparent straightforwardness:

Her life is about climbing mountains. Everything else falls into place around that. She goes up a mountain, she comes down again, she moves on to the next. Her only worry is running out of them. It makes her a living and supports her family. If her ego is big, it is also simple. The child-faced figure in the summit pictures seems to know no mortal fear, has no concept of her own possible death. Perhaps that's why she can do it.

Alison's simplistic response when people asked her if she felt equivocal about the risks of climbing, or even why she did it, is revealing. It was not, as Brooker speculated, that her ego was simple or she had no conception of her own death. In private, she had questioned her decisions and wondered whether she was doing the right thing throughout her life. Before leaving for Pakistan, she had confessed to Susan she was having doubts, and now she would put herself through agonies of indecision at Base Camp.

But she wouldn't allow others to see those doubts because it would have undermined the fragile structures she was building up for herself. She grabbed at the things she wanted and then stuck to them; moving in with Jim was perhaps the greatest example. Much as she hated to be seen as a failure, her greatest fear was of being judged a fraud. She could conceive of her own mortality, but she could not begin to articulate it, let alone in public. Alison admitted to moments of peril and the knowledge that she could have died on certain mountains, but she was no existentialist. She had guessed, like many high-altitude climbers, that it needed a mental trick to get up big mountains. You understood the risks and planned for them, but assumed that somehow they wouldn't apply to you. That is why she could tell Emma Brooker:

If I was frightened, I wouldn't go. If I thought it was desperately dangerous, I wouldn't do it. Look, I drive on motorways at night, I consider that risky.

Quite a few people have been killed on [K2] but that's because people have got caught in storms. The trick is not to be up high when a storm comes.

However poignant her words seem now, in a literal sense she was right. And while the general public might think the odds insane, Alison knew that the majority of people who go climbing in the Himalaya, even on the biggest peaks, come back alive. In the same way that accepting a small amount of risk liberates car drivers, accepting a much bigger risk liberates a mountaineer. She was strong, fit, had a great deal to live for and fully expected to come back to her children. Any number of mountaineers who had climbed with her in the past have since acknowledged that she was entirely capable of climbing the mountain. When she arrived at the Strip on the afternoon of June 24, she had every right to be there.

Already in residence for the past two weeks, the rest of the team had set up an advanced base to cache supplies and a first camp on the Abruzzi Spur itself. The route is named after the Italian noble-man, Luigi Amedeo di Savoia, Duke of Abruzzi, who had come within 200 miles of the North Pole and had climbed mountains from Africa to Alaska as well as in the Himalaya. He took a well-equipped expedition up the Baltoro in 1909 and settled on the southeast spur of the mountain as the most likely route. The Duke of Abruzzi's attempt soon petered out low down on the ridge as the climbers realized the scale of the difficulties ahead of them: thou-sands of feet of challenging climbing on brittle outcrops of rock and steep snow and ice, far more difficult than the uniform snow slopes found for long sections on the normal routes on Everest. The worst problem was an 80-foot chimney of rotten rock at 21,600 feet. It took Bill House four dangerous hours to overcome it in 1938, and the feature was known from then on as House's Chimney, giving climbers another name to mythologize. This pitch was the hardest climbing done in the Himalaya before the Second World War. As the number of expeditions to K2 increased in the 1980s, a metal-runged rope ladder was fixed down its length for convenience.

Three camps are usually placed on the Spur, which ends at a sloping shoulder at about 25,600 feet, a featureless, tilted, icy ocean, prone to avalanches and violent winds, where hypoxic mountaineers lost in the mist have struggled in vain to find shelter. It was here that the victims of the storm in 1986 were trapped. From the Shoulder, the site of Camp IV, the view of the top is incredibly foreshortened, making it seem closer than it actually is, luring climbers on. The K2 summit day, for even the fittest and best acclimatized mountaineer, is a much more serious proposition than the ascent of Everest from the South Col or the final camp on the North Ridge.

Rob Slater, the leader of Alison's expedition, was also determined to add his name to the list of those who had climbed K2. A native of Wyoming from a traditional and conservative family, early on he determined a life plan of epic proportions and proceeded to carry it out, including making a million dollars on the floor of the Chicago Board of Trade. In terms of adventure he was no less ambitious, deciding on objectives before he had acquired the expertise to stand a chance of success. He climbed several hard routes on the 3,000-foot granite walls of Yosemite, and then learned to parachute so he could jump off them when he got to the top. During an expedition to a slender, vertiginous granite tower above the Baltoro glacier, he became bored with high-altitude rock climbing and, abandoning his partners, trekked up the glacier to study K2. There and then he conceived a desire to climb it. Perhaps he recognized that the cachet associated with K2 was far greater than anything he had done so far. He had told friends in his hometown of Boulder, Colorado, that he would reach the summit or die.

"It was the only mountain he ever needed to climb," says Kevin Cooney, who had trekked into base camp with Alison and Alan Hinkes. "He was a driven individual and I had a real problem with his summit-or-death attitude. When he asked me to come, I decided I needed someone else I could partner up high." That someone was Scott Johnston, a long-standing friend of Cooney, from Bend, Oregon. Cooney was concerned when he heard that Alison would be joining the team. He knew little about her beyond her sudden rise to fame and was worried they would have a prima donna on their hands. "I was very pleasantly surprised," he recalls. "High-altitude mountaineering is not about glamour, it's about grunt work. She was determined and prepared to do the dirty work. There are very few women who could have carried an equal share of the gear the way she did."

Nor would she tolerate the squalor that many male climbers exist in while camped at the foot of a mountain. "Things were in a bit of a mess when we arrived," recalls Hinkes. "Rob could suffer having rubbish everywhere, but Alison set about tidying up." She also wrote several letters home, relying on the satellite communications of a Dutch expedition that was also already there to attempt the Abruzzi. "I am greatly missing all the family and look forward to returning to the U.K. to start to straighten things out," she told Sue on June 28. To her parents she was even more open, apologizing for the problems she felt she had caused them and reflecting on her uncertain future: "I have a lot to sort out—in some ways it is just the beginning and right now I am unsure how it will work out."

Her uncertainty was exacerbated by the fragmented nature of the team she was climbing with. As soon as they arrived, the expedition doctor had quit. Al Hinkes describes a group short on high-altitude experience trying to prove themselves and being "gung-ho." As for Alison, she was exhibiting doubts about the widely assumed plan that she and Hinkes would climb together.

At the very end of June the two carried loads up to the first camp at 19,000 feet, spending the night to improve their acclimatization and getting used to the terrain. This first part of the climb is steep and exhausting, and it is threatened by stones falling from above, often knocked down by climbers higher on the mountain. On the following day Alison and Hinkes continued up ropes previously fixed by other climbers to the second camp, just below House's Chimney. Above the chimney was a section known as the Black Pyramid, an area of icy gullies and slabs of rock. It wasn't technically extreme, and Alison's passage was made easier by the ropes already fixed in place. But the angle was unremitting, the exposure immense, with few places to rest; tent sites for Camp III were limited to shallow ledges improved by hacking out more rock.

With the first stage of their acclimatization plan completed, Alison and Hinkes came down to recover. Hinkes assumed they would rest together at Base Camp for a couple of days, so when Alison said she would be going back up after only one day in camp with the Americans, Hinkes realized that she meant she was breaking their partnership. "It was obvious after that, that she didn't want to climb with me," he says. "There was no falling out. All she said was she was going up the next day." She must have believed that by climbing with the others, she would maximize her chance of success. At the same time, Hinkes says, she may have feared that if she reached the summit with a fellow Briton, this would diminish the impact of her climb with the media.

On July 4 Alison and Kevin Cooney returned to Camp One without Hinkes. Johnston and Slater followed a day later. They worked on the route, gaining height, ferrying supplies and fixing more rope. "She was always a team player," Cooney says. "When I came down [from fixing rope to Camp III] on the evening of July 6, she had everything sorted out in camp and had a brew on. Hinkes wasn't always helpful in that way. He was there to get to the summit and not to be a member of a team."

For a few days the weather turned, confining everyone to base camp. Then, on July 14, Alison, Slater, Cooney, and Johnston returned to the mountain, reaching Camp II that night, and moving on up the Black Pyramid to set up Camp III the next day at 23,650 feet. Hinkes, accompanied by another American, Richard Celsi, the man who'd invited Alison to K2 in the first place, followed a day behind. The weather looked promising, but it was just three weeks after the expedition's latecomers—Alison, Cooney, and Hinkes—had arrived at Base Camp. None of the Americans felt sufficiently acclimatized to the altitude to continue. Most people who climb K2 take at least four or six weeks to acclimatize, and they judged it was still too soon to push on up to Camp IV.

Hinkes felt differently. He had attempted the Abruzzi once before, in 1993, and had also been on K2 a year later, when he tried to climb the mountain's North Ridge from over the border in China. With his experience of the mountain, he sensed that his chance had come. Perfect days in the Karakoram are rare, but Hinkes had a feeling that one was coming. He passed Alison and the others descending from Camp III, but the following day, instead of descending to base camp as the others had done, he took a tent and stove and continued to the Shoulder at 25,600 feet.

The Dutch team also reached Camp IV that day, so Hinkes knew he wouldn't be alone on the upper reaches of the mountain. He crawled into his tent to try to sleep and then, at 3 a.m., he struggled out into the night to assess the conditions. "The weather was absolutely perfect, very little wind, no clouds but bitterly cold. The other guys were determined to make a bid for the summit. I felt that the time was right for me." He set off after the four others across the Shoulder and up the steepening slope to a narrowing beneath a huge, hanging ice cliff, the Bottleneck, at over 27,000 feet. It took him more than eight hours of effort to reach this point, fighting for breath and stopping every few steps to slow his wildly beating heart. From here the climbers traversed left, fixing ropes on stretches that might prove difficult later on. "The weather was still good," Hinkes recalls. "You could see it was clear all around. I wouldn't have done it if the weather was changing."

He reached the summit at 6 p.m., shortly after the last of the Dutch climbers, Ronald Naar. When Naar started descending, Hinkes was on his own on the summit of the world's second highest mountain with dusk creeping in. "I knew from two years before that three people had died descending from the top in perfect weather in daylight. And I was going to do it in the dark." He soon overtook Naar and continued past, trying to get as far down the mountain as he could before darkness overtook him. There was little communal effort; at such extreme altitudes, there was not much they could do for each other. When he reached his tent at Camp IV, the Dutch were still three hours behind him.

As he climbed down next day, Hinkes met Alison and Rob Slater rushing up from Camp II. They were trying to take advantage of the good weather, having woken on Hinkes's summit day to discover they had been caught at Base Camp during what would be the best day of the entire season. But now, as they greeted Hinkes, a gray lenticular cloud shrouded the summit, heralding a change in conditions. Alison congratulated him, but she was visibly devastated to have missed her chance. "She had a bit of a tear," Hinkes recalls. "She could have done it then, she was strong enough." In opting to climb with the Americans, she had made a serious misjudgment.

Rob Slater soon abandoned their hurried summit bid, but Alison went on to Camp IV despite the threatened change in weather and spent the night there. It was an act of desperation. The following day the weather broke. Alison found herself alone at 25,600 feet, on the threshold of the anoxic Death Zone, the best part of two vertical miles from safety. Outside her tent conditions were deteriorating and she couldn't be sure how bad they would get. To stay on the Shoulder was to risk the fate that had befallen Julie Tullis and Al Rouse in 1986. Her lifeline, the string of fixed ropes that snaked down the Black Pyramid, down House's Chimney and down the broken, shattered spur beneath, began some way below Camp IV. She had no choice but to find it. Before she became trapped in her tent, she forced herself to get ready and left the Shoulder. Then came a long and lonely descent. Time after time she repeated the routine she had practiced on crags and mountains for so many years: clipping her belay device to the rope; checking everything was in order; then starting to rappel, trusting herself completely to the rope and equipment, controlling her speed by gripping the line with her mittens. She had started her period, and felt physically and mentally low. Even her body, it seemed, was letting her down. She must have thought on every abseil what she might have achieved if she had stuck with Alan Hinkes. She could have been on her way back to her children, her future and fame secured, ready to start a new life. Instead, if she still wanted K2, she faced coming back to this dangerous, grueling climb and weeks of uncertainty.

As Hinkes rested and prepared to go home, the weather closed in again, dumping snow on the mountain. The storm lasted for 11 days straight. "By the end of it we were making snowmen and snow sculptures at Base Camp," Cooney recalls. "There wasn't a whole lot for anyone to do except drink coffee and stay away from avalanches." Johnston talked of being "jerked around" by the mountain, that they were all frustrated and "about to go off at the deep end." For Alison, the enforced rest tightened her spiral of fear and doubt. In a letter to her parents dated July 22 she wrote:

> *The Dutch expedition (who arrived two weeks before us) managed to put two climbers on top five days ago. Al Hinkes (pushing the boat out) tagged behind them; they are all now leaving and it makes me even more want to come home.*

Her sentences reek of tension. The Dutch, she explains, reached the top because they had been on the mountain two weeks longer than she had. Hinkes had only succeeded by taking a risk and letting the Dutch work for him, breaking trail to the summit. None of it altered the bald fact that he had reached the top and she hadn't. "She was envious," Hinkes says. "She was frustrated that she'd missed her chance."

The rational thing to have done was remind herself that the mountain would still be there next year, that she had put in a creditable performance and could be happy with her achievements. It had taken Hinkes three tries to climb the mountain. But in her state of confusion and loneliness, she was losing her perspective. She found K2 a remote and harsh experience, and had told Hinkes that she wouldn't come to the Karakoram again, preferring the easier-going style of expeditions in Nepal. Paradoxically, her unhappiness only increased her determination to succeed. "I've been missing Tom and Kate today," she wrote in her diary as early as July 3, "probably because I have had time to think about them. I've half felt like not wanting really to stay and finish this 'job off'—but I don't know if or when I'll get another chance, so I might regret it."

"She was desperate to get the climb done and get home to her kids," Scott Johnston said afterward, a view shared by most others who talked with her that summer. "She said she'd never go on a long trip again without her kids. She was so torn, she was at her wits' end." Cooney remembers her returning in tears on July 11 from one of the agonizingly short telephone calls she made on the satellite phone to her children. "I spoke for two and a half minutes," she wrote miserably in her diary. Nor did she made any secret of the fact that her marriage was over. "It was obvious there was a split," Hinkes says. "It was only the kids she would talk about. She made it clear things were not right."

In her diary Alison wrote that she had been dreaming of Derbyshire. At altitude, where sleep patterns are more broken, dreams seem brighter and more real and have a greater impact on the conscious mind. When she wrote: "I dream of days gardening and hiking with the children, the Derbyshire hills and holiday skiing," she was recreating her own childhood, but idealized, with only the good memories remaining. It was the childhood she wanted to give her own children. Waking after dreams like that, in a frozen tent beneath the looming presence of K2, must have been a dismal blow to her spirit. The gloom that surrounded her and the others during the bad weather affected even Al Hinkes as he left for home. "I knew there was going to be a tragedy," he says, adding that he told a number of people about his doubts when he got back to Britain. "I just had a feeling that things were going to go pear-shaped." His fears, shared by some of her friends at home, were not some kind of surreal premonition. Five climbers had been killed on K2 the previous year, five the year before that. It was natural that many who knew Alison feared for her safety.

However torn she felt, the tangible pressures on her to stay and concentrate on the mountain were increasing. Hinkes had contacted his sponsors from Base Camp, and back in England they issued a press release with news of his success. It was inevitable that journalists started asking why she hadn't been to the top with him. "She was getting faxes asking: 'Hinkes got up, why not you?' Cooney says. After Alison's death, Joyce Hargreaves said: "She was fearless about climbing a mountain because she knew it was a fear she could control. But she hated the fear she felt about her marriage problems, because it was out of her control." Now she had an additional pressure beyond her control: a judgmental and largely ignorant media that would be watching everything she did. "I am feeling pressure back home," she wrote in her diary on August 5 at the height of her crisis. "Why I failed, what went wrong. Personally it doesn't matter, but I worry how everyone else will see it." Except, of course, that how others saw her was very important indeed to her self-esteem, and for Alison failure was bitterly personal.

On August 1 the weather finally relented. There was barely time for another attempt at the summit; porters would be arriving on August 5 to carry the expedition's equipment back down the Baltoro Glacier. Alison planned to go with them, although she had told Susan and others that her flight could be changed if she needed another chance.

Johnston and Cooney left Base Camp aiming to get to Camp II, but the heavy snow had buried the fixed ropes and they were forced to descend to Camp I, where Alison, Slater, and Celsi planned to spend the night. Camp I was now overcrowded, so Cooney and Johnston suggested that the others go down to sleep and let them clear the ropes between Camps I and II next day. Slater, who according to Celsi had become paranoid, accused them of trying to sneak ahead and grab the summit without them. Alison was also worried that they were being left behind. "They both became very afraid that Scott and I would go to the summit without them," Cooney says. In the end they acknowledged that Johnston and Cooney were making sense and descended back to base camp.

The following day the two Americans set to work clearing the snow off the fixed ropes. Cooney says that in sections the snow was so deep that he had to use his shovel to make progress. When they reached the site of Camp III, they discovered their tents had been crushed and buried by snow. As far as Cooney was concerned, his attempt to climb K2 was over. On August 3 he and Johnston descended to base camp to prepare to leave, meeting Slater, Celsi, and Alison on their way back up to Camp III.

When Alison and Slater got there the following day, they set to work trying to find their tent in the deep snow. When Celsi arrived after the long and exhausting climb up from Camp II at around 6 p.m., he discovered that the others had appropriated a sleeping mat he had left weeks before. Standing at 24,000 feet on the tiny campsite poised above the steep ridge, the teammates argued before Alison and Slater returned to their digging, asking Celsi to help.

After a further 20 minutes, there was still no sign of the tent, and Alison began to think it was gone. The 46-year-old Celsi had been slightly slower on the ten-hour trip up the ropes from Camp II, but he remained essentially fit. However, ambition now overcame friendship. Because of the storm, Slater and Alison were missing vital items of equipment that had been cached at Camp III. Looking at Celsi, Slater told him he seemed ill and ought to go down. He also told him to leave behind his sleeping bag, down suit, food, and stove. He and Alison only had one sleeping bag and one down suit between them. It was clear Slater simply wanted his equipment. "I couldn't believe what they were talking about," Celsi says. "I thought, I'm just not staying here, there are bigger things than this."

Celsi was facing a long descent alone, with 34 consecutive rappels down the Black Pyramid. Some of the ropes were frozen solid, and Celsi was already exhausted. He climbed a little way down to the tents of another expedition, the mainly New Zealand team led by Peter Hillary. Alison followed him, and Celsi thought she was going to offer him some assistance, perhaps her water bottle, an act of generosity that would, according to Celsi, have been entirely in character. Instead she asked to borrow his overboots. Celsi refused. Sitting in his tent, Peter Hillary was aghast at what was happening and tried to talk Celsi out of going down, but he was now determined to quit the mountain. Later, with considerable magnanimity, he explained Alison and Slater's reasons to the writer Alison Osius: "Without the equipment, their summit bid was over. These people were my friends. We shared a lot. I tend to believe they got completely focused in a very selfish way. There's a fine line, with the need on big mountains to succeed, between focused and selfish."

It was unacceptable behavior for a mountaineer, and it colored Hillary's impression of Alison and Rob Slater. It was just the sort of behavior Alison would have normally criticized. Alison believed that Celsi really was ill, but if that was the case, then he should have been accompanied or given bivouac equipment. Instead he was sent down a dangerous mountain from a relatively high altitude alone and ill prepared to spend the night out.

There's no doubt about Alison's motivation for such extreme behavior. She had barely two or three days to reach the summit and make the flight home to see her children, and the urgency of the situation had eroded her usual generosity and safe practice. She could have both, the mountain and her children, if she just pushed a little harder. With Slater taking the initiative, it was easy enough to follow his lead, even if under normal circumstances she would have known it to be wrong. During the long, tedious days of the storm in late July, she had given an interview to Matt Comeskey for the New Zealand Alpine Club's newsletter. The boredom and frustration show in her more cynical remarks about mountaineers, and, not for the first time when things were going badly, she discusses giving up professional climbing. "I'm so pissed off with the way things are going in climbing," she told Comeskey. "I think people have always been competitive, but people are getting so dishonest about things and it just pisses me off, basically." It is possible she was thinking enviously of Alan Hinkes again, now on his way home. But she may also have been thinking of herself, caught up in something constructed and artificial, designed more to catch the media's interest than satisfy her needs. What had been magical had become workaday. No wonder she was dreaming of her childhood.

Celsi's equipment notwithstanding, Alison and Slater made no bid for the summit. Once again they were driven off K2 by bad weather. Back at Base Camp, there was more wind and snow. They were living inside a cold, gray cloud. The porters arrived as arranged, and for Alison and Slater success on K2 seemed to be slipping away. For the other three Americans there was no choice to make. Kevin Cooney and Scott Johnston had jobs to go back to, firm commitments that prevented any equivocation, and Cooney was getting married. They were not professional climbers who depended on the mountain for their living, and neither had told their friends that it would be "the summit or death." Richard Celsi had simply had enough.

In her last letter to Jim on July 22, Alison said that she would be leaving Base Camp on August 6 to catch her flight on August 13. "I don't think I can face any longer here than that," she wrote. Yet even before the incident with Celsi and their abortive attempt on the summit, there were signs that both Alison and Slater were changing their minds. On July 29 they had dropped by the New Zealanders' camp to ask if they could join their expedition when Cooney, Johnston, and Celsi left. However, after their summit bid failed, Alison packed her gear along with the rest of the American team, making up loads of her personal belongings for the porters. On August 5, with the porters ready to start carrying her equipment down the glacier the next day, she wrote of how she missed the children. She'd now spent more than a hundred days of 1995 away from Tom and Kate. Yet there was still a desire for the mountain, too. "It eats away at me—wanting the children and wanting K2," she wrote. "I feel like I'm being pulled in two. Maybe they'd be happier if Mum was around but maybe summiting K2 would help make a better future for them. Long term, having me back safe and sound is surely more important."

In weighing her decision, Alison's chief preoccupation wasn't danger but whether she could cope with being away from her children for a few weeks longer. Going on the mountain was not the difficulty for her. Mountains were the one place she felt confident about what to do. Going home meant finally resolving her relationship with Jim and surviving as a single mother. Still unaware of the full impact of her ascent of Everest, she believed that her route to future security was via the top of K2, and that by reaching it, she would finally achieve a position where she need never be away from her children for so long again.

When she woke up on August 6, she was still in agony over whether to leave. As rain fell outside, she sat in the Base Camp mess tent and talked things over with Celsi, drinking coffee and waiting for the appointed hour of departure. Fifteen minutes before they were due to leave, she changed her mind for good. She was staying. She recovered her gear from the two porters who were to have carried it, and gave some letters and a fax to Richard Celsi to send when he could, so that those at home would know what she had done. As the Americans left, Alison was crying. "She couldn't let herself go home and do what she really wanted to do," Scott Johnston said. Unlike Hinkes, Cooney says he wasn't overly concerned for her safety, and he fully expected to meet her again.

"I feel like a lead weight has gone from my shoulders," she wrote when the others had gone. "I'm sitting here with the Kiwis—I'm happy my decision is the right one. I feel much more content, restful and happier now." When Matt Comeskey, sitting next to her over a late breakfast, asked why she had changed her mind, she deflected his question. "It's a woman's right," she said.

Ghulam Rasool, the expedition's cook, would later tell Scott Johnston that he heard Alison sobbing in her tent on the evening before her final attempt on K2, but her mood in the available portions of her diary is optimistic, confident, and even happy. Comeskey says: "If she was [unhappy] I don't remember her showing it." The New Zealanders, their Pakistani staff, Alison, and Rob Slater spent the next few days of bad weather playing frisbee with aluminium dinner plates, each climber marking their favorite plate with their name and, in their boredom, creating a kind of obstacle course they could guide their frisbees round. Each evening a team of Spanish climbers, the only other expedition still left on the Strip, would stroll down from their camp to chat and discuss plans. If she was unhappy at night, then during the day Alison hid it well.

At long last, on August 9, the weather cleared, and although there was trepidation about fresh snow high on the mountain, all the climbers agreed to try for the summit. Alison had asked for porters to be sent up for her gear on August 16. After weeks of indecision and doubt, her immediate future was settled. She had a plan. She had time to give K2 one more try and then she would go home to her children. "We don't really know what the weather is doing but hope it holds for long enough," she wrote. "Can we possibly be offered the chance to summit? God willing."

Early next morning, at around 4 a.m., Alison zips the door of her tent shut and leaves Base Camp with Rob Slater. Wrapped warmly against the cold night, they race to get high on the mountain before the sun rises. All of the New Zealand team also heads for the Abruzzi Spur. Matt Comeskey is one of them, despite being worried about his health, and he is joined by Peter Hillary, Bruce Grant, Kim Logan, and Jeff Lakes, a Canadian who has been on K2 before. They are all strong climbers, all of them excited by the sudden release from waiting and the promise of good weather. The climbers rope up across some crevasses below the first camp and then follow marker wands stuck in the snow, pacing steadily up the snow and ice slopes. Comeskey finds himself vomiting but continues, hoping his condition will improve. He shares part of the day with Alison, chatting easily as they follow the line of ropes up to Camp II. Slater says he hopes never to have to sweat up those slopes again, but the route is familiar now, the mood relaxed.

The following day the good weather holds and the climbers continue, using the fixed ropes to climb through House's Chimney. Kim Logan and Bruce Grant break trail for much of the day, wading through steep fresh snow on the slopes above the chimney. Rob and Alison bring up the rear, carrying a spare tent in the likely event that the one they have previously used has been crushed by new snow or high winds. At least they have footsteps to follow, where the snow has been compacted by those in front. And on the fixed ropes there is no need to think about where to go. They have only to slide their Jumar clamps up the line and plod steadily up.

When they reached Camp III, both teams find the tents and equipment buried, and the long and exhausting process of digging out and reerecting the tents begins. Alison is keen to continue on to Camp IV, which she alone of the climbers still on the mountain has reached that season, and after reestablishing their camp, most of the New Zealanders follow her. Comeskey, who is still feeling the effects of his stomach illness, stays behind on his own.

On the morning of August 12 Comeskey wakes to another clear day. It is his birthday and he is feeling better, but he feels his chance of going to the top is gone. He is sure that the climbers must have continued on for the summit in such good conditions, but when he makes a prearranged radio call to Kim Logan he is surprised to find that the climbers are still at Camp IV. Two days of wading in deep snow has left them exhausted, and so despite the good weather and the dubious value of resting at such high altitude, they have all opted to stay in camp.

Five of the Spanish climbers are also relaxing at their tents high on the Shoulder that morning. Unlike the other expeditions that summer, they have been climbing a different route, the south-southeast spur, a line parallel to the Abruzzi, which reaches the slopes of the Shoulder a few hundred feet farther up, where the Spaniards have pitched their own Camp IV. But they have climbed through much of the previous night: like Alison, Slater, and the New Zealanders, they also decide to rest. Led by 38-year-old Pepe Garcés, all the Spaniards have previous Himalayan experience. Lorenzo Ortiz, the youngest of the group at 29, climbed the giant Nanga Parbat in Pakistan the year before. Javier Escartín, 46, and 42-year-old Lorenzo Ortas have been to the summit of another 8,000-meter peak in the Karakoram, Gasherbrum I. Garcés himself climbed Everest four years before. The fifth Spanish climber high on K2 today is 39-year-old Javier Olivar. Like the New Zealanders, they are on the mountain for one last effort, and are expecting porters to arrive on August 14.

Later five figures emerge from the camp above the Abruzzi Spur. Moving slowly in the thin air, the five climb the gentle snow slope up to the Spanish tents: Alison Hargreaves and Rob Slater, and three New Zealanders, Peter Hillary, Bruce Grant, and Kim Logan. They have come up to get a better view of the upper slopes. The weather is fine with a few clouds brushing the mountain but otherwise settled, as it has been for the previous two days. After several hours discussing plans and watching the mountain, the five return to their camp to prepare for tomorrow's attempt on the summit.

After his morning radio call, Matt Comeskey rouses himself, and toward dusk he reaches Camp IV. The group's two tents are now in cloud, a smaller one shared by Hillary and Lakes, and a larger dome structure that houses Alison, Slater, and Logan. Bruce Grant is outside the dome tent telling the others of Comeskey's arrival, who glances inside and sees a mass of arms and legs. He jokingly asks for some room and is directed down to the little tent. The team are in fairly good spirits. A few of them are coughing, but that's to be expected at high altitude.

As he walks down to the other tent, Comeskey is sick again, as he has been during the climb from Camp III. Each time he vomits, his legs buckle underneath him. Fearful that it might happen on the steep summit slopes above Camp IV, or that he is becoming too dehydrated and risks a stroke after losing vital fluid, he decides to retreat the following day. The other 11 climbers at the two high camps will be going for the summit.

Alison and the others sharing the dome tent struggle in the darkness, bumping into each other as they pull on their outer boots, adjusting their clothing in slow motion as they breathe heavily in the thin air. The blue flame of the stove that has been melting snow in the endless battle against dehydration is turned off, and without its steady purr the night seems suddenly quiet. They unzip the door and leave the tent at 2 a.m. Alison is wearing everything she has, yet the cold drills through her body and into her bones. She doesn't expect to return for at least 18 hours.

Alison, Rob Slater, Kim Logan, and Bruce Grant set out together, the yellow light of their head lamps dancing on the white snow as they walk up the gentle incline of the Shoulder, trying to orient themselves. With the lamps shining just in front of their feet, it's harder to see the black shapes of the peaks around them and K2's summit pyramid above. Matt Comeskey stays in the tent alone, suddenly colder without the bodies of his friends to help him stay warm. Peter Hillary and Jeff Lakes have already been gone for two hours. Alison's crampons crunch and squeak on the hard snow, and the climbers shuffle off into the night.

At the Spanish camp, Lorenzo Ortas dozes inside his tent. He has felt ill all night and has chosen not to go with his friends. An hour later he hears three climbers pass by, following the Spanish tracks. The fourth, Kim Logan, has already returned to Camp IV, complaining of illness. The rest are moving strongly, heading toward the ice cliff, the Bottleneck, at 27,000 feet. As they grind up the slope, resting often on their ice axes, bending double to haul on what little air there is, Hillary and Lakes pass them coming down. Hillary tells Alison that he has become too cold and has decided to descend and warm up in the Spanish tents. Alison says simply: "I'm going on." Then Pepe Garcés passes them as he also descends. His feet are numb and he is nervous that he already has frostbite. When he reaches his camp, Ortas tells him to come in with him because their other tent is already occupied by Hillary and Lakes, who are still recovering from the intense cold.

For Alison and the others, time passes in an intense, hypoxic blur. Dawn comes and at last the cold recedes. As she gains height, Alison feels euphoria mixed with doubt and caution. The day seems brilliant beyond imagining. They are above every glacier, every glittering spire. The Karakoram mountains, which towered over them as they walked up the Baltoro Glacier, are now all beneath them, even the triple-summited Broad Peak, and the shapely pyramids of the Gasherbrums—all of them more than 26,000 feet high. There is no more gray, only white and the radiant blue on the fringes of the stratosphere. K2's summit seems so close. The climbing is not so difficult; no more rocks, only snow and ice. Slowly the slope to the Bottleneck steepens, but nowhere is it vertical. Were it not for the crippling altitude, it would be easy. As on Everest, Alison feels a sudden certainty. She has only to keep going, and she will climb K2, the joy of reaching it all the greater for the suffering and unhappiness of the past few weeks. In the end, up here, in the death zone, her willpower will see her through. As she works up the white slopes, her mind can only manage half-thoughts, impressions of the weather, her desire to keep going, her need to go home. Perhaps she says a silent prayer, as she has so often in her diary after great days in the mountains.

At 7 a.m. Hillary borrows the Spanish team's radio and speaks with Grant. He is still on the long slope that sweeps up to the Bottleneck. Conditions are perfect, Grant says, and Lakes and Hillary decide to continue, despite their delay at the Spanish camp. It is already too late for them to reach the summit and come back before dark, but they may not get a better chance to climb K2.

As they get close to the Bottleneck, Hillary becomes aware of a thick layer of cloud to the north of the Karakoram, over China. Two colossal weather systems are meeting. The vast depression of the monsoon is driving northward, crashing into an anticyclone over China, to the north of the mountains. If the anticyclone advances south, the Karakoram will be the battleground, and the cloud is its harbinger. The vast surreal landscape, the depths of space above his head, add to Hillary's sense of vulnerability. Clouds have crept across K2 now, and though the weather is still generally good, there are flurries of light snow. Doubt defeats his desire to climb. He tells Lakes he's decided to descend. Lakes says he'll go on a little while longer and see how things go. He has been on K2 before and doesn't want to need to return.

There are now seven climbers above Hillary in the region of the Bottleneck. When they reach the ice cliff, they will traverse left and around it, reaching the long summit slopes above. Ortiz, Olivar, and Bruce Grant are moving fast, but they wait as Alison, Escartín, and Slater start the long traverse. Jeff Lakes is still some way behind. In the still air, Hillary can hear Alison shouting down some information to one of the other climbers about which of the fixed ropes to use to climb across the steep ice. Then he turns his back on the summit.

As Logan and Comeskey reach III Three in the late morning, Comeskey looks across to Broad Peak. He sees massing, heavy clouds to the north of the mountain, but feels sure the climbers above him will be coming down before the storm hits. But to the climbers higher on K2, the weather doesn't seem so threatening. Only Lakes, still far behind the others, at last turns round to descend. The Spaniards at Camp IV receive a radio message just before midday from their companions struggling up the summit pyramid. They are at an obvious triangular rock, less than 800 feet from the summit and believe that conditions are good enough to continue. They feel too close to go back now, but the snow is deep, and they sink in to their knees or thighs. The hours tick by like minutes; the climbers are losing their grip on time. Hypoxia slows everything down, movement, thought, progress. And now, like their friends beneath them, they can see the bad weather brewing.

Alison knows this feeling, a tightness in the stomach, an awareness that the outcome, so recently certain, is suddenly in doubt. She looks at the cloud and tries to judge whether it's moving, and if so, how fast. They don't know how bad it will be or when it will fall, and in the meantime they just grind on, slowly lifting their feet and steadying themselves on the slope with their mittened hands or an ice ax. Perhaps she says another prayer. Please God, let it be all right.

As Hillary descends for the second time to the Spanish tents, thick cloud engulfs him and he finds it difficult to navigate. Garcés and Ortas give him a drink and Hillary borrows the Spanish radio and speaks to Comeskey and Logan, who are now descending to Camp II. He decides to carry on down, and again he loses his way on the blank ground below Camp IV, before the start of the fixed ropes. The clouds swirl around the mountain, obscuring the route. At around 5 p.m. the weather system pushing down from the north finally reaches him. The storm, he will tell reporters afterward, turns on like a tap and "just roars." Above him, however, the air remains completely still. Even now, the climbers are still on their way to the summit, wading up deep snow, unaware of the maelstrom building below them.

Ortas and Garcés, waiting nervously at Camp IV but still not experiencing the winds that are blasting Peter Hillary, hear from the others at around 6 p.m. Ortiz and Grant, who have clearly been the strongest on the mountain, have reached the top first. Half an hour later they hear from Olivar. He and Alison have reached the top as well. All four of them will soon be descending, he says. Below them, Escartín and Slater are still crawling up toward the summit. Olivar doesn't doubt that they will make it.

Alison stands on the summit of K2 as the day fades and looks about her. To the south, along the fringes of the distant monsoon, rain clouds are swelling deep inside Pakistan. Much closer, from among the jagged peaks of the Karakoram, more clouds are bubbling up from the darkening valleys. Cocooned in fleece and down and windproof nylon, her eyes thickly shaded from the glare of the evening sun, she stands with her companions and sucks the thin air into her lungs. Turning her sunburnt face to the north, she looks down on the Shaksgam region of China. From here, the thick bank of alto stratus is moving toward her. There is no reason to think it will overtake them before they reach shelter. For the moment the air is perfectly still. It is shortly after 6:30 p.m. on August 13, 1995. She can go no higher.

Inside their tent at Camp II, Matt Comeskey and Kim Logan are sheltering from the storm. They feel sure everyone must have abandoned plans for the summit and be rushing down the mountain. Then comes the radio call from Ortiz. With their radio tuned in to the same frequency as the Spanish team, they can hear their Pakistani Base Camp crew, the cooks and liaison officer, cheering the success. It only deepens their sense of horror. Shortly afterward, as the storm reaches Base Camp, the same crew are battening down tents to stop them from being torn away by the wind.

Peter Hillary reaches Camp II at 7:30 p.m. He has spent the last two hours fighting his way down, struggling in savage conditions to stay with the line of fixed ropes. And he is 7,000 feet lower down the mountain than Alison and the others. As Matt Comeskey and Kim Logan help him into their tent at Camp II, they tell him the others reached the summit an hour earlier. "Oh my God," he says. Then he shuts the tent behind him and they wait for the night to end.

CHAPTER 10

AFTERMATH

When wind strikes the bottom of a mountain it has nowhere to go but up, and as it searches for escape, it accelerates. Peter Hillary and the others at Camp II understood that anyone caught high on the mountain in that savage wind would have little chance of surviving. Garcés and Ortas discovered this a little over half an hour after Hillary reached the safety of his tent when the winds struck Camp IV at the shoulder. They described the storm as hurricane-force, and soon they found themselves being blown off the mountain inside the tent. Ortas rushed outside, grabbing the poles with his bare hands to prevent the tent taking off with Garcés inside it. They then crawled into the second tent, which was better secured. Taking out a penknife, Ortas cut a slot in the top of the fabric to let the wind through and they crouched at the bottom of the tent to wait for dawn. Later, at 11 p.m., this tent would also be flattened by the hurricane, and they would huddle in the lee of its base, waiting helplessly for the storm to abate.

The Spaniards estimate that the storm reached them at 26,000 feet some time between 8 p.m. and 9 p.m. It would have struck the summit area soon after, with winds in excess of a hundred miles an hour. There was no snow and the skies above were clear. Later the Spanish would argue that this showed the winds had originated to the north, from the anticyclone that sits over China. It had moved south in the evening, nudging back the monsoon system to the south and blasting the six climbers crawling down from the summit slopes. Allowing for their latest departure time from the summit being 7 p.m., the climbers would have got perhaps a third of the way down, past the rock at 27,500 feet from which the Spanish had made a radio call nine or ten hours earlier. Faced by the sudden and violent onrush of freezing air, they were either blasted from the ridge or frozen wherever they tried to take shelter. Nobody knows exactly how they all died, only that they did.

Next morning, as dawn broke, the winds had subsided. The storm had moved on, and the eerie calm that followed gave the survivors a chance to escape. Garcés and Ortas, frozen by their ordeal, waited for the sun to warm their exhausted bodies before starting the long descent. At the lower Camp IV on the Abruzzi spur, Jeff Lakes also roused himself. He had called at the Spanish tents much later than Hillary, having turned back from his summit bid too late. He was tired, the Spanish said, and they gave him a drink before he descended. As he sat inside his tent at the lower Camp IV it was flattened by wind, and he was forced to dig himself out and sit outside through the night, the bitter temperature and strong winds chilling him further.

In the morning, in the warm sunshine that resurrected the Spanish, Lakes tried to recover the equipment he needed to help him climb down, scraping at the snow to find his crampons and ice ax, his harness and the crucial metal device he needed to rappel the fixed ropes. He found none of it, and at 11 a.m. he carried on down as best he could without being able to make himself a drink. At Camp III he found the tents buried by avalanche debris. Comeskey recalls the desperate radio conversations they shared as Lakes struggled to survive. The climbers at Camp II urged him to dig out the tent at Camp III, uncertain how Lakes would cope on the Black Pyramid. They wanted time to recover and climb up to him with more equipment, making his passage over the steep rocks easier. Lakes could not tolerate the thought of another night sitting out in the snow and so, cutting a length of cord to tie himself into the fixed ropes, he fought his way down to Camp II, falling inside the tent at 1:30 a.m., exhausted, dehydrated but now in the care of his friends.

"Incredibly," says Matt Comeskey, "he had no frostbite." Every time Lakes reached a belay point where the fixed ropes were secured to a piton or ice screw, he had had to untie the short length of rope he had used as a makeshift harness and then retie it on the other side of the belay, and to keep doing that on dozens of occasions for thousands of feet, his body and mind stretched to breaking point. "All day we had been in radio contact, never really knowing what the outcome would be," Comeskey says. "A number of times when we lost radio contact, we thought we had lost him too. We put him in the tent with me, and after a prolonged bout of dry wheezing, he seemed to get his breathing under control. I assumed his wheezing was due to dehydration. It was very similar to an asthma attack. After he had got this under control, he lay down and went into a sleep he never woke from."

Comeskey and Logan tried to administer cardiopulmonary resuscitation, but it was no use. The storm on K2 had claimed its seventh victim. They buried him in the snow on the morning of August 15 on slopes near Camp II. From Base Camp they heard that there were no sightings of any of the climbers who had been to the summit, only of Ortas and Garcés who had remained at Camp Four.

The Spanish were also close to the edge, suffering from frostbite. At 4 p.m. on August 14, as they continued to retreat down their route, at an altitude of around 24,000 feet, they spotted some clothing well across from the line of their descent in the middle of the huge south face of K2. Ortas moved toward it to get a better view and found an empty boot. It had a heating device, powered by battery. The only climber using such a device was Alison; she had shown him how the boots worked only days before at base camp. Ten feet below the boot he found an anorak and a harness, which he recognized as Alison's. Both items were bloodstained. Looking up from this point into the broad gully above him he could see three distinctive tracks in the snow, each also stained with blood. Looking up again to the summit ridge, he guessed that the three had fallen from about 27,600 feet, well above the Bottleneck. There was no avalanche debris and Ortas assumed that the wind had simply prised the climbers from the slope. He took the harness, intending to give it to Alison's family, but later, as his descent became more difficult, he was forced to abandon it.

Ortas then followed the gully down a little way and spotted a body lying in a hollow at the edge of a massive band of ice cliffs that form one of the most obvious features of the South Face. It was level with the Spanish Camp III, at about 23,000 feet, but there was no way that he could reach it from above. Ortas, after seeing the body's distinctive clothing, believes it was Alison's. He climbed back to Garcés and the two descended to Camp III with the intention of reaching her from there. They soon gave up the plan. Camp III was stripped of equipment and provisions. They would have to go lower at once to reach safety. Alison remained where she had fallen.

Pepe Garcés and Lorenzo Ortas continued to Base Camp next day, the latter helped down by Manuel Ansón, who climbed up to meet them and offer support. It was 9 p.m. before Ortas finally made it back to the tents. At Base Camp they learned of the death of Jeff Lakes from the New Zealanders, who had also descended after burying their friend. The following day, August 16, Hillary, Comeskey, and Logan trekked down the Baltoro to the Base Camp at the foot of Broad Peak, where an American guide, Scott Fischer, had led a group to that mountain's summit on the same day as Alison and the others had climbed K2. There they scanned the mountain with Fischer's telescope, hoping to catch some glimpse of the missing climbers. Fischer reported seeing an unidentified body that "appeared to have fallen 1,500 feet." Comeskey, also looking through the telescope at the huge glacial area above the serac band, recalls: "I couldn't tell conclusively from what I saw that there was a body there, but given that whatever it was, was lying surrounded by a large area of glacial snow, I doubt if it was a rock. I'm inclined to believe that the Spanish were correct, that it was Alison's body they saw. They were familiar with what she had been wearing." Given the period of time since the accident and the evidence of the Spanish, it was obvious that all six were dead. It was time to tell the world, and Hillary asked Fischer to use his satellite communications to file a report to Outside Online, an internet information service.

As soon as the story was published the news spread, even before the bereaved families were told what had happened. The head of the Press Association's bureau in Scotland called Jim Ballard for confirmation. He had heard nothing and phoned *Climbing* magazine in Colorado. "He spoke quietly," wrote Alison Osius, the magazine's senior editor, "so as not to be heard by the children, yahooing in the background."

The first public media reactions were of grief and shock. In the London *Times* on August 18, Jan Morris wrote:

> To hear of her death is like a slap in the face from a malevolent force, resentful that we had all been given pleasure by a feat of entirely harmless, essentially uncompetitive, totally individualist courage.

But information about her death was still in short supply, and the same factors that had worked in Alison's favor during her life, the "good story" of the mother alone on Everest, now began to work against her. The K2 Motel in Skardu was filling with journalists. Most knew little about her, and less about mountaineering. With her success on Everest so fresh in the public's mind, the temptation was to see Alison, while quietly sidelining those with her, as an overreacher, someone who flew too close to the sun.

When Peter Hillary arrived in Skardu a few days later, he appeared to provide all the required evidence. In an interview with the *Independent*, he criticized those who had gone to the summit:

Summit fever had developed in that group. There was a chemistry in there that meant they were going for the summit no matter what.... They were all driving each other on. These people came together and because of the place and the atmosphere and their personalities, they became blinkered and simply focused on the top.

Of Alison and Rob Slater, he was particularly critical:

Alison was a brilliant climber but she had tremendous commercial pressures on her and she became obsessed. When you spoke to her, it was clear that climbing came first and everything else was secondary.

This was not the complete picture her friends or family recognized. Alison's primary concern was always her children. Nor was she governed simply by commercial pressures.

In truth, Hillary and the other New Zealanders were exhausted and in a state of shocked grief. Two of his own expedition members had died on the mountain, one of them more or less in front of him. Later on, after the story had dropped out of the news, Hillary would admit to wondering as he turned to descend if he'd done the right thing: "My decision to turn back still fills me with wonder. I felt it strongly, but I also felt I may be making the wrong decision." But now his words only fueled an avalanche of speculative comment, much of it hostile to Alison.

A procession of experienced mountaineers from all over the world was asked for their views, and most of them agreed that to succeed at high-altitude mountaineering, you had to take risks. They had all done so and survived; to criticize Alison for doing the same would have been hypocrisy. "Sure she was driven," the American mountaineer Greg Child said, recalling his own success on K2. "But everybody who goes to the summit of K2 is driven."

Child's insight wasn't shared by the majority of commentators who had no understanding of mountaineering's appeal. The news that a mother of young children had lost her life climbing a mountain provoked moral outrage. Alison had already been attacked for climbing Everest by the *Times* columnist Nigella Lawson, with her accusation of a "reality-denying self-centeredness." Now, after her death, others picked up this theme. Alison, it was claimed, was not only reckless but selfish, a woman who had paid the ultimate price for indulging her ego. Polly Toynbee, an influential liberal commentator, wrote:

> Danger for its own sake seems to me no better than drug-taking as a social activity. Danger can be powerfully addictive, and those of us with no taste for it at all consider it as appalling as a taste for crack. It would be better not to glamorize danger, not to prize foolhardiness.

In Toynbee's view, tolerance of a way of life beyond the conventional was not to be allowed. The most powerful sentence in Toynbee's column, however, was also the most revealing of the criticisms made about Alison. "What is interesting about Alison Hargreaves," she wrote, "is that she behaved like a man." By considering her behavior as typically male, Toynbee was able to condemn it. Risk-taking, she argued, is purely a male choice, to do with testosterone and machismo.

Within a few days of Alison's death, her memory had become a battleground. The person Alison had really been became irrelevant; she was now a symbol, an icon, to be fought over and discussed. At the opposite end of the twentieth century, the story of Robert Scott and his disastrous expedition to the South Pole acquired a similar mythic status. His death and those of his companions became the quintessential symbols of an age of collective goals, of Empire, of greatness achieved through Nation. Eighty-four years later, Alison was being alternately vilified and venerated, held out as the ultimate representative of an age that had replaced shared glories with the primacy of self.

Of course she had taken a risk. Merely being on K2 is risky. To press on when she and the others could see the gathering cloud was more risky, but had they survived, then the criticisms would have been lost in the plaudits offered by the same newspapers that were now judging her. Part of the problem was that the press had only Alison's forthright, intense public image from which to draw conclusions about her motivation. The picture of a woman possessed fitted what little was known about her. Her self-doubt, her periods of low self-esteem, the crushing isolation she felt during the more difficult periods of her marriage, were all undiscovered country. To many journalists who met her, she seemed pretty much as Hillary described her.

However, there was a deeper level to Alison's posthumous condemnation. In the West, as life expectancy becomes more predictable, premature death seems a greater tragedy than ever, and those who take risks are judged to have behaved not just irresponsibly but immorally. They have broken a modern taboo. But it is precisely because society seems controlled and diluted that people seek out such challenges. Many men and women in society find freedom in the hills, an escape from the mundane, a way to achieve fulfilment. Alison Hargreaves was alive among mountains as she was nowhere else, and she brought that energy and joy to her children. She could be manipulative and ambitious, even self-centered; she did not always empathize strongly with the problems of others. But those are common human failings, not restricted to mountaineers.

Even more instinctive was the feeling that the mother of young children should not have been taking such risks. Plenty of fathers have died in the mountains, and a few days before Alison disappeared, Paul Nunn and Geoff Tier, both talented British mountaineers and both fathers, died on a mountain called Haramosh II, close to K2 itself. But the response to Alison's death was visceral, and many commentators believed that a mother taking such risks was morally more culpable than a father doing the same. Alison herself was only beginning to explore these arguments, and it's ironic that she never really had the debate within herself that the press had after her death. At the climbing festival in Canada she attended in late 1994, she had met well-known women mountaineers who challenged her to think again about her attitude to risk, and after Everest, with a world-class achievement completed, there are signs that she was developing and maturing from the intensity and burning ambition of her youth. It is quite possible that after K2 she would never have gone on such a climb again. The claim that she was in some way a bad mother was not remotely true, and would have caused her deep unhappiness.

Alison Osius wrote after the events on K2:

Hargreaves was public property; her death, news round the world. It was especially painful to women climbers, many of whom had been trying to sort out their own conflicting obligations to self and family. We felt for her, trying to pursue her dreams. Some thought and wondered, well, had she been selfish? But we cannot judge that. We can only draw our own lines.

Ultimately, those around Alison understood her passion for the mountains and the risks she faced there, and they accepted both. Alison's triumphs were public, but her tragedy is more personal, and it is borne by those who loved her. Behind the cliché and moral censure that surrounded her death was an ordinary woman with an extraordinary talent and determination, with hopes, fears, loves, virtues, and faults, who did great things and made some terrible mistakes. It is not too much to hope that in the moments before the hurricane closed around her, as she started home from the summit of K2 with the world beneath her feet, Alison was happy.

Alison Hargreaves 1962—1995

- The fifth British ascent of K2, August 13, 1995.

- The first unsupported ascent of Everest by a woman, without bottled oxygen, May 1, 1995.

- The first female solo ascent of the Croz Spur on the Grandes Jorasses in the French Alps in 1993. A steep, technical ice climb, Alison's ascent of the Croz Spur was completed in a day.

- A new route on the northwest face of Kangtega in Nepal, climbed with Mark Twight of the U.S.A. in 1986.

- The first female solo ascents of several north faces in 1993, including the Aiguille du Petit Dru in the French Alps, the Cassin Ridge on the Cima Grande in the Dolomites, and the Matterhorn.

- The first ascent by a British woman of the Eiger's notorious north face, July 1988.

- Several first female British ascents of difficult Alpine climbs such as the north face of Les Droites and the Supercouloir on Mont Blanc du Tacul, both in the Mont Blanc Range above Chamonix.

INDEX

AUTHORS' NOTE

Many people have helped us in the preparation of this book. We wish especially to thank John and Joyce Hargreaves, Alison's parents, and her sister, Susan Stokes. Their support and cooperation is the rock on which this project was founded.

Among the many others who require our gratitude are: Steve Aisthorpe, Julie Allen, Richard Allen, Sir Chris Bonington, Russell Brice, Ian Brown, Richard Celsi, Daphne Chalk, Greg Child, Dr. Charles Clarke, Peter Clarke, John Cleare, Matt Comeskey, Kevin Cooney, Simon Currin, Catherine Destivelle, Julianne and Phil Dickens, Leo and Mandy Dickinson, Xavier Eguskitza, Cally Flemming, Liz Hawley, Peter Hillary, Alan Hinkes, Dawn Hopkinson, Martin Howarth, Paul Howarth, John Hunt, Ted and Jackie Johnson, Michael Kennedy, Pat Lewis, Gerry Lidgett, Jeff Lowe, Bernadette McDonald, Bev Marshall, Bonny Masson, Nick Morely, Bernard and Janine Newman, Bill O'Connor, Alison Osius, Margaret Osman, Ian Parsons, Andy Perkins, Jim Perrin, Tom Prentice, Audrey Salkeld, Doug Scott, Nigel Shepherd, Sally Skinner, Andrew Spencer, Mark Twight, Stephen Venables, Geraldine Westrupp, Tim Wilson.

Alison's diaries provide a record of her life that is well in excess of a million words. For the period 1973-92, the quotations from them found here were copied by us from the originals, which were left at Meerbrook Lea when the house was repossessed in 1993 and rescued by her parents. Later diary entries were published in her own *A Hard Day's Summer* (Hodder and Stoughton, 1994) and Jim Ballard's *One and Two Halves to K2* (BBC Books, 1996).

David Rose
Ed Douglas